SARMIENTO
AND HIS ARGENTINA

SARMIENTO
AND HIS ARGENTINA

edited by
Joseph T. Criscenti

Lynne Rienner Publishers • Boulder & London

Frontispiece: courtesy of Ambassador Carlos Keller Sarmiento. Jacket: front cover art
courtesy of the Columbus Memorial Library of the Organization of American States,
Washington, D.C.; back cover photo of the statue of Sarmiento in Boston courtesy of
Milton I. Vanger.

Published in the United States of America in 1993 by
Lynne Rienner Publishers, Inc.
1800 30th Street, Boulder, Colorado 80301

and in the United Kingdom by
Lynne Rienner Publishers, Inc.
3 Henrietta Street, Covent Garden, London WC2E 8LU

Library of Congress Cataloging-in-Publication Data
Sarmiento and his Argentina / edited by Joseph T. Criscenti.
  Includes bibliographical references and index.
  ISBN 1-55587-351-0 (alk. paper)
  1. Sarmiento, Domingo Faustino, 1811–1888. 2. Argentina—
History—1817–1860. I. Criscenti, Joseph.
F2846.S26S27 1993
982′.05′092—dc20   92-38372
                                                                          CIP

British Cataloguing in Publication Data
A Cataloguing in Publication record for this book
is available from the British Library.

Printed and bound in the United States of America

The paper used in this publication meets the requirements
of the American National Standard for Permanence of   ∞
Paper for Printed Library Materials Z39.48-1984.

To

Jackie and Louise

Contents

Introduction
Joseph T. Criscenti

In 1988, on the centennial anniversary of his death, Argentines honored the memory of Domingo Faustino Sarmiento, essayist, journalist, educator, polemicist, and former president—a talented self-made man who had contributed immeasurably to the formation of modern Argentina. The Argentine government observed the occasion abroad by sponsoring scholarly symposia on Sarmiento. The Argentine Embassy in Washington, D.C., asked Georgette M. Dorn to organize a one-day conference at the Hispanic Division, Library of Congress, and asked me to organize a two-day symposium at Harvard University. Both of us accepted the challenge of putting together panels that would present an up-to-date look at Sarmiento, his ideas, and his significance for Argentina. The present volume contains most of the papers presented at these two meetings. A paper that Dorn read at the Sarmiento Centennial Symposium, University of Ottawa, Canada, and one that I have written specially for this book are also included.

Sarmiento was a prolific writer, but he established himself as a literary figure with *Civilización i barbarie* (1845), more familiarly known as *Facundo,* and *Recuerdos de provincia* (1850), both written while Sarmiento was living in exile in Chile and serving the Chilean government in various capacities. *Facundo* first appeared in serial form in *El Progreso,* a Chilean newspaper with which Sarmiento was closely associated, and was later published in book form by its press. Its sales were not impressive. *De la educación popular* (1849), *Recuerdos de provincia, Viajes en Europa, África i América* (1849–1851), *Arjirópolis* (1850), and *Vida de Facundo Quiroga* (1851) were all published by Sarmiento's business partner and son-in-law, the Frenchman Julio Belín.[1] Belín, who opened his printing shop in January 1849, paid some of the publishing costs associated with Sarmiento's works, and Chilean government subsidies reduced or eliminated the balance. Belín also published a French edition of *Argyrópolis* (1851), but other printers released French translations of *Vida de fray Félix Aldao* (1847) and *Facundo* (1853). *Campaña en el ejército Grande de Sud América* was published in Spanish in its entirety in Rio de Janeiro (1852). *Facundo* appeared in English in 1868 in both New York and London, but Sarmiento's report on education in the United States and his life of Abraham Lincoln, both published in Spanish in New York in 1866, never appeared in English.

In his thoughtful essay, which opens our own *Sarmiento and His Times,* Solomon Lipp notes that Sarmiento's writings were primarily political and reflected his desire to transform Argentine society. As Lipp observes, Sarmiento was not always logical or consistent. Still, he held steadfast to some basic tenets that set him apart from most men of his generation. Yet Sarmiento was also typical of his times in that his native province of San Juan was his native country (*patria*), and its concerns were uppermost in his mind. "Local affections," he once said, "are part of our existence."[2] When José de Oro taught him "to love liberty and the fatherland," the provinces in the former Viceroyalty of the Río de la Plata were already emerging from the War of Independence as military republics.[3] Love of *patria* explains Sarmiento's persistent interest in the economic well-being of San Juan and its citizens. San Juan and the other interior provinces would benefit, he believed, if the restrictions on their transandean trade with Chile and Bolivia and on navigation on the Paraná and Uruguay rivers were removed. This idea permeates much of his early writings.

Another of Sarmiento's early beliefs, one expressed by Bolívar, was that "all Americans should have only one fatherland."[4] Initially, this concept was widely shared by visionaries, but by 1829 it had lost its appeal. In the former Viceroyalty of the Río de la Plata, there was a continuous process of amalgamation and disintegration of political units, of making and remaking new patrias, as provinces groped for economic survival and well-being. These political units had short lives, for they overextended their limited military and financial resources or their alarmed neighbors formed alliances that overwhelmed them. In this environment the provinces always remained the primary *patria*, but the intellectuals, the educated, and businessmen dreamed of a larger nation. They had few precedents to follow and were unprepared for the tasks that faced them. Their ideal nation-state changed with the alterations experienced in the regional political and military arenas. At first the ideal was the entire South American continent, then it was reduced to a combination of two or more of the large colonial administrative units or small republics. The final version, reluctantly accepted, was all or part of the former Viceroyalty of the Río de la Plata.

In this evolving situation familiar words took on new meanings, family relationships were strained, and institutions were created, in law but not always in fact, based on competing European and North American models. Once created, these formless institutions acquired a life of their own. They became facades that camouflaged reality. At the cultural level, as Nicolas Shumway points out in his essay, Sarmiento and his followers wanted to change reality, albeit not completely, to conform to their foreign model. Sarmiento went one step further. As Tulio Halperín Donghi notes, Sarmiento announced in *Recuerdos de provincia* that he was a candidate for the presidency of the as yet unconstructed nation that would emerge from the overthrow of Rosas. He was prepared to lead the provinces out of the collapsing colonial world into one of civilization and progress. This new nation would be a reconstructed Viceroyalty of the Río de la Plata, an unrealizable dream as long as the República Oriental del Uruguay and Paraguay remained independent. In his provocative essay, William Katra examines Sarmiento's hatred of José Artigas, the leader of the Orientales. Sarmiento blamed Artigas for the refusal of the Provincia Oriental del Uruguay and four Argentine provinces to join the United Provinces in South America created at the Congress of Tucumán in 1815.

Size would not be the only dimension of greatness of Sarmiento's nation. He had tremendous faith in the transforming value of trade, immigration, education, and democratic institutions. This faith was not solely the result of his reading of the French philosophers. It also came from growing up in San Juan, a place more open to outsiders than Sarmiento's own writings suggest. San Juan was the home of numerous British soldiers who had been captured during the ill-fated invasions of 1806 and 1807, of survivors of shipwrecked merchant ships off the coast of Chile, and of deserters, discharged sailors, or passengers from foreign ships stopping in Pacific ports. Foreigners also arrived with San Martín's Army of the Andes. Some of these same elements settled in the neighboring provinces of Mendoza and San Luis, but most travelers felt that San Juan was the best interior province for immigrants.[5] Another source of immigrants was foreign merchants who opened their shops in Chile in the early 1820s. A decade later ship captains overcame their fear of Cape Horn and were able to ship more goods to the Province of Cuyo (the union of San Juan, San Luis, and Mendoza from 1813 to 1820). A monthly courier service between Chile and San Juan was established, and there were always messengers and travelers in town. Local merchants, in turn, traveled to Santiago de Chile, Valparaiso, and Coquimbo.[6]

In the 1820s, when Sarmiento was a teenager, San Juan had the reputation as the most progressive province outside Buenos Aires.[7] It, along with Mendoza, fostered religious tolerance, and permitted interfaith marriages.[8] Foreigners helped establish schools for boys and girls in San Juan (as well as Mendoza). There was also a lively interest in the United States. One widely read and discussed book was a biography of

Sarmiento's hero, Benjamin Franklin. Villavicencio's translation of the U.S. Constitution, probably published in Lima about 1812, and Vicente Rocafuerte's translation of the Articles of Confederation (1821) were also available.[9] Another source of information about the United States were North Americans who established permanent or temporary residences in the Province of Cuyo. One of them was Dr. Aman Rawson. He had married into a prominent San Juan family, and his son, William, was a friend of both Sarmiento, whom he inspired to learn Italian, and Bartolomé Mitre. Growing up in San Juan, then, contributed to Sarmiento's interest in the United States. This topic is discussed by Michael Aaron Rockland, who describes Sarmiento's initial reactions to the United States, and Georgette Magassy Dorn, who reminds us of the reception and accomplishments of the U.S. teachers who Sarmiento attracted to Argentina.

How successful was Sarmiento in transforming Argentina? Ricardo Piglia and Noel F. McGinn look closely at Sarmiento's belief in civilization and progress. Piglia sees in Sarmiento an effort to compare and contrast Argentine culture with other cultures in order to distinguish between the civilized and the barbaric. McGinn compares Sarmiento's development theory with what actually happened in Argentina and explains why its application fell short of expectations. What happened in Sarmiento's own lifetime was not what he had expected or witnessed in the United States. Samuel L. Baily calls for a closer look at the results of the immigration policy Sarmiento advocated, and Kristin H. Ruggiero demonstrates the failure to successfully integrate immigrants into Argentine society. Efraín Kristal analyzes Sarmiento's debate with Lastarria and Bello, which began as a discussion of what teaching method would most effectively reduce illiteracy in Spanish America and eventually centered on the desirability of Spanish America declaring its cultural independence from Spain. Laura V. Monti describes Sarmiento's positive attitudes toward women, and Diana Sorensen Goodrich looks closely at the manner in which an Argentine nationalist used *Facundo* to further his own program. Kristine L. Jones effectively compares the Indian policies of Argentina and the United States. Her chapter focuses on the Indians who never became allies of the Spaniards and never established families among them. Under Spanish law, caciques and their children had all the rights of pure-blooded Spaniards, which is why the family members of Juan Eugenio de Mallea, married to the Indian queen of Angaco, were regarded as "mestizos of pure and noble blood."[10] In my own article I focus on the early stages of the Argentine nation.

As the chapters presented in this volume indicate, Sarmiento's program for civilization and trade had mixed results. Taking the United States as his model, he encouraged immigration and the expansion of public education. Immigrants arrived, schools were built, and teachers trained, but the immigrants never became Argentines. The U.S. experience with immigrants was not repeated in Argentina.[11] Argentine democratic practices were very feeble. The opening of the Río Paraná to international trade, as Sarmiento anticipated, benefited the interior provinces, which reoriented their economies toward the Atlantic Ocean. Sarmiento struggled throughout his life to build the *patria común*, and he completed its formation during his presidency.

This volume would have been impossible without the encouragement of His Excellency Enrique A. Candioti, the former Argentine ambassador to the United States, and the support of friends such as Professor Milton I. Vanger and his wife, Elsa Oribe de Vanger. Professor Vanger took the picture of Sarmiento's statue on Commonwealth Avenue, Boston, which was made by the Argentine sculptor Ivette Compagnion, and was given to the city of Boston by the city of Buenos Aires in 1973. Dr. Celso Rodríguez located the portraits of Sarmiento in the Columbus Memorial Library of the Organization of American States, which appear here through the courtesy of that institution. Harvard College Library granted permission to reproduce two maps of Argentina found in its collection. Kristin L. Jones ably assisted me in translating the two chapters that were presented in Spanish. Finally, I want to thank Lynne Rienner and her assistant, Kate Watts, for their patience and thoughtful suggestions.

NOTES

1. Domingo F. Sarmiento, *Obras de D. F. Sarmiento,* vol. 14, *Los emigrados (páginas póstumas)* (53 vols., Buenos Aires: Moreno, 1887–1900), 365. I have followed Sarmiento's spelling of his titles.
2. Domingo F. Sarmiento, *Convención de San-Nicolás de los Arroyos* (Santiago de Chile: Imprenta de Julio Belín i Cia., 1852), 5.
3. Domingo F. Sarmiento, *Memoria enviada al Instituto Histórico de Francia, sobre la cuestión décima del programa de los trabajos que debe presentar la 1ª clase, "Quelle est la situation actuelle des Républiques du centre et du Sud de Amérique"* (Santiago de Chile: Imprenta de Julio Belín i Cia., 1853), 16; Domingo F. Sarmiento, *Viaje a Chile del Canónigo Don Juan María Mastai-Ferreti oi sumo pontifice Pio, Papa IX,* trans. from Italian, includes an appendix (Santiago de Chile: Imprenta de la Opinión, 1848), 40.
4. Quoted in Enrique de Gandía, "Conferencia del Guayaquil; El fracaso y los mitos," *Historia,* (Buenos Aires) año II, 11, no. 44 (December 1991–February 1992): 62. Unfortunately, I have not seen Dr. Gandía's *Historia política argentina,* in which he describes San Martín's plan to build a large republic in South America.
5. Charles Brand, *Journal of a Voyage to Peru: A Passage Across the Cordillera of the Andes, in the Winter of 1827, Performed on Foot in the Snow; and a Journey Across the Pampas* (London: H. Colburn, 1828), 81; N. A. R. Mackay, *Las relaciones entre Gran Bretaña y la República Argentina entre los siglos XVIII y principios del XIX*

(Buenos Aires: Asociación Argentina de Cultura Inglesa, 1962), 60–61; Conrad Malte-Brun, *Universal Geography, or A Description of All Parts of the World* (6 vols., Philadelphia: A. Finley, 1827–1829), 3:365; J. C. Brigham, "South America. Mr. Brigham's Journey from Buenos Ayres to Mendoza and Chile," *Missionary Herald,* 22 (February 1826): 42–47 and (March 1826): 75.

6. Alcide d'Orbigny, *Voyage pittoresque dans les deux Amériques; Resumé général de tous les voyages* (Paris: Chez L. Tenré , Libraire-Editeur, 1836), 317–318 and 326; Th. Pavie, "Passage des Andes en Hiver," *Revue des Deux Mondes,* 4th ser., 3 (1835): 482 and 494.

7. D'Orbigny, *Voyage pittoresque,* 317–318.

8. "South America, Buenos Aires," *Missionary World,* 21 (October 1825): 320–321; Isaac C. Strain, *Cordillera and Pampa, Mountain and Plain. Sketches of a Journey in Chili, and the Argentine Provinces, in 1849* (New York: H. H. Moore, 1853), 205 and 241.

9. *Constitución de los Estados-Unidos de América. (Noticia de la Población)*, trans. Dr. Villavicencio (Lima?: n.p., 1812?); "Artículos de Confederacion, y Constitucion de los Estados Unidos de America," Vicente Rocafuerte, *Ideas necesarias á todo pueblo americano independiente, que quiera ser libre* (Philadelphia: D. Huntington, 1821).

10. Domingo F. Sarmiento, *Recuerdos de provincia* (Buenos Aires: Editorial de Belgrano, 1981), 92.

11. The extent to which the United States was used as a model is succinctly described in "Yankee-mania," *La Prensa* (Buenos Aires), 9 June 1870, p. 2.

Sarmiento Revisited:
Contradictions and Curiosities
Solomon Lipp

This chapter deals with some perceived contradictions and conflicts that constitute part of the tempestuous career of Domingo Faustino Sarmiento. Perhaps contradictions and inconsistencies are to be expected. One who is passionately involved in a mission cannot always be logical.

Few men have spoken about themselves at such great lengths, nor have many men had so much written about them. Quite a few pages written by Sarmiento himself reveal his unbridled confidence, coupled with doubts and perplexities, militant aggressiveness, and insecurity.

Sarmiento was a man of action. Having decided to link his own destiny with that of his country, his writings are primarily political and instrumental. For him, literature had to serve a utilitarian purpose. Content was more important than form. Improvement in writing techniques, he felt, would develop eventually, but at any given moment there were more pressing problems. "To write just for the sake of writing," he said, "is the profession of the vain and pretentious, those who are indifferent, without principles or true patriotism."[1] And so Sarmiento used his pen as a weapon. As Unamuno put it: "His stiletto is his style."[2]

Sarmiento's autobiographical writing reveals a conflict between a personality that strives constantly to achieve and an environment that resists his efforts. Possessed of a messianic complex, he wrote: "I was born in 1811, in the ninth month after May 25, i.e., Independence."[3] He thus saw himself as a historical event, an embryo gestating nine months in the womb of his mother country. Imbued with a romantic conception of history, Sarmiento merged the highly emotional overtones of his own life with his interpretation of Argentina's social condition. Influenced by the French Enlightenment in his youth, and subsequently overwhelmed

Solomon Lipp is professor emeritus of Hispanic studies, McGill University, Toronto, Canada.

by the waves of romanticism, he was determined to act as a catalyst as he described the forces of Argentine society with a view to effecting a radical measure of improvement.

The very reality in which he found himself must be transformed. But how? He would do it by means of a political program of national reconstruction, public education, European immigration, technical and economic progress, and, finally, the establishment of civil liberties and representative democracy. Sarmiento would teach freedom as one would teach a pupil how to read.

Education, then, was a political instrument. Sarmiento endeavored to plant the seeds of European and U.S. educational practices in Argentine soil, but he evidently failed to see that it was first necessary to create favorable social conditions so that these seeds might fructify. And these conditions did not exist.

Facundo is the feverish result of his restless energy, the first study of its kind—neither history nor novel nor sociology—utilizing geography as a point of departure to explain the author's thesis. Sarmiento's treatment of his subject matter is reminiscent of the ideas of Hippolyte Taine and Charles Darwin, an approach characteristic of the period. In this context of continuous evolution, the country, as opposed to the city, represents disorder and barbarism. The inhabitants of the pampas do not know the meaning of law and civilization. The pampas's vastness produces a feeling of insecurity and a stoic resignation in the face of death. In contrast, only those living in cities are aware of the guiding principles of social solidarity, of the rights and duties of the nation's citizens. The educated classes in the city represent civilization. They are viewed with disdain by the gaucho. Although they may have read many books, they do not know how to bring down a fierce bull and slaughter it. The nature of Argentine history is explained by the physical and social environments and by the way these mold the rural inhabitants. Men like Facundo and Rosas are but manifestations of a social condition, of an underlying barbarism. In fact, if Rosas had not existed, it would have been necessary to invent him.

The antinomy of civilization-barbarism gradually assumed additional characteristics, nuances, and symbols. To the polarity city-country were added: Unitarians-Federalists, Buenos Aires–Río de la Plata, Rosas-Rivadavia, Europe–Latin America, and *frac-chiripá*. Barbarism, in Sarmiento's thinking, became equated with the Americanism and anti-Europeanism represented by Rosas. The *salón literario* of Buenos Aires, engaged in reading predominantly French works, was synonymous with civilization. In short, Argentina's Europeanized future was locked in battle with the backward Americanism of past and present.

The polarity eventually broadened into a conflict between commerce and progress, on the one hand, and economic and cultural stagnation, on the other. Subsequently, too, barbarism was associated with economic nationalism, Spanish feudal institutions, Jesuit education, nomadic tribes in Africa, and the *montonera* (guerrilla fighters). Similarly, civilization assumed equally diverse garb, often represented by some political, economic, and social reform.

At times there appears to be an irresistible oscillation that takes hold of Sarmiento—an oscillation between the political and the aesthetic. On the political side, he wanted to attack the centers of barbarism that he believed existed in the vast plains of the interior and in the customs and institutions of rural society. But on the aesthetic side he pays homage to the natural environment and picturesque way of life of his native country. The men of the pampas should have been poets and dreamers. From a practical point of view, Sarmiento condemns the gaucho as a retarded social element; yet his romantic impulses well up as he describes, with no small measure of admiration and in the most colorful of terms, the life-style of the various types of gauchos. Sarmiento even expresses occasional admiration for Rosas, putting him in the same class as Napoleon.[4] With respect to Facundo, Sarmiento sees him not as a petty villain, but rather as a great man, a victim of determinist forces. Facundo is a historical figure who lends himself to a variety of interpretations. In the hands of Sarmiento he is a semifictional character who acquires quasi-mythical overtones.

Perhaps Sarmiento himself realized that his formula was not hard and fast. The truth was that the plains were not so barbaric, nor the cities so civilized as he made them out to be. He tried to reconcile opposites by claiming that he felt like a provincial in Buenos Aires and a porteño (someone from Buenos Aires) in the provinces. Sarmiento knew that Facundo, the symbol of barbarism, wished to organize the country and provide it with a constitution, nevertheless the author chose to ignore this in order not to spoil his agenda.

If *Facundo* is antigaucho, anticaudillo, and prourban, what is the appeal of the gaucho image? Sarmiento placed more emphasis on the very forces he felt were destructive to his country. Reason made Sarmiento shun the caudillo, but instinct made him admire the gaucho's horsemanship. Sarmiento's enemies claimed that his own ruthlessness equaled Facundo's and that he used gaucho methods against opponents like El Chacho.[5] Yet the essence of *Facundo's* message is that the gaucho must go, as well as the caudillismo engendered by him.

El Chacho, a political enemy of Sarmiento during the latter's administration as governor of the Province of San Juan, was executed because he was an outlaw according to Sarmiento. The incident caused a violent controversy. For example, José Hernández, author of *Martín Fierro*, and Juan Bautista Alberdi, Sarmiento's political adversary, did not share Sarmiento's opinion that El Chacho was an outlaw. According to Alberdi, Sarmiento represented El Chacho as a common bandit only because he feared him as a political rival. The case of El Chacho raises a basic question: In the fight against lawlessness, must humans descend to the level of barbarism in order to triumph?[6]

There is a certain irony in the fact that Sarmiento is best known for portraying Facundo, a character he wanted removed from the Argentine scene. As suggested, he succeeded in immortalizing those whom he wanted to destroy.

The *Facundo* thesis was attacked vigorously by Alberdi. Sarmiento, he argued, did not understand the role played by economic factors. In Alberdi's view, Sarmiento believed that the Argentine revolution for independence was a movement inspired by ideas, rather than material interests; that the countryside, i.e., the provinces of the interior, were devoid of ideas; and that only the cities (chiefly Buenos Aires) played host to educational endeavors.

Alberdi stepped in to defend the hinterland. It is there that raw materials are produced and wealth is created. The provinces thus provided the necessary power to promote the independence movement. Alberdi does not mince words: "If only Sarmiento had suspected that the nature of political power resides in the power of finance, then he would not have wasted his time, prattling his stupid and ridiculous theories of civilization and barbarism, of city and country."[7]

Perhaps the bitter dispute between Sarmiento and Alberdi might have been dissipated if a clearer definition of terms had been established. It should be remembered that there are two sides to the campo (countryside): cattle-grazing and agriculture. Only the former has the potential of giving birth to "barbarism." The latter, by virtue of its power to transform nature, is the matrix of the beginning stages of civilization. According to Alberdi, Sarmiento confuses "desert" with "countryside," and, therefore, barbarism for him begins the moment one leaves the city. Argentina is thus barbaric as a rule and civilized only in exceptional cases.

Alberdi also hastened to the defense of the gaucho. The producers of wealth are the rural communities. "Where wealth and opulence exist, civilization exists."[8] The services of the gaucho should be utilized, stressed Alberdi. "It is necessary to civilize the gaucho instead of offending him. He who does not understand this is inept."[9]

Neither *Facundo* nor its author inspired Alberdi. The book, he thought, was pernicious. It oozed satire and calumny against Argentina. Alberdi's criticism is vitriolic. "The gaucho whom Sarmiento labels 'barbarian' . . . is a better representative of European civilization than Sarmiento; the latter is a sterile, nonproductive worker who makes a pretense of being a lifetime employee of the State, which pays him to behave like a lackey to his boss."[10]

It is difficult to find epithets that are more unpleasant than those used by Alberdi to describe Sarmiento. Sarmiento, in Alberdi's lexicon, was a madman, an educated barbarian, Facundo II, servile, bilious in his writing, a disrupter of the nation, incapable of freedom, of indisputable mediocrity, a renowned author who did not know how to write because he did not know how to think.

Sarmiento was quick to respond and presented a veritable anthology of insults. Alberdi was a "dead soul" (*alma muerta*), possessed of a "dissipated nature," an "old maid in search of a husband," a shyster lawyer with a woman's voice, a scared rabbit, a political eunuch, the rickety hunchback of civilization.

On one occasion, perhaps without realizing the kind of impression that would be created, Sarmiento wrote the following: "I was the only officer in the Argentine army who sported European trappings: a saddle, spurs, polished sword, buttoned-up frock coat, gloves, French kepi, *paletot* instead of a poncho."[11] Of course, this was all the result of his craving for Europeanization or civilization. Alberdi, upon reading this, reacted accordingly:

> An officer in a South American army, wearing such an outfit, is a most curious figure . . . probably a source of great entertainment for the troops. A whole army of gauchos, dressed in this fashion, would probably produce a comedy so hilarious as to make them all split their sides laughing, and cause their guns to fall from their hands.[12]

On another occasion, Alberdi surpassed himself in his venomous criticism of *Facundo:*

> The book . . . is equivalent to a slaughterhouse, unfortunately, not of cattle, but rather, akin to a butcher shop of human flesh which, notwithstanding the neatness and flowers, and the white apron worn by the salesman in order to mask the horror of the blood, exudes a nauseating odor which completely upsets anyone unfamiliar with the business.[13]

Alberdi admitted that in all countries of the world the rural population is, generally, less advanced than its urban counterpart. Nevertheless, he was quick to point out that elements of progress and backwardness appear in varied proportions in *both* cases. In this connection it should be noted that, initially, *Facundo* created the impression that the pampas and the interior provinces were practically synonymous in that the provinces were also isolated and thus unable to benefit from the norms and values that prevailed in Buenos Aires.

In addition, it should be remembered that in the provincial cities, as opposed, for example, to Buenos Aires, a sort of "prebourgeoisie" arose. This class never developed fully because of the penetration of European and U.S. capitalism. It thus remained stagnant as an oligarchy, associated with foreign interests.

Perhaps this brings us to a more realistic view of the movement for independence, one that would be couched in terms of social and economic class conflict. Independence was the work of the rising bourgeoisie, and not of the city as such. The caudillos were opposed to the commercial class, not to the city. The class factor is corroborated by the fact that the lowest strata of the urban working class (the "lumpen proletariat") supported the caudillos.

It should also be recalled that historical factors that go back to the heritage of the mother country served to further complicate the differences between the Unitarians, who pressed for the hegemony of Buenos Aires, and the Federalists, who were in favor of autonomy for the provinces. Some Federalist "barbarians" were absolutists in the sense that they were opposed to the liberal Constitution of Cádiz, as were the Spaniards, who were the followers of Ferdinand VII. Rosas was called "Restorer of the Laws" (*Restaurador de las Leyes*). What laws, if none had been abolished? Restorer of absolutism would be more to the point. Other Federalists were liberals and proconstitution, but not in accord with the liberal Unitarians.

Sarmiento was not too attentive to these ideological differences. Was he aware that many inhabitants of the cities supported Rosas and that many individuals in the rural areas were opposed to the Restaurador and to absolutism? Many caudillos of the provincial cities were opposed to the policies of Buenos Aires, not because they were enemies of civilization but because they favored the federal idea of more autonomy for the provinces.

History has shown that cities, generally speaking, have been the transmitters of Western civilization in the New World. It has also been demonstrated that the American city tends to be more Europeanized or cosmopolitan than the countryside, and that the rural areas maintain for a much longer period of time the so-called authentic national character of the country. The true or ideal personality of a country (if this is at all a viable concept)—the true character—is a synthesis of the indigenous and the imported.

A curious sidelight, a contradiction perhaps, is the fact that Sarmiento, who painted the Argentine pampas and its inhabitants with such masterful strokes, had never—until he wrote *Facundo*—seen the pampas. Seven years later, he visited it as an army officer and noted with satisfaction the accuracy of his description.

Because of the vastness of the pampas and the scarcity of population, Sarmiento stressed the need for European immigration, thus coinciding with Alberdi's view. However, Sarmiento realized that this could easily lead to barbarism instead of contributing to civilization. Immigration had to be a carefully selective process, he maintained subsequently, thus predating José Enrique Rodó by more than half a century.

It may be the case that Sarmiento and Alberdi had more in common with each other than they believed. They both favored immigration for the good of the country. Alberdi's famous slogan, "to govern is to populate" (*gobernar es poblar*), complements Sarmiento's "educate the sovereign" (*educar al soberano*). It would seem, also, that the term "civilization" had more legal and cultural meaning for Sarmiento, whereas for Alberdi it was more economic and technical in its implications.

In spite of being so pro-European or pro–United States, Sarmiento argued heatedly in defense of the historic character of Argentine nationality in the face of a rootless cosmopolitanism, which he saw as a threat in the final decades of the nineteenth century. He insisted on the nationalization of the European immigrant, as though anticipating the criticism by nationalists, which developed subsequently.

Sarmiento's home environment was Federalist-oriented. However, he soon realized that the activities of the local caudillos were not at all in harmony with the federalist principles he had nurtured. He likewise concluded that the old hostility between Federalists and Unitarians was by then an anachronism, impatient as he was with the fanaticism of both parties. Rejecting the utopianism of the Unitarians, as this no longer satisfied him, his thinking gradually evolved toward a new kind of federalism; not that of Rosas, but more in keeping with the federalist ideas emanating from the United States. In this way, Sarmiento's brand of federalism could coincide, without much difficulty, with the progressive ideas of such Unitarians as Rivadavia. As far as Sarmiento was concerned, Rosas was neither a Federalist nor a Unitarian. Rosas represented the war waged by barbarism against civilization, not the conflict between Federalists and Unitarians. In spite of this, Sarmiento confessed on one occasion that the slogan "civilization and barbarism" was not always adequate or applicable "to all phases of the struggle, at all times and to all men."[14] On another occasion he observed that in the course of day-to-day existence, and when the chips are down, a person does not really know where one begins and the other ends.[15] And, as though to drive the point home, he repeated the observation when he saw Mrs. Horace Mann's English translation of *Facundo*, in which the phrase "Civilization and Barbarism" had been omitted from the title page. Perhaps this had been done, he mused, because one cannot always be certain as to exactly where barbarism is to be found.[16]

At times Sarmiento considered *Facundo* his best work. On other occasions he denigrated it, stating that he would gladly cast some of its pages into the fireplace. Continuing his ambivalence, he affirmed that *Facundo* was inspired in a moment of lyrical ecstasy, similar to the one that had produced a Moses or a Garibaldi. A strange work, he concluded, "without feet or head."[17] The man against whom *Facundo* was aimed,

Rosas, also had an opinion of the book. After reading it, Rosas was known to have exclaimed: "The book by that crazy Sarmiento is the best that has been written against me. That's the way to attack!"[18]

A final inconsistency must be considered. In accordance with the romantic temper of the times, Sarmiento attacked Spain violently. Only a Spaniard could criticize the mother country in such a fashion, or as the popular adage maintained: "If a man speaks ill of Spain, he must be a Spaniard."

Ricardo Rojas has written that Sarmiento was proud of the Spanish blood that coursed through his veins in spite of the diatribes he launched against the country of his forebears. Sarmiento thinks like an old hidalgo of Castile, writes Rojas, but speaks like a hero of republican Argentina.[19]

When Sarmiento visited Spain, he had some very unkind things to say about bullfights. Yet, after he had attended one, he wrote:

> I have seen the bulls, and experienced all their sublime attraction. A terrible, barbaric, bloody spectacle, but nevertheless, highly seductive and stimulating. Oh, what emotions! Man has need of emotions. A need which only the bulls can satisfy. . . . Much more so than any civilized spectacle can.[20]

Some of his impressions of U.S. cities seemed curious to him and are amusing to us. For example, he writes: "If you quietly smoke a cigar, a passerby will take it to light his own, and if you are not ready to take it back, he will personally put it back in your mouth.[21] On another occasion, when four individuals seated around a marble table invariably put their eight feet on it, Sarmiento concluded that North Americans have a cult for feet.

His observations concerning Montreal—a city where I have lived for the past two decades—drew my immediate attention. Sarmiento admired Montreal and considered it the most advanced city in the world, although he found the people embittered by what he thought was a futile battle between French and English elements.[22]

A rereading of some of Sarmiento's last pages reveals additional contradictions. As already mentioned, he who condemned the gaucho as being the epitome of what he called barbarism, prided himself on being the "gaucho of ideas." In the battle against the *montonera*, Sarmiento himself exhibited all the manifestations of a *montonero*. Although he detested caudillos, he boasted that they were all marked with his brand.

Sarmiento defended the Europeanized party of the Unitarians with all the aggressiveness and violence of the nativist, "barbarian" Federalists. Symbolically, underneath his swallow-tailed coat, he wore the *chiripá* used by the gaucho. In short, he was less the cultivated European that he wished to be, and more the gaucho than he knew. He liked to think of himself as a free thinker, yet he maintained that without religion there could be no ethics. He placed all his faith in elementary education as a panacea for the nation's progress, for which he was strongly criticized by Alberdi. Schooling was not enough to ensure material progress and civil liberties, Alberdi believed. The majority of the male inhabitants of Chile and Paraguay, e.g., know how to read, he argued, but they are far from being cultured individuals—a statement that could well be applied to the North American continent also.

There are several ways of reading *Facundo*. The first method utilizes the older, so-called liberal view, which speaks in terms of economic and educational reform. Then there is the revisionist orientation, which rejects this liberal ideology and considers Sarmiento a tool of foreign interests. Finally, there is the exclusively literary approach, which removes the text from the sociopolitical realm.

In this chapter I have cast aside the third approach. It appears to me to be a sterile exercise not to take into account the social milieu in which a work is produced. Instead, I have tried to combine elements from each of the other two approaches.

Sarmiento will continue to be criticized and reevaluated by friends and admirers and reviled and attacked violently by enemies and detractors. All strong-willed personalities are destined to suffer this fate. On this one hundredth anniversary of his death, after decades of turmoil, war, and dictatorship, Sarmiento's place in his country's history is still assured.

NOTES

1. Juan Pablo Echagü, *Páginas selectas, extraídas de sus obras* (Buenos Aires: Ediciones Argentinas S.I.A., 1945), 360.

2. Ibid., 359.

3. Quoted in Enrique Anderson Imbert, *Estudios sobre escritores de América* (Buenos Aires: Editorial Raigal, 1954), 53.

4. Cyril A. Jones, *Sarmiento: "Facundo"* ([London]: Grant and Cutler, 1974), 81.

5. Francis G. Crowley, *Domingo Faustino Sarmiento* (New York: Twayne Publishers, 1972), 72.

6. Ibid., 82.

7. Juan Bautista Alberdi, *Proceso a Sarmiento.* Foreword by León Pomer (Buenos Aires: Ediciónes Caldén, 1967), 9.

8. Ibid., 11.

9. Ibid.

10. Ibid., 33.

11. Luis Alberto Murray, *Pro y contra de Alberdi, y otros ensayos.* Foreword by Fermín Chávez, [2d ed.] (Buenos Aires: Editorial Sudestrada, 1969), 120–121.

12. Ibid.

13. Elizabeth Garrels, "El *Facundo* como folleto," *Revista Iberoamericana* 143 (April–June 1988): 426, n. 15.

14. Quoted in José S. Campobassi, *Sarmiento y su época* (2 vols., Buenos Aires: Editorial Losada, 1975), 1:221.

15. Milcíades Peña, *Alberdi, Sarmiento, el 90; Límites del nacionalismo argentino en el siglo XIX* (Buenos Aires: Ediciones Fichas, 1970), 71.

16. William H. Katra, *Domingo F. Sarmiento, Public Writer: Between 1839 and 1852* (Tempe: Center for Latin American Studies, Arizona State University, 1985), 129.

17. Campobassi, *Sarmiento,* 1:226.

18. Ibid., 1:227.

19. Conrado E. Eggers-Lecour, *Sarmiento; Estudio y antología* (Madrid: Compañía Bibliográfica Española S.A., 1963), 199.

20. Quoted in Dardo Cúneo, *Sarmiento y Unamuno,* 3rd ed. (Buenos Aires: Editorial Pleamar, 1963), 79.

21. Domingo F. Sarmiento, *Viajes* (3 vols., Buenos Aires: Hachette, 1955–1957), 2:358.

22. Crowley, *Sarmiento,* 96.

The Old Order and Its Crisis as Theme of *Recuerdos de Provincia*

Tulio Halperín Donghi

What is the intent of *Recuerdos de Provincia*?[1] Since its publication, readers have refused to believe what Sarmiento stated in the introduction, that it is addressed "Only to my compatriots." In fact, it was difficult to take seriously his claim that the presence in Santiago of an agent of the government of Buenos Aires, empowered to seek his extradition (something everyone knew had little prospect of success), represented a threat to his future in Chile. Those readers doubted that this laughable threat could force Sarmiento, already a successful public figure, to repeat the defense that he had offered in his first biographical sketch in 1843, when he was a newly arrived individual in the small journalistic world of Santiago. Discarding that scarcely believable justification, they preferred to see in *Recuerdos* a tremendous self-portrait with which Sarmiento was inaugurating the political campaign that, he was sure, would carry him to the pinnacle of power in the post-Rosas epoch—an epoch he thought was just about to begin in Argentina.

But the book itself is not organized along the lines that could be expected if its theme were the glorification, and not the defense, of its author; only half-way through it does Sarmiento begin to concern himself with himself. Unkind readers easily ascribed even that incongruence to his megalomania. They saw in it instead an exaggerated pause before he glorified his lineage in an excessively thorough evocation of the outstanding figures who had adorned it since the sixteenth century. Still, the version Sarmiento offers of "the colonial history of my family" does not accomplish particularly well the task that those unkind readers assigned to it.

To grasp this one needs only glance at the so-called "Genealogical chart of a family of San Juan de la Frontera, in the Argentine Republic."

Tulio Halperín Donghi is professor of history, University of California, Berkeley.

This "index to the book," which follows the introduction, succinctly presents the trajectory of the Sanjuanino lineage, founded at the beginning of the colony by Bernardino Albarracín, "Maestre de Campo." The family was currently represented, on one side, by Paula and Rosario Sarmiento, "workers in embroidery, textiles, etc.," and on the other, by Procesa Sarmiento, "artist, disciple of Monvoisin"; Bienvenida Sarmiento, "director of various girls' schools"; and, of course, Domingo F. Sarmiento, member of learned societies and public service associations of the Old and New Worlds, director of and contributor to newspapers, and author "of a series of works on elementary education adopted by the University of Chile."[2]

This summary of three centuries of family history does not invoke enjoyment of the pride derived from an exalted ancestry. Rather, it clarifies the problems produced by a trajectory that started at the summit of San Juan society and that at present dangerously approaches its most intimate fringes.

Thus, it is not necessary to conclude that those readers had erred in recognizing among the central objectives of *Recuerdos* the exaltation of the figure of its author. This objective would be achieved less obviously precisely by exploiting the problem that, though revealed through his family history, does not affect it alone. The very title of the genealogical chart—presented not as the author's, but as that of "a family of San Juan de la Frontera"—regains for Sarmiento that broader significance.[3] *Recuerdos* is an unceasing defense of the "memory of *his* kin who deserved the gratitude of the fatherland," his province, and the "humble home in which he *was* born." It is also—as the last pages affirm—an example of the biographical genre to which *Facundo* belongs. The fact that the principal biographee is this time the author himself does not establish a difference in essence between the two works.[4]

Saying that *Recuerdos* and *Facundo* are two examples of the same genre does not do complete justice to the extremely complex relations between the 1845 work and the 1850 one. This is not surprising, given Sarmiento's disinclination to spend time critically examining his own work. He shows little interest in its literary quality, as can be observed in his commentaries on its successes. These commentaries are characterized by a conciseness entirely anomalous with him. (Thus he limits himself to mentioning in passing that his *Apuntes biográficos* of Father Aldao is a "little work very well liked by the intelligent as a literary composition.")[5] He does not even occupy himself with providing an adequate account of the motivations and justifications that underlay it. Among the reasons Sarmiento gives in the introduction to *Recuerdos* for prefering the biographical genre is that biography is "the most adequate cloth on which to print good ideas" and whoever writes one "exercises a type of judgship, punishing triumphant vice, encouraging hidden virtue."[6] This characterization, valid for the one on Aldao, but already inadequate for *Facundo,* once more defines very poorly the purpose of *Recuerdos.*

The function of the biographical narrative is, in reality, quite different in Sarmiento's two major books. Both deal, by means of a character or group of characters, with unlocking a totality of feeling that is the creation of a collective historical experience. But it is not only the ultimate goal of *Recuerdos* that puts it on the same level as *Facundo.* In the latter, Sarmiento had elaborated an entire set of expository resources suitable to that goal, which revealed an unexpected literary skill, quickly appreciated as such by his readers. Sarmiento does not fail to notice that, although he sees himself primarily as a political publicist, many of his readers regard him above all as a producer of literature, and he glories in that in *Recuerdos.* That public offers him not only applause but also indications about which features of his work it best appreciates. Among these is the evocative force that Sarmiento gives to the description of an individual or collective way of life and to the setting in which it unfolds.

In fact, it would be dangerous to ignore what Sarmiento tells us about his relations with the public (and, in particular, the Argentine) just because what moves him to say it is the desire to exalt himself. Thus, his claim that Don Pedro de Angelis, the erudite Italian in Rosas's service, was proclaiming his admiration for the precise description of the pampas in *Facundo,* becomes more credible when one learns that the young Doctor Bernardo de Irigoyen was trying to obtain from Mendoza a copy of *Recuerdos* in order to send it to that other promising member of the rosista intelligentsia—his then-friend Rufino de Elizalde, an official in the Ministry of Foreign Relations of Buenos Aires.[7] Sarmiento was more disposed to continue producing the descriptive and evocative *pezzi di bravura* that the public admired mainly because these offered the best vehicle for the historicosocial vision he wished to communicate to them. In this way, the prestige that *Facundo* acquired as a literary model in the eyes of its author is confirmed in its role as a model for *Recuerdos* at levels that now are no longer those of literature.

But the weight of that model does not prevent the exploration undertaken in *Recuerdos* from traveling a very different road from that of *Facundo.* This is reflected in the different way in which they each work to combine an eminently practical objective, that make them both instruments of the fight against the rosista dictatorship, with the theorist ambition of uncovering the secret of what the first work had called the Argentine sphinx. In both, the articulation between those two objectives is not free of problems. However, in *Facundo* they originate in the unresolved contradiction between the announcement of universal reconciliation inscribed in the third part (which has the eminently practical purpose of persuading those who support the regime that Sarmiento opposes that they have nothing to fear from its downfall) and the grand evocation in the two first parts of a reality split down to its roots into irreconcilably hostile hemispheres. In *Recuerdos* it is less easy to mark the precise point at which the problem becomes evident. More than by any contradiction, the relation between those two objectives seems affected here by the doubtful relevance that the knotty problem explored in the new work presents for the obligations of political battle.

This discontinuity between Sarmiento's practical and theoretical objectives occurs in part because the latter do not appear in *Recuerdos* as clearly as in *Facundo*. It is perhaps revealing that the 1850 book lacks something equivalent to the invocation of Quiroga's shadow that opened *Facundo* and that had hidden under its excited oratorical flight a coherent "idea of the book." This announced the precise itinerary of the exploration undertaken in it to uncover the secret of the Argentine sphinx.

True, attenuated and unconnected echoes of the interpretive effort so vigorously sketched and justified in *Facundo* crop up again in *Recuerdos*. They appear in excessively concise sentences like the one in which Sarmiento points out that "the appearance of the soil has shown me at times the physiognomy of the men, and these almost always indicate the road that events have had to take." Notations like this seem to forecast the return to the route followed in 1845. Beginning the book with the description of a specific place (that corner of semidemolished houses, dominated by a few giant palms, stronghold in the past of the "first families which made up the old colonial aristocracy") reminds us of the descriptive and evocative techniques of *Facundo* and seems also to promise a route parallel to the one followed then.

But it is a promise destined not to be fulfilled. This time geography makes only a fleeting appearance in that initial picture, to yield the foreground immediately to history. In fact, the very brief evocation of a place leads to a summoning of the now almost-erased footsteps. In these we can trace a vanished past, from the palm trees themselves, brought from Chile by the first conquerors, to "a broken down . . . door . . . where there were once encrusted lead letters, and in its center the sign of the Company of Jesus," and in the nearby house of the Godoys, equally ruined, a folder whose label reads: "This file contains the 'History of Cuyo' by the Abbé Morales, a topographical and descriptive map of Cuyo, and the testimonies of Mallea," though it now contains only the latter.[8]

In *Facundo* the evocation would have served as a point of departure to explore the configuration of an equally precise way of life. In *Recuerdos* it gives way immediately to the complaint about the damage done by time, reflecting very well all that will separate the dominant perspective in *Recuerdos* from that of *Facundo*. In *Facundo* the literal and metaphorical keys referred to a spatial key. Even when the conflict that was tearing apart the Rioplatense provinces was presented as being that between the eleventh and nineteenth centuries, those two periods designated two historical configurations that were strictly contemporaneous in Argentina. They were rooted, in turn, in two rival places, and were understood in a totally literal sense as two spaces in which the very body of the nation was divided: the city and the rural interior. This conception of a spatial key to the conflict will never lose its importance for Sarmiento. Even in his writings at the end of the decade, from *Viajes* to *Educación popular*, he resorts to the metaphor of the siege of the fortress of civilization that is the city by a barbarous mass settled in the outskirts (whether it is the ever swelling ocean of the poor in a rapidly growing Santiago or of the then submissive droves mobilized by the Industrial Revolution in Europe).

Alongside this interpretative perspective it is possible to discover at a second level another—one that sought its clues to the same problem on a temporal rather than a spatial axis. Thus, *Facundo* does not avoid the theme of the decadence of the city of La Rioja. But in *Facundo* this decadence is the unfortunate result of the defeat of a historical subject rooted in a space—the city, the territory of civilization—in its battle with another subject that is its irreconcilable rival, the other space, that of the rural interior, the redoubt of barbarism.

It is precisely this relationship between these two interpretative outlooks that has been inverted in *Recuerdos*. The theme elicited by the destroyed and fragmented testimonies of a brilliant past with which the work opens is again that of decadence. Now, however, decadence is not the result of external defeat, but the punishment that time implacably inflicts on those who do not know how to go forward with it. In this way, an aspect of the Argentine catastrophe that certainly had been considered in *Facundo*, but was decidedly relegated to second place, comes to the foreground. In *Facundo*, Sarmiento deplored the opposition in the very bosom of the cities that arose in response to the innovations introduced during the revolution and he deplored the reforming fickleness of the Unitarian party. But he then had reproached that opposition less for its misoneistic orientation than for the factious obsession that had made it initiate a suicidal alliance with the barbarous besieger.

In *Recuerdos* the decadence is not the result of a defeat from ambushes from outside, and Sarmiento is so persuaded of the validity of this perspective that he does not notice that the first example he offers to validate it is inappropriate. The example is that of the Huarpes, an "important and large" nation of indigenes, that inhabited the valleys of Tulum Mogna and Jachal and the Guanacache lakes.

> The historian Ovalle, who visited Cuyo sixty years after [the conquest], speaks of a grammar and a book of Christian prayers in the Huarpe

!anguage, of which the only vestiges that remain among us are the cited names, and Puyuta, name of a neighborhood, and Angaco, Vicuña, Villicún, Huanacache, and a few others.[9]

In order to deduce from the Huarpes' history the moral that already can be guessed, Sarmiento is willing to forget the role the Spanish conquest played in their ruin. It is not surprising that in exploring San Juan's decadence he does not attribute the decisive role in the city's conquest that he had assigned in the past (and would assign again in the future) to Quiroga's guerrilla plainsmen. On the contrary, this decadence acknowledges the same roots as its predecessors who controlled the land of San Juan, and the book states further:

> Ay to the nations that don't progress! They do not only stay behind! Three centuries have been sufficient for the Huarpes to be erased from the catalogue of nations. Ay to you, colonists, backward Spaniards! Less time is needed for you to have descended from a confederated province to a hamlet, from a hamlet to a vineyard district, from a vineyard district to an inhabited forest. Before you had wealthy people among you. . . . Now you are all poor! Wise men . . . theologians . . . politicians . . . governors . . . today you do not even have schools, and at the top the very people who govern you parade their own barbarism. Down from general ignorance there is another step, general poverty, and you already have taken it. The step that follows is into the shadows, and peoples disappear at once, without it being known where they went and when they left![10]

This was not the first time that Sarmiento found that this hard corollary of his faith in historical progress required incorporation into its constantly more frenetic rhythm a condition of collective survival. In 1843, he had commented on *Research on the Social Influence of the Conquest and the Colonial System of the Spaniards in Chile*, by his friend, J. V. Lastarria. Sarmiento was convinced that progress occurred in accord with "immutable laws." In obedience to these laws, through countless crimes and injustices, "the strong races exterminate the weak, the civilized nations supplant the savages in the possession of the land." This did not prevent Sarmiento from proclaiming the spectacle, whose gloomy underside he did nothing to dissemble, as "providential, sublime, and grand."[11]

That vision, at once desolate and enthusiastic about the march of history, is again dominant in *Recuerdos de provincia*. It offers a central argument for a work that is nostalgic about a dead world, which seems paradoxical at first sight. As soon as one examines how that attitude is articulated in *Recuerdos*, with this passionately futurist argument, it is clear that both reciprocally support each other. The old San Juan had been the victim of its inability to change as rapidly as the new times demanded. It is undeniably a fault, but any alternative explanation of the decadence that Sarmiento proposed to explore would have required a confrontation with San Juan's other more serious failings.

That nostalgic ambiance makes Sarmiento's resistance to criticizing the descendants of the now abolished San Juan entirely understandable. It is apparent in one of the first chapters of *Recuerdos*, entitled "The Sons of Mallea." In it is a narrative of the history of old Don Fermín Mallea and his clerk, *"the young Oro . . . so honest and laborious* that Mallea . . . had to make him a partner in his business." After ten years, during which Don Fermín withdrew funds without counting them, and his partner *"had touched nothing,"* a balance sheet reveals that all of the business now belonged to the former clerk. Don Fermín, desolate and furious, began an interminable suit against his former protégé, whose *"suave and loveable nature* could not resist such a difficult test"; *"the sad [one] died of sorrow seeing the injustice done to him by his friend and protector,"* who for his part found in insanity a refuge against remorse. Sarmiento believes he knows who is to blame for the tragic conclusion of that provincial tragedy—the courts of justice: "in them, in the general ignorance, in the torpor of the judges, in the unbridled passions that a system of iniquity which has crime written on its forehead, starting all of its acts with the ritual *mueran . . . ,* incites instead of containing."[12]

This scarcely convincing conclusion doubtless reflects the already noted distance between the practical political purpose and the theoretical ambition of *Recuerdos*. It makes it more difficult for Sarmiento to find good maxims to be thrown in the face of the enemy in the polemics of the day. But the aprioristic decision to blame political enemies is outweighed by the need to defend at any cost the innocence of a descendant of old San Juan. To proclaim Mallea's innocence, Sarmiento will assert unconvincingly that Mallea possesses certain generic qualities in his heart that his behavior fails to confirm: he is (as he does not hesitate to tell us) "of gruff character and unbearable temper," and "he had made it obvious in his youth." Sarmiento refuses to see in the stubbornness with which the irascible old man rejects the rendition of accounts presented by his former clerk and later very honest partner anything worse than "the obstinacy of character and unrestrained passions that the injustice and ineptitude of the judges he did not know how or wish to restrain." Sarmiento even limits the significance of these more attenuating negative features by presenting them as "temperamental characteristics that did not go as far as tarnishing some very laudable endowments of the heart," again not a very convincing conclusion but not for that less significant.

This is not the only occasion in which such personal traits are invoked to dispel shadows on the portraits of survivors of the colonial elite. (They occupy an even more prominent place in the more detailed portraits of Don José and Don Domingo de Oro.) The price is that it reduces the most characteristic features of an individual to mere eccentricities. Such arbitrary irrationality makes the characters inaccessible to the analytical focus that in *Facundo* had permitted reading in them the revealing signs of the peculiarities of the historicosocial context in which they had been forged. Nothing less than this renunciation of the most powerful hermeneutic tool that Sarmiento relied upon to unveil the mystery of the Argentine sphinx was required to secure the monolithic innocence of the heirs of the San Juan of yesterday in the misfortunes that followed its decline.

Sarmiento's refusal to interpret the characteristics that define the Sanjuanina elite who survived the revolutionary torment from a historicosocial perspective has more limited consequences than that which equally hobbled the exploration of colonial San Juan. Sarmiento did not give it the same scrutinizing look he directed at post-revolutionary Argentina in *Facundo* because his beloved San Juan was branded by the iron of Spanish colonization. Sarmiento had always condemned the colonization and in *Recuerdos* it is still the object of a decidedly negative judgment. In its pages, as in those of *Facundo*, a preferred argument presents rosista Argentina as the revenge of the colony, the legacy of which the revolution has not been able to eradicate.[13]

To protect this golden isle of memory from a determined attempt to trace the roots of its present degradation to the Spanish past is less easy than to present its surviving heirs in the abominable Argentina of 1830 or 1850 as misguided innocents in a world whose intrinsic iniquity they have the good fortune of not understanding. The accomplishments of colonial San Juan, which Sarmiento evokes nostalgically, are those of a civilization upon which he continues to cast his condemnation. Thus, his impassioned identification with a founding elite composed of landowners, *encomenderos,* and theologians can only be maintained by enveloping in a charitable cloud features that he has used to build images more filled with historical substance than when he focuses on realities with which he feels less tied. It would therefore be useless to look in *Recuerdos* for a picture of the old San Juan—like that of Córdoba in *Facundo*—without failing to do justice to the prodigious and articulated complexity of the object that Sarmiento evokes. He maintains a punctilious critical distance, which makes it less surprising to see him burst into a passionate appeal for its destruction. He invokes all of this with an intuitive immediacy that is capable of giving the reader the illusion of reliving it from within.

To elude a similar exploration, which might reveal to him what he perhaps would prefer not to find out, Sarmiento will take a path that is somewhat different from the one based on a personal, nontransferable arbitrariness. This explains the conduct of Don Fermín Mallea and is especially clear in the discussion of the episode that dragged Friar Miguel Albarracín to the courtrooms of the Inquisition of Lima. The episode opens with a rich and precise description of a historical frame presented now as absolutely relevant. Friar Miguel, pride of the maternal family of Sarmiento, is a son of that "Middle Ages of the colonization of the Americas [in which] the letters were sheltered in the monasteries." As might be expected, the characterization of his dreaded antagonist, the Tribunal of the Holy Office, is less cursory. Long paragraphs examine the role it filled in cloistering the Hispanic world from foreign influences as well as the weight that its legacy maintains in the Hispanic America of 1850, especially in rosista Argentina.

Sarmiento looks at that tribunal with the eyes of a fervent believer in the liberal civilization of the nineteenth century. As such, he emphasizes it so as to condemn both the role it performed as the agent of the colonial regime and of Spanish xenophobia:

> The Inquisition of Lima was a phantom of terror which Spain had sent to America to intimidate *foreigners*, the only heretics it feared . . . among whom there is a Juan Salado, French, who was burned without any other rational cause than the novelty of being French.

The tribunal's role was revealed by the pompous cruelty of its spectacles, marked with the stamp of "the horribly puerile customs of that epoch."[14]

Even in this presentation, however, we see gradually emerging dissonances from the somber and pathetic tone preferred in the middle of the nineteenth century for evoking the Holy Tribunal and its victims. These will come together at the end in an arrangement, as a sort of sarcastic counterpoint to the contrite recreation of the crimes of fanaticism. As Judaizing and heretical foreigners were not abundant, Sarmiento tells us,

> the Inquisition fed itself from time to time on some old pious woman who sought communication with the Virgin Mary, through the intermediation of angels and seraphims, or some other less delicate type who preferred to deal with the fallen angel. . . . When the reputation of holiness or devilry reached its peak, the Holy Tribunal fell on the unhappy wretch, and after a long and erudite process, made of her thin body an agreeable and lively nourishment for the flames to the great contentment of the populace, employees and high clergy, who attended the ceremony by the thousands.[15]

This ironic language reflects a rejection of what Sarmiento now presents as a ludicrous exercise of gratuitous cruelty rather than as a crime of fanaticism. It does not prevent Sarmiento from slipping from one to the other interpretive key as he did when he postulated personal character as the basic reason for certain characteristics of the San Juan elite that he found difficult to justify otherwise. He again refuses to look for the key to that capricious cruelty in the secret rationality of the historical setting. Only when Sarmiento's subtle labor has deprived a good part of the Spanish historical background of much of its clarity does he decide to introduce into his narrative the encounter of Friar Miguel Albarracín and his inquisitorial judges.

In presenting the reasons that brought Friar Miguel to the attention of the fearful superior Lima tribunal, Sarmiento displays an attitude that is even closer to the one that dominated the history of Don Fermín Mallea and his clerk. Sarmiento again explicitly considers the presence in the historicosocial field of an area of stubborn arbitrariness impenetrable to the hermeneutic instruments masterly employed in *Facundo*.

> There are rare manias—we read in the passage that introduces us at last to the episode—that trouble the human spirit in certain epochs; curiosities of thought that come without one knowing why, as if in the presence of events was indicated the ability to satisfy them. The philosophers' stone, which chemistry produced in Europe, was followed in America by the famous question of the millennium, in which even a Saint Vincent Ferrer had been left bewildered.

Friar Miguel himself had "applied his sagacity to solve so arduous a problem," in a folio whose "daring doctrines" he now had to defend in the courtrooms of the Holy Office.[16]

What follows suggests that what is important here is Sarmiento's disinclination to analyze the sudden rebirth of speculations about the millennium. True, he stresses that "a few years after the appearance of the millenarians, the revolution for the independence of South America appeared, as if that theological longing had been only a presage of the next commotion,"[17] but the path that this observation invites taking will not be followed. Sarmiento is not interested in unveiling the secret rationality perhaps hidden behind that rare mania, since he discards the idea that it would have enlightened the protagonists of the episode or endowed their conduct with meaning. Only retrospectively, in fact, would the ties between those ravings about the *ultimissima* and the crisis of the Spanish empire be made evident.

Sarmiento admits that in the intensity of the debates about the millennium a symptom of the future revolution can be recognized. However, he insists that in spite of that the rivals in those debates were disputing about what was for them pure nonsense. In the case of Friar Miguel, "according to what I believe," Sarmiento tells us, "neither he nor the Inquisition *understood* above all one iota about all that medley of conjectures."[18] That does not prevent him, though, from including the victory achieved by Friar Miguel on the terrible stage of the Lima tribunal in that inventory of family glories that *Recuerdos de provincia* wants to be.

If the inclusion is not strictly justified, it is because it need not be. It is as if—thanks to the replacement of an authentically critical distance by another very different distance that protects him under the double veil of nostalgia and irony—Sarmiento had succeeded in seeing the episode with the eyes of the protagonists and their contemporaries. It is the criteria that they share that he invokes to explain the triumph that Friar Miguel reaped in Lima: "Fortunately, they say, the friar was as eloquent as a Cicero, whose language he possessed without rival; profound as a Thomas, subtle as a Scotus." Notice how that nostalgic identification, far from renouncing ironic distance, is built on it. The readers of *Recuerdos* did not need to be reminded that Sarmiento did not appreciate any more than they the subtlety of Duns Scotus or the profundity of Saint Thomas Aquinas. Further, he had never concealed how completely he considered it noxious to waste effort in learning dead languages. But this ironic distance, rather than opening the way to a critical attitude, becomes an effective barrier against it. That is apparent as soon as one examines the point at which Sarmiento judges it necessary to assume an explicit distance in the face of the collective pride inspired in his family by the memory of the great Friar Miguel.

Sarmiento's family was convinced that the San Juan region had been fraudulently deprived of the leading role in the rebirth of millenarian speculations by the exiled Chilean Jesuit Lacunza, whose *Return of the Messiah in Glory and Majesty* had been published in London. Recalled Sarmiento,

> My uncle Friar Pascual, seeing me an able child and anxious for knowledge, explained the work of Lacunza to me, telling me with indignant pride: "Study this book, which is the work of the great Friar Miguel, my uncle, and not of Lacunza, who stole the authorship, taking the manuscript from the archives of the Inquisition, where it remained deposited." And then he showed me the allusion which Lacunza makes to a work about the millennium by an American author that he did not dare to cite. Afterwards I have come to believe that family vanity made my uncle unjust with poor Lacunza.[19]

The most notable aspect of this distance taking is the firmness with which Sarmiento refuses to submit to a historicocritical perspective the material that family tradition has fashioned to augment its own glory. That perspective would have been less concerned with knowing whether those apocalyptical commentaries were Lacunza's or Friar Miguel's and more in explaining how it was possible that, in a country that ten years earlier had adopted the political language of the representative republic, and where for a quarter of a century the intellectual elites had begun to articulate a new vision of society under the notion of the nascent political economy, those texts could have been recommended as valid objects of study for a boy "able and anxious for knowledge." The counsel of Friar Pascual is based on criteria that lend themselves admirably to examination from a perspective analogous to the one that dominated the description of Córdoba presented in *Facundo,* but of course they were not so examined.

If the description of the encounter of Friar Miguel with the Inquisition still requires an ironic distance, in the passages that follow in the chapter entitled "The Albarracines," admiration now overcomes all reticence. The discussion is that of the wealthy Doña Antonia Irarrazábal and her incomparable life-style, which shows her surrounded by a

> covey of Negro slaves of both sexes. In the gilded bedroom of Doña Antonia two young slave girls slept to watch over her sleep. At meal time, an orchestra of violins and harps, composed of six slaves, played sonatas to enliven the banquet of their masters. . . . [She] frequently rode horseback, preceded and followed by slaves, to look over her vineyards. . . . Once or twice a year . . . the great patio [was] covered with hides on which thick layers of blackened *pesos fuertes* were put out in the sun, to clean the tarnish from them, and two old Negroes . . . walked from hide to hide carefully turning over the clinking silver grains.[20]

Here Sarmiento appears to anticipate that his reader may find shocking what he himself finds admirable. Without taking explicit responsibility for the skeptical reactions that his idyllic portrait of an order based on slavery might provoke, Sarmiento answers them implicitly in his commentary on that incongruous scene in which slaves grown old in servitude still devote themselves to restoring luster to the wealth of their mistress. This invites admiration for the presence of the "patriarchal customs of those times in which slavery did not debase the good qualities of the loyal Negro!"

The refusal to take any critical distance is also maintained in the face of the economic criteria that underlay the life-style of Doña Antonia. Once more her capricious arbitrariness makes them impenetrable to any historical analysis. ("It was the mania of the colonists to hoard peso upon peso and to be proud of it."[21]) That impenetrability makes it impossible, and therefore unnecessary, to explore the possible nexuses between the modalities of past opulence and the recent fall into the most extreme penury, such as had already begun to appear in some examinations of the problems of independent Hispanic America. Rather than exploring possible continuities between colonial splendor and a present of ruin and decadence, Sarmiento prefers to underline the contrast between both. They are symbolized by him in the homes of the *Dulce nombre de María,* which offered "sumptuous lodging to the rich and powerful Doña Antonia," and are "degraded today by necessity to being used, because of their large size, as barracks for the troops." This permits repetition of a moral that we have already heard: "What has happened, oh settlers, to that wealth of your grandfathers? And you, federal governors, military executioners of the people, could you gather by crushing, torturing, an entire town, the amount of pesos that no more than sixty years ago was contained on just the patio alone of Doña Antonia Irarrazábal?"

Common sense suggests why Sarmiento refused to examine historically (that is, critically) the family legacy that unites him with the Albarracines, Oros, and Irarrazábales. Together with an affective identification too deep to permit it, the least tolerant readers of *Recuerdos* could not fail to notice Sarmiento's wish to wrap himself in his inherited glitter. This wish is reflected in the tone of dynastic pride that stands out in passages like this:

> The heads of this family [the Albarracines] founded the monastery of Santo Domingo in San Juan, and even up to today has maintained its patronage and the feast of the Saint, whom we all have been accustomed to call Our Father. There is a Domingo in each of the branches in which the family is subdivided . . . and until the closing of the monastery in 1825, there was among its choristers a representative of the patron family of the order.[22]

Here is a conclusion that would be inconvertible evidence, were it not that it is precisely in the passages dedicated to his parents that this bond reaches its maximum intimacy. At this point, Sarmiento suddenly abandons the reticence that had prevented him from paying fuller attention to the historical context of his family story.

The discontinuities in this attention are incomprehensible when one seeks to explain them exclusively by basing them on the sentimental identification with that past that Sarmiento would retain, or of how he uses it to develop the image of himself presented in *Recuerdos*. But they are better understood when one remembers what aspects of his legacy are protected by such reticences from any historicocritical scrutiny. Under its cover will remain, as already indicated, all that makes San Juan a typical example of Spanish colonization in America. Because he speaks of old San Juan with the voice of the family tradition that he had sucked in his infancy, Sarmiento can present an out-of-focus image made from those controversial aspects of the colonial experience of San Juan. It is an image by someone who views it from—if one can put it that way—too close up.

That image of colonial San Juan does not sketch in those characteristics of the civilization forged by Spain in the old land of the Huarpe that the new liberal civilization would most quickly find upsetting. Thus, Sarmiento can identify himself unhesitatingly with a prominent lineage. He sees its eminent position in the hierarchical and unequal society of the Old Order reflected as much in the somewhat tenuous ties of the exploits of the Great Captain, General José de San Martín, in Italy, as in the immense deserted *latifundias* and the *encomiendas* of Indians that brought luster at the onset of the San Juan phase in his family history and the civil and ecclesiastical prebends accumulated later.

In such a way the image of the setting that would have made this trajectory of his lineage historically intelligible was corroded. It offers only the gorgeous, ennobling backdrop for a family that only reached the real level of history when it was integrated into the context of the final crisis of the Old Order. In that context, finally explored in all of its ambiguity and contradictory richness, we now look for the key to the complex equilibrium that reigns in the home founded by Paula Albarracín and José Clemente Sarmiento. Sarmiento describes the equilibrium as the tension between the still firm colonial heritage and the fragmentary outlines of a new way of living together that appears fugitively throughout the revolutionary storm. Sarmiento explains that he was attracted simultaneously in his childhood by "contradictory impulses"; "through my mother . . . the colonial vocations; through my father the ideas and preoccupations of that revolutionary epoch slipped in." While she expected to see him become a "cleric and priest of San Juan, in imitation of my uncle, [I saw on] my father uniforms, galloons, sabers, and other trifles."[23] Those two rival influences are far from being of equal force in Sarmiento's immediate surroundings. On the contrary, the short text cited here anticipates what Sarmiento's story of his childhood and youth will confirm: that he is above all the son of his mother.

In a world divided by the revolution into irreconcilable hemispheres, the predominant maternal influence had inscribed him in that of the colony. Sarmiento's recognition of this is prepared by, and made less disagreeable to a public little disposed even in its most conservative fringes to receive any open apology for the colonial order, the examination (performed now with the same hermeneutical instruments employed in *Facundo*) of the impact that the crisis of the Old Order had produced on his most immediate family, even before the revolution itself would impose a violent outcome on it. In "The Story of My Mother," this perspective, fully historical for the first time, will dominate the exploration of "the genealogy of those sublime moral ideas that were the wholesome atmosphere that my soul breathed while it was developing in the family home."[24]

Sarmiento wanted to find out "who had educated *his* mother," and he was going to find the answer to that question in "the history of a man of God," Don José Castro, Sanjuanino cleric and author of a "religious reform attempted in an obscure province, where it is still well preserved in many privileged souls."[25] That reform was not only religious. This "ascetic saint," adorned with "the piety of a Christian of the most beautiful times" was at the same time a philosopher, the nature of whose conversations leads Sarmiento to suspect that he knew "his eighteenth century, his Rousseau, his Feijóo." Castro, while he purified the life of the devout of "absurd, cruel, and superstitious practices," resistant until then to "sane reason," also swept away the superstitious beliefs "pursuing them with ridicule and patient, scientific explanation, made from the pulpit, of the natural phenomena that gave rise to those errors." Castro's action even extended to other spheres: "Perhaps with *Emilio* hidden under his cassock, he taught mothers how to raise children, the practices that were harmful to health, the way to care for the sick, the concerns that the pregnant women should keep in mind." The miracles of this saint were those of science. In a scene that evokes the resurrections referred to in the Gospel, he ordered a magnate at whose solemn funeral he was officiating to rise up, because he trusted in the correctness of the conclusions that "his knowledge of the art of healing" suggested to him upon examining the face of the supposed cadaver.

In *Recuerdos*, the Old Order only begins to be seen historically when it undertakes, under the aegis of Rousseau, its own redemption in the crucible of the reform in whose "healthy atmosphere" Sarmiento's soul is going to be formed. This Old Order therefore contains its own revolution within itself, and through it has validated the legitimacy of the life-style forged by colonizer Spain. Perhaps for this reason Sarmiento, who wants to be a man very much of his time, will lavish in this chapter allusions to behaviors that are part of that style. When the premonition of his mother's death struck him on his trip to Vesuvius, he tells us, he bought "in Rome a requiem Mass," so that it would be sung in her honor by "my pupils, the boarding students of Saint Rosa," whose school had its headquarters in the old convent where his family had exercised the patronage in colonial times. And when—after telling how he found a way of pouring out his pain and his filial piety in ways prescribed by the Old Order—he asks for a posthumous recognition of the Socrates of San Juan, he again proposes a way of honoring him that is very much in the same line: "I recommend to my uncle, the bishop of Cuyo," Sarmiento in fact says upon concluding his evocation of Don José Castro, "to get hold of this relic and keep it in a place of worship."

Surrounded now by a devotion born of the most traditional piety, Castro also deserves to receive the devout homage of the combatants for the new liberal civilization. (Without perceiving any irony in it, Sarmiento notes that Castro's sister has been exhibiting the remains of the disciple of Rousseau "to people who obtained so much grace" and edified themselves by confirming that "the action of the tomb [had] respected his body, as it usually does with the bodies that had sheltered the soul of a saint."[26]) The moral genealogy that Sarmiento has constructed thus suggests a continuity between an Old Order in the process of self-regeneration and the future Argentine regeneration of which the author of *Recuerdos* presents himself as leader.

That continuity has been broken, however, and what broke it was the war of independence. The story of the priest Castro, whose preaching of a peaceful revolution of the spirits was brutally interrupted by the less peaceful political revolution, threatens to cast an ambiguous light over the latter. Sarmiento tells us that

> when the revolution broke out in 1810, still young, liberal, well-educated as he was, [Don José Castro] declared himself openly in favor of the king, excoriating from the pulpit that had been his instrument for popular education, against disobedience to the legitimate sovereign, predicting wars, demoralization and disasters, which unfortunately time has confirmed. The patriotic authorities found it necessary to impose silence on that powerful counterrevolutionary; the persecution fattened on him; for his obstinacy he was exiled to Brucas of sad memory, and from there he returned to San Juan on foot, and there, in poverty, in obscurity, forsaken and ignored by all, he died kissing alternatively the crucifix and the portrait of Ferdinand VII, the Desired.[27]

It is that neglect that Sarmiento invites his uncle the bishop to remedy by giving a place in his cathedral to the remains of the Sanjuanino saint, "so that his ashes receive reparation for the offenses that the fatal necessities of the times made to his person."

This long passage, which culminates in the vindication of a posthumous triumph for an enemy and victim of the revolution, appears even more significant because it is the only one in *Recuerdos* that confronts the central knot of the conflict that ended the Old Order. Should it be therefore deduced that *Recuerdos* contains a secret counterrevolutionary moral? This was clearly not Sarmiento's intention. Even more than the polemic against the federalism in power, which by denouncing federalism as responsible for the postrevolutionary decadence of Argentina distracts attention from the search for any other less obvious source of blame the irreversibility of the revolutionary process (the incontrovertible point of departure and term of reference for any viable political enterprise in independent Hispanic America) prevents such a counterrevolutionary moral. It is not surprising that Sarmiento, in order to justify his resistance to undertake a different type of exploration that might also open him up to some not very pleasant surprises, once more invokes the presence in the sociohistorical reality of a zone of capricious arbitrariness for which it would be idle to look for any hidden rationality. He only mentions the antirevolutionary position of Castro—he assures us—"to point out one of the rare combinations of ideas."

By underlining the hesitations and contradictions present in the image of the Old Order that *Recuerdos* offers, and the image it suggests of the revolution, is not to suggest that these corroded images poorly conceal the power of another image that Sarmiento did not perhaps dare confess even to himself. In this image, nostalgia for the colonial past would have found its corollary in identification with the Old Order. It is more likely that the confusion that these images reflect expresses the frustration awakened by everything that the first retrospective look at the revolutionary epoch discovers. It reveals equally the ambiguities of the emancipating process and those of its relation to an Old Order, the memory of which is still capable of being recalled as quite different from those of the brutally simplified portraits offered by the publicists of the cause of independence.

But it does not seem sufficient to conclude that Sarmiento has resigned himself to the presence of an uneliminable element of ambiguity in both his image of the Old Order and the revolution. It could better be said that he treasures this ambiguity. And it is understandable: *Recuerdos de provincia* is simultaneously the introduction of a candidate and of a program for action. Because it is the former, it dedicates so much space to exalting the legacy that Sarmiento has received from the Old Order and from the revolution. As for the latter, it is precisely the contradictions that tear at each one of them and the absence of a reconciliation between them that open a wide field of action to the one who offers himself as a future protagonist of the history whose threshold Argentina is about to cross, once the prehistoric phase evoked in *Recuerdos* is closed. The role that Sarmiento demands for himself is that of purifying and then reconciling those traditions of which he is equally an heir. In *Facundo* he had taken de Tocqueville as a model; now he was taking Lamartine, "that last scion of the old aristocratic society who, under the maternal wing, is transformed well afterwards into the angel of peace who was to announce to anxious Europe the arrival of the Republic."[28] The insufficiencies of the historical legacy with which Sarmiento identifies himself are revealed as being as necessary as its accomplishments in order to justify the protagonistical ambition that makes him offer himself to his compatriots through *Recuerdos de provincia.*

NOTES

1. This paper was presented at the Symposium on Domingo F. Sarmiento held at Harvard University, 14–15 October 1988. It later was published in the *Boletín del Instituto de Historia Argentina y Americana "El Dr. Emilio Ravignani,"* 3d Ser., 1 (1989): 7–22. An English translation of it is published here with the permission of that journal's editor. In addition to the editor, Kristin L. Jones was involved in translating the article into English.

2. Domingo F. Sarmiento, *Recuerdos de provincia* (Buenos Aires: CEAL, 1979), 10–11.

3. That this decline of the first families is general is affirmed explicitly in ibid., 39. "Carriles, Rosas, Rojos, Oros, Rufinos, Jofrés, Limas, and so many other powerful families, are living in misery and descending day by day to the level of the destitute rabble."

4. Ibid., 9.

5. Ibid., 216–217.

6. Ibid., 9.

7. Bernardo de Irigoyen to Rufino de Elizalde, Mendoza, 8 November 1850, in Instituto de Historia Argentina y Americana "Dr. Emilio Ravignani," *El doctor Rufino de Elizalde y su época vista a través de su archivo* (4 vols., Buenos Aires: University of Buenos Aires, 1967–1974), 2:304. The passage in which Irigoyen informs Elizalde of this aim reads: "This miserable reprobate has put out a new publication titled *Recuerdos de Provincia;* I will try to send you one if I obtain it; so far I only have had a copy I sent to the minister. Let us hope that this publication becomes well-known, because [this] means that this crazy man, [a] ridiculous mixture of all that is repugnant, becomes known." The reason for sending it to Elizalde is, of course, not very convincing. In view of the polemical uses it suggests, the by now habitual practice of publishing in the rosista press the passages that best suited it seems much more reasonable than the massive diffusion of the exiles' publications. The reasons why Irigoyen uses this argument also are not mysterious: he has been sending Elizalde materials published by the exiles in Chile, in addition to sending them to Minister Arana, and it evidently makes him somewhat uneasy. In his previous letter of 8 February, Irigoyen writes Elizalde: "I am surprised to learn that you have not received the packet of printed matter which included the 'Crónicas' [the newspaper that published Sarmiento's articles on Argentine politics] and the letter of Arcos: . . . I repeat try to inquire into the whereabouts of the 'Crónicas' that I sent you by the November mail, without mentioning the name of the newspaper, because you can ask about a package and nothing more." Ibid., 2:303.

8. Sarmiento, *Recuerdos,* 12.

9. Ibid., 17–18.

10. Ibid., 18.

11. Domingo F. Sarmiento, *Obras completas,* vol. 2, *Artículos críticos y literarios* (53 vols., Buenos Aires: Editorial Luz del Día, 1948–1956), 220–221.

12. Sarmiento, *Recuerdos,* 27.

13. After evoking the condemnation and posthumous rehabilitation of Juan de Loyola, falsely accused of Judaizing, Sarmiento again emphasizes the tie between the Spanish past and the Argentine present by pointing out that "Colonel Ramírez has called me *Jew* to flatter the Argentine inquisitor." Ibid., 33–36.

14. Ibid., 34.

15. Ibid., 32.

16. Ibid.

17. Ibid., 37.

18. Ibid., 36.

19. Ibid., 37.

20. Ibid., 37–38.

21. Ibid., 39.

22. Ibid., 31.

23. Ibid., 152.

24. Ibid., 119.

25. Ibid., 122.

26. Ibid., 125.

27. Ibid., 124.

28. Ibid., 118.

Civilization and Barbarism and Sarmiento's Indian Policy

Kristine L. Jones

The contradiction between the image of Sarmiento as a progressive statesman and the harsh record of the military conquest of the Indians under his administration is not a comfortable topic to broach on the occasion of a centennial commemoration.[1]

In retrospect, it is easy to criticize the record of treachery, land grabbing, and violence that characterized the actions of all involved in the decade preceding the ultimate "conquest of the desert" in the 1880s. I will not discuss that issue in this chapter. Instead, I will examine the rationale of that conquest within the context of those times and will suggest how closely Indian policy under Sarmiento's administration mirrored the U.S. lead in justifying dispossession of the Indians with an ideology of civilization.

THE DISCOURSE OF CIVILIZATION: NORTH AND SOUTH AMERICA

When Sarmiento first visited the United States in the 1840s, and so enthusiastically embraced the progressive ideas circulating along the eastern seaboard, he arrived in the midst of the implementation of the Indian Removal Act that had been signed in 1830. Public debate on Indian policy revolved around the idea of civilizing the aborigines, and the removal policies that were enacted explicitly sought that end. It was easy to laud this great social experiment in civilization in Boston, a city far removed from the shame and disgrace of the Trail of Tears, where over one hundred thousand Cherokee, Shawnee, Seminole, and other southeastern tribes were forcibly removed from their verdant homelands

---

Kristine L. Jones is in Chile continuing her research on the Indians.

to the harsh and arid expanses of the newly created Indian territory.

Some of the strongest support of Indian opposition to removal was centered in the Northeast, but the ultimate bureaucratization of the policy allowed President Andrew Jackson to authorize the negotiation of the removal treaties in the Southeast under the guise of civilizing the Indians. U.S. Indian policy equated education with civilization, and the first commissioner of Indian Affairs in 1838, T. Hartley Crawford, explicitly outlined these objectives. He wrote: "The principal lever by which the Indians are to be lifted out of the mire of folly and vice in which they are sunk is education." And what was the nature of this mire of folly and vice? The commissioner was clear in this respect. "Unless some system is marked out by which there shall be a separate allotment of land to each individual . . . you will look in vain for any general casting off of savagism. Common property and civilization cannot co-exist."[2]

The parallels between the public discourse on civilization and education in North America and Sarmiento's discourse on civilization and barbarism can hardly be missed. In fact, Sarmiento explicitly linked the literary tradition of North and South America in the development of his theme. He cited James Fenimore Cooper's genius in "removing the scene of the events he described from the settled portion of the country to the borderland between civilized life and that of the savage, the theatre of the war for the possession of the soil waged against each other, by the native tribes and the Saxon race." Sarmiento continued to draw the analogue:

> When I came to the passage in Cooper's *Last of the Mohicans,* where Hawkeye and Uncas lose the trail of the Mingos in a brook, I said to myself: "They will dam up the brook." When the trapper in *The Prairie* waits in irresolute anxiety while the fire is threatening him and his companions, an Argentine would have recommended the same plan which the trapper finally proposes—that of clearing a space for immediate protection, and setting a new fire, so as to be able to retire upon the ground over which it had passed beyond the reach of the approaching flames. Such is the practice of those who cross the pampa when they are in danger from fires in the grass.[3]

In Sarmiento's depiction, the categories of civilization and barbarism depended on the presence of the Indian, but hearkened to classical ideas about civilization. On the one hand, Sarmiento's categories were firmly planted in a distinctly New World context. On the other hand, they were deeply rooted in classic Roman and Greek ideas about civilization and savagery. Sarmiento collapsed the characteristics of the native tribes, of nature, into the image of the gaucho, the "white-skinned savage, at war with society and proscribed by the laws."[4] He implicitly identified with and appropriated some of the indigenous cultural influence, but rejected other aspects, particularly the rootlessness. In this way, the barbarisms of the savages of nature now became the attributes of the forces against civilization at work in Argentina—and the Indian all but dropped out of the picture in the story of Facundo. Sarmiento's criticisms of barbarism spoke most explicitly of the Creole world in Argentina, but he was left without a clear category of the other, the "American Bedouins," as he called the Indians.[5]

INDIAN POLICY IN ARGENTINA IN THE 1840s

Sarmiento's vagueness with respect to the various native tribes in Argentina in the 1840s and 1850s mirrors Argentine Indian policy at that time. Some of the vagueness has to do with the confusing development of intertribal and interprovincial political relations among competing Indian tribes in the southern grasslands. The boundaries were *not* clear between caudillo armies, Mapuche Indian hunting and war parties, Pampas Indian bands, or even Tehuelche foragers. Indeed, a cultural continuum linked the "savagery" of the least-settled aborigine to the "civilization" of the city, and an exchange of goods and ideas circulated throughout the pampas. Fluid political and territorial boundaries allowed this interchange, as competing forces struggled for territorial and political control in the southern frontier of Creole settlement.

Local conflicts were sometimes resolved with pacification treaties that included annuity payments to the Indians in exchange for peace. Local cattlemen's associations worked out the terms of the agreements, most notably in the Province of Buenos Aires.[6] These locally arranged alliance structures ensured the economic and political dependency of the Indians involved and denied nonallied groups access to local commerce.[7] When Juan Manuel de Rosas moved into prominence in the 1830s, he built upon the local alliance structures within the Province of Buenos Aires. His successful military campaign of 1833 pitted locally recruited Creole militia units and loyal and pacified Indian groups against nonallied Indians. Dependence on annuities, rather than ethnicity, tied the allied Indians geographically to specific territories in alliances with specific local caudillos, most of whom were loyal to Rosas.[8] The military campaign of 1833 pitted band against band, family against family, as military actions forced the pacified Indians against competing groups of Pampas, Tehuelches, and Araucanians.

Jockeying his popularity as a military hero, Rosas took steps to consolidate his political power when he became governor of the Province of Buenos Aires. He moved quickly to transfer responsibility for the annuity payments from the local frontier livestock associations to the provincial government. Between 1835 and 1859 (annually until 1851) the provincial government authorized payments from the General Commissary to allied Pampas and Araucanian tribes. These payments were recorded in the books under the heading "negocio pacífico con los indios."[9]

Much as Rosas, based on his cagey understanding of frontier conditions, was able to transfer his locally constituted power to the provincial arena, Indian leaders moved to consolidate their own political power. Distinctive tribal unities emerged out of pre-existing band organizations. Powerful personalities developed into prominent political and military leaders. The most powerful of these was the Vorogano leader Calfucurá,[10] who understood the annuity agreements for the limited palliatives that they were, and who began negotiations with opposition Indian and Creole caudillos, including General Justo José de Urquiza, the Federalist opponent of Rosas. Between 1847 and 1852, Calfucurá consolidated his position, taking advantage of any military distraction to carry out raids (*malones*) into undefended regions.

While he was building his empire, Calfucurá conducted diplomatic overtures with a variety of Argentine caudillos. During the brief existence of the Argentine Confederation, he sent ambassadors to meet with Urquiza in Paraná, its capital, or at his home, the Palacio de San José. He even established an embassy in Buenos Aires. After the battle of Pavón, Calfucurá formed an alliance with President Bartolomé Mitre of the Argentine Republic. His official correspondence carried a diplomatic seal bearing an insignia depicting the sacred circle of *colihue* (a sturdy reed that was used for weapons and symbolically enclosed ceremonial gatherings) and the crossed lanzas and boleadores of warfare. Calfucurá had clearly picked up some of the trappings of civilization. He encouraged the education of his dependents and sent his son Namuncurá to mission schools in Chile to learn to read and write. In October 1857 another son was expected to enroll in the Colegio del Uruguay.[11]

When Rosas was overthrown in 1852, the new provincial leaders no longer deemed it necessary to continue the annuity payments, which, after all, protected only the southern ranching interests, and the "negocio pacífico con el indio" came to an end. There followed three more decades of military hostilities along the southern frontier that reached unparalleled excesses in terms of economic and social costs.

INDIAN POLICY IN SARMIENTO'S ADMINISTRATION

While Argentine military efforts centered on the costly War of the Triple Alliance with Paraguay (1865–1870), Indian raids into the undefended southern frontier picked up. Great confederations forged by Araucanian, Ranquel, and Pampas tribes sent war parties to raid the southern frontier. They captured hundreds of thousands of head of cattle and thousands of women and children in highly organized *malones*. Indian warrior societies very strongly mirrored the professionalization and militarization of the Argentine army.

Sarmiento's administration corresponded with the apex of Calfucurá's dynastic rule (which his son Namuncurá assumed after his death on 4 June 1873). Only after the conclusion of the Paraguayan War was it possible to concentrate efforts on resolving the frontier issue. Speculators and landowners pressured the national government to regain territory that had been reclaimed by the Indians after the overthrow of Rosas. Plans to build the transcontinental railroad to Chile and railroads into the southern pampas heightened speculative interest. Between 1869 and 1873 military operations were carried out by leaders such as Teodoro García, Luis María Campos, and Manuel Baigorria. These operations, backed with the assistance of the Sociedad Rural Argentina, did succeed in pushing the frontier slowly back, but not without great cost. The policy of issuing annuity payments was reinstituted; this time originating in the General Commissary of the Department of Army and Navy. Payments began in 1867, continued for the following two years, and then lapsed until 1875. Dropping this policy was costly; while the payments had amounted to no more than 4 percent of the Army and Navy Department budget, the greater cost lay in defending the frontier, not to mention the losses due to the war.[12] *Malones* carried out by the forces of Calfucurá, who had depended on the annuities, caused havoc in the frontier settlements. In one *malon* six thousand warriors invaded the districts of Alvear, 25 de Mayo, and 9 de Julio; they carried away over two hundred thousand head of cattle and five hundred captives and left more than three hundred dead.[13] The continuum between savagery and civilization no longer existed.

THE NORTH AMERICAN INFLUENCE IN SARMIENTO'S INDIAN POLICY

Sarmiento clearly had an Indian problem to resolve, and it was natural that he turned to the U.S. example for ideas. He found many parallels there. Responsibility for Indian affairs in the United States had been transferred from the War Department to the Department of the Interior in 1849. The convulsions of the Civil War (1861–1865) had diverted military attention away from defending the frontiers, which allowed the resurgence of uprisings among the Plains Indians in the 1860s, including the Minnesota Sioux uprising of 1862. Military relations on the frontier were harsh, and the depredations were not limited to the infamous and bloody campaigns of Kit Carson against the Navajo and Apache in the Southwest or to the notorious Sand Creek Massacre in Colorado. The

Indian response (seen in cases like the Fetterman Massacre) solidified the enmity of the local settlers. At the same time, public outcry in the East against the treatment of the Indians led to the creation of the Indian Peace Commission in 1867. So it was that in the midst of the most violent, extensive, and centralized military campaigns to subjugate and dispossess the remaining sovereign Indian nations in the United States, President Ulysses Grant inaugurated a peace policy and Congress appropriated funds for Indian education. Once again, the goal of the policy was civilization.

The peace policy turned over the assignment of Indian agencies to religious denominations, with the intent to "watch over them and aid them as missionaries, to Christianize and civilize the Indian, and to train him in the arts of peace." In his second annual message to Congress (5 December 1870), President Grant justified his action:

> I entertain the confident hope that the policy now pursued will in a few years bring all the Indians upon reservations, where they will live in houses, and have schoolhouses and churches, and will be pursuing peaceful and self-sustaining avocations, and where they may be visited by the law-abiding white man with the same impunity that he now visits the civilized white settlements.[14]

SARMIENTO AND CIVILIZING THE ARGENTINE INDIANS

Sarmiento clearly shared the vision of an educated and civilized populous, as his record in bringing public instruction to Buenos Aires shows. His efforts to promote farming colonies in the southern frontier also reflect the dream of the yeoman farmer so dear to U.S. statesmen. Less successful than schemes for public instruction, Sarmiento's policies in support of the colonization efforts met the resistance of local landowners, who found such colonies useful mostly in serving as buffers along the frontier. As for the Indians, Sarmiento and the landowners alike shared the notion that civilizing them now remained the sole option. The only question was the method.

By this time, the categories of civilization and barbarism were no longer confused. The gauchos—Sarmiento's "white-skinned savage"—had been fully tamed and settled into a comparatively docile rural labor force. Although many rural Creoles had escaped military service by joining Indian groups like the Ranqueles, the social fluidity that characterized frontier relations in the 1820s and 1830s and into the 1840s no longer existed. The boundaries were very clear, and the conflict coalesced into, and was debated as, a clear struggle between civilization and the savages. One contemporary observer summed it up: "The Indians robbed because they need what they rob. There are only two [sic] courses of action: their extermination, putting them beyond the reach of the bait that attracts them, or their Christianization."[15]

In this commonly shared ideology, only the details concerning how to civilize the Indians remained to be worked out. Sarmiento sent delegations from the Army and Navy Department to Washington, D.C., where they met with representatives of the Indian Bureau (which many in the United States felt should be transferred back to the War Department).

In Argentina the *Anales* of the Sociedad Rural Argentina became the most ardent supporter of civilizing the Indians. In 1870 the provincial government of Buenos Aires formed a commission made up of Manuel Belgrano, Adolfo Reyes, and José María Jurado to deal with the Indians near Tapalque. The appointees reported on their mission in the *Anales*, where they discussed their offers to construct schools and to establish police forces, all in an effort to civilize the Indians. As in the United States, the notion of common property was considered by the Argentines as the crux of the problem of savagery.

> We believe it is indispensable in order to civilize the Indians, to persuade them to change their roaming habits, incompatible with all social progress, to make them property owners of a given tract of land, broken into small lots, so that its distribution can reach the largest possible number of Indians.[16]

People such as General Julio A. Roca began to argue that the government adopt the ideology of civilization and take possession of the eastern side of the Andes in a conquest of the desert. In a letter to the Buenos Aires newspaper *La República* in 1876, General Roca outlined his justification for the ultimate conquest of the desert. He cited the example of Sidney Johnson's campaign against the Indians in the Rocky Mountains in 1847, a campaign ordered by President James Buchanan, and argued that the Argentine case called for different measures. General Roca opposed the creation of a reservation system, which some generals favored, and called attention to the difficulty of dealing with the Indians because the boundary with Chile had not been determined. He cautioned against the dangers of common property, and argued for government possession of the territory the Indians held. General Roca defended Sarmiento's proposal to support a scientific expedition to define and establish a clear frontier in the Andes.

In this way, Sarmiento's progressive ideas ultimately were used to justify the military campaigns of the 1880s that subjugated and dispossessed tens of thousands of Argentine Indians. Although not anti-Indian, Sarmiento's ideas contributed in an important way to a public discourse in Argentina that equated civilization with the conquest of the Indians.

NOTES

1. Some of the material presented here appeared earlier in the following article of mine: "Calfucurá and Namuncurá: Nation Builders of the Pampas," *The Human Tradition in Latin America: The Nineteenth Century*, ed. Judith Ewell and Williams H. Beezley (Wilmington, Del.: Scholarly Resources Inc., 1989), 175–186.

2. Francis Paul Prucha, ed., *Documents of United States Indian Policy* (Lincoln: University of Nebraska Press, c1975), 74.

3. Domingo F. Sarmiento, *Life in the Argentine Republic in the Days of the Tyrants, or Civilization and Barbarism. With a Biographical Sketch of the Author by Mrs. Horace Mann* (New York: Hafner Press, 1971), 26.

4. Ibid., 40.

5. Ibid., 15.

6. Records of these agreements were kept by the local authorities and can be found in the Archivo Histórico de la Provincia de Buenos Aires "Ricardo Levene," La Plata, under the heading "Negócio Pacífico con el indio (1825–1828)."

7. Kristine L. Jones, "Indian-Creole Negotiations in the Southern Argentine Frontier, 1750–1859," paper originally presented at the annual meeting of the American Historical Association, December 1987.

8. Juan Carlos Walther, *La conquista del desierto: Síntesis histórica de los principales sucesos ocurridos y operaciones militares realizadas en la pampa y Patagonia contra los indios, años 1527–1883*, 2d ed. (Buenos Aires: Círculo Militar, 1964), 71.

9. "Negocio Pacífico con los indios, rendiciones de cuentas, 1835–1839," Archivo General de la Nación, Buenos Aires, *sala* 3, leg. 17-8-5, and "Negocio Pacífico con los indios, rendiciones de cuentas, 1840–1858," *sala* 3, leg. 17-8-6.

10. This is the Argentine spelling of his name. In Mapuche it is Kalfukura, and the final syllable is not accented when spoken.

11. Walther, *Conquista del desierto*, 571.

12. "Memorias y estados de la comisaria de guerra de 1867 y 1868," in *Memoria presentada por el Ministro de Estado en el Departamento de Guerra y Marina al Congreso Nacional en 1868* (Buenos Aires: Imprenta del "Plata," 1868), annex C.

"Memorias y estados de la Comisaria de Guerra," in *Memoria presentada por el Ministro de Estado en el Departamento de Guerra y Marina al Congreso Nacional en 1869* (Buenos Aires: Imprenta Americana, 1869), annex D.

"Comisaria de Guerra," in *Memoria presentada por el Ministro de Estado en el Departamento de Guerra y Marina al Congreso Nacional en 1870* (Buenos Aires: Imprenta Americana, 1870), annex F.

"Memoria de la Comisaria de Guerra," in *Memoria presentada por el Ministro de Estado en el Departamento de Guerra y Marina al Congreso Nacional en 1871* (Buenos Aires: Imprenta Americana, 1871), annex D.

"Memoria de la Comisaria de Guerra," in *Memoria del Ministro de Guerra y Marina, 1872* (Buenos Aires: Imprenta de la "Unión," 1872), annex E.

"Memoria de la Comisaria de Guerra," in *Memoria del Ministro de Guerra y Marina de la República Argentina presentada al Congreso Nacional en 1873* (Buenos Aires: Imprenta Americana, 1873), no. 5.

"Comisaria general de guerra," in *Memoria del Ministerio de Guerra y Marina presentada al Congreso Nacional en 1874* (Buenos Aires: Imprenta, Litografía y Fundición de Tipos de la Sociedad Anónima, 1874).

"Comisaria de Guerra y Marina," in *Memoria presentada por el Ministro Secretario de Estado en el Departamento de Guerra y Marina Dr. D. Adolfo Alsina al H. Congreso Nacional en 1875* (Buenos Aires: Imprenta "Nueve de Julio," 1875), chap. 13.

"Comisaria general de guerra," in *Memoria presentada por el Ministro Secretario de Guerra y Marina Dr. D. Adolfo Alsina al H. Congreso Nacional en 1876* (Buenos Aires: Imprenta del Porvenir, 1876).

Memoria presentada por el Ministro Secretario de Estado en el Departamento de Guerra y Marina Doctor Don Adolfo Alsina al Honorable Congreso Nacional en 1877 (2 vols., Buenos Aires: Imprenta, Litografía y Fundición de Tipos de la Sociedad Anónima, 1877).

"Comisaria general de Guerra y Marina," in *Memoria presentada por el Ministro Secretario de Estado en el Departamento de Guerra y Marina al Honorable Congreso Nacional en 1878* (Buenos Aires: Imprenta Moreno, 1878), chap. 4.

Memoria de Departamento de Guerra presentada al Honorable Congreso por el Ministro de Guerra y Marina Jeneral D. Julio A. Roca (Buenos Aires: Imprenta de El Porteño, 1879).

13. Walther, *Conquista del desierto*, 452. This is the *malón* of 5 March 1872.

14. Quoted in Prucha, *Indian Policy*, 135.

15. Archivo Museo Roca, Buenos Aires, carta 001128.

16. Sociedad Rural Argentina, Buenos Aires, *Anales*, 28 February 1870, p. 451.

4

Sarmiento's Views on the United States

Michael Aaron Rockland

A s everyone knows, Sarmiento was a great admirer of the United States. Seeking a model for a developing Argentina—and after his disillusionment with France—Sarmiento enthusiastically fastened on the United States. In doing so, he honored this country as much as any foreign commentator on the United States, surely more than any other Latin American commentator. Sarmiento's views on the United States, in a nutshell, were not "Yankee Go Home"; they were that Latin Americans could learn much from a visit to the home of the Yankees.

At the same time, Sarmiento's admiration for the United States was, as an editorial in *La Prensa* of 1870 (when Sarmiento was president) pointed out, more than a little excessive. He avoided recognizing the defects of the United States because if he had to recognize them, it might not have been quite as easy for the United States to serve Argentina as a model.

For example, in his *Viajes* Sarmiento virtually ignores slavery in the United States and, when he does speak of it, he goes out of his way to insist that the North Americans are not responsible; it is the fault of the English. "Should we throw the perpetuation of slavery in the face of the Yankees?" he asks. No, he answers, for "slavery is a parasitical vegetation which English colonization has left glued to the leafy tree of American liberty."[1]

In a similar manner, Sarmiento chooses to ignore another aspect of U.S. policy that is certainly a defect from a Latin American point of view: its notions of manifest destiny or expansionism. Here, too, Sarmiento tries to cast a decidedly negative feature of the United States in a positive light. "I do not mean to make Providence an accomplice in all American forward movement," he writes, "since at another time this theory might

---

Michael Aaron Rockland is professor of American studies, Rutgers University.

be used to justify attempts at attracting politically or uniting with (or 'annexing' as the Americans say) Canada, Mexico, etc." Nevertheless, he continues, "if that day comes, the union of free men will begin at the North Pole and, for lack of further land, end at the Isthmus of Panama."[2] Sarmiento's enthusiasm for a wider application of U.S. liberty, as compensation for its imperialism, seems at this vantage point more than a little ingenuous.

If Sarmiento was naive about the United States in some areas, he was also less than prescient in others. Some of his views on the United States have not stood the test of time well. For example, he tells us that "Americans live without a government, and their permanent army amounts to only 9,000 men. It is necessary to make a trip to special places to see anything of the army's equipment or of the soldiers themselves, and there are families and towns in the Union which have never seen a soldier."[3] Would that this were true now. Today those in the United States are far from living without a government, however much candidates for political office ritually promise that, if they are elected, that will change. And the nation's massive defense budget has surely guaranteed that there cannot be a town or family in the United States that has not seen a soldier.

Sarmiento's almost adoring view of the U.S. government was, at least from a contemporary perspective, also wide of the mark. He writes, "As a government, the United States is irreproachable in its public acts, while the individuals who make up the country suffer from repugnant vices."[4] After Vietnam, after Watergate, after Iran-Contra, few in the United States view their government as irreproachable. Precisely because of the occasionally scandalous behavior of the federal government, the U.S. citizenry tend to place considerable faith in the common sense of the individual—vices or not—as well as in the media and in local government. They feel that these forces must remain strong as a counterbalance to the excesses of the federal government.

Sarmiento's views on individual freedom in the United States no longer hold up. He writes,

> The Yankee stands on his own two feet, and if he wants to commit suicide no one will hinder him. If he wants to run after a train and dares to jump aboard, grabbing hold of a bar to save himself from the wheels, he does it. If a little urchin newsboy, in his eagerness to sell one more paper, has allowed the train to pick up speed before jumping off, all will applaud his skill as he lands on his feet and walks away. Here is how nations' characters are formed and how liberty is applied. There may be a few more victims and accidents, but on the other hand there are free men and not disciplined prisoners whose lives are administered.[5]

Surely the United States is *not* today a country where, if one wishes to commit suicide, one can do so unhindered. And whatever one's sympathies for the view that a country is better off if it has a few more victims and accidents and not "disciplined prisoners whose lives are administered," I doubt that many of my compatriots would agree. Surely our extraordinarily powerful insurance companies would not agree.

Sarmiento's own Argentina might today more closely fit his description of unbridled freedom than the United States. In the United States we have a whole species of laws that control citizens' behavior even when the rights of other citizens are not affected. It is not likely that mandating the use of seat belts and of motorcycle helmets is part of a United States to which Sarmiento would have been attracted.

But if some of Sarmiento's ideas about the United States seem passé in the 1990s, others are as fresh and brilliant as when he wrote them. Sarmiento believed, for example, that decentralization is the fundamental idea that animates the United States. It explains our system and guards our liberty. The fact that we are fifty distinct and powerful states; that the governments of our towns and cities are vigorous; that we not only have freedom of religion but strive to ensure that all of our religions enjoy equal status; and that, ethnically, we are the United Nations in miniature, all creates, as Sarmiento saw clearly, a pluralism of peoples, ideas, and values that is the best guarantor of freedom.

If Sarmiento's views on liberty in the United States were perspicacious, his views on equality were similarly so. He believed that equality, the lack of social classes, is responsible for U.S. economic power. "You have here," he writes, "the origin of the unbridled American passion. Twenty million human beings are, all at once, creating capital for themselves and for their sons."[6]

At the same time, Sarmiento saw that liberty and equality are a double edged sword. They guarantee that individuals need not accept their current status as permanent, but they raise competition to the level of crime. "Avarice," Sarmiento writes, "is the legitimate daughter of equality, while fraud comes (strange as it may seem) from liberty itself."[7] Thus, while Sarmiento celebrated U.S. liberty and equality, he saw them as part and parcel of a stressful society in which everyone competes with everyone else, not always mindful of moral scruples.

In such an environment, precisely *because* everyone is theoretically the equal of everyone else, manners are almost nonexistent. Says Sarmiento, "The Yankees are the most uncivil little animals under the sun. At least," he continues, "that is what such competent judges as Captain Marryat, Mrs. Trollope, and other travelers have said about them. But then," he concludes,

if in England and France the coal miners, woodcutters, and tavern keepers were to sit down at the same table with artists, congressmen, bankers, and landowners, as is the case in the United States, the

Europeans would form another opinion of their own culture. In civilized countries, good manners have their limit. The English lord is uncivil out of pride and contempt for his inferiors, while the masses are uncivil out of brutality and ignorance. In the United States, civilization holds sway over such great numbers that, slowly, improvement is coming about. The influence of the gross masses on the individual forces him to accept the customs of the majority and creates, finally, a kind of national consensus. . . . Europeans make fun of these rude habits, which are more superficial than profound, and the Americans, for the sake of argument, become obstinate and justify them as going hand in hand with liberty and the American way of life. I do not mean to defend or excuse these characteristics. Still, after examining the chief nations of Christendom, I have come to the conclusion that the Americans are the only really cultured people that exist on this earth and the last word in modern civilization.[8]

Thus, while Sarmiento believed North Americans have no manners, he writes that they are more truly cultivated or, at least, have come by their cultivation more honestly than other peoples for whom manners may be largely a means of obscuring social ills.

It is in his description of manners that Sarmiento is most engaging as a commentator on U.S. civilization. Although the Frenchman Alexis de Tocqueville, in his *Democracy in America,* is more sagacious when he writes of U.S. politics, no foreigner is more delightful than Sarmiento when he describes everyday life. Here is Sarmiento discussing the inability of North Americans to sit in a normal way:

Among a people who advance their frontier a hundred leagues each year, set up states in six months, transport themselves from one end of the Union to the other in a matter of hours, and emigrate to Oregon, the feet would naturally enjoy the same esteemed position as the head among those who think and the chest among those who sing. In the United States you will see evidence everywhere of the religious cult which has grown up around that nation's noble and worthy instruments of its wealth: its feet. While conversing with you, the Yankee of careful breeding lifts one foot knee high, takes off his shoe in order to caress the foot, and listens to the complaints that his overworked toes make. Any four individuals seated around a marble table will infallibly have their eight feet on top of it unless they can get seats upholstered in velvet, which, because of its softness, the Yankees prefer to marble. In the Fremont [*sic:* Tremont] Hotel in Boston I have seen seven Yankee DANDIES in friendly discussion seated like this: two with their feet on the table; one with his feet on the cushion of an adjacent chair; another with a leg hooked around the arm of his own chair; another with both heels dug into the edge of the cushion of his chair so that his chin rested on his knees; still another embracing or "legging" the back of his chair in the way that is usually only reserved for the arm (this posture, impossible for all other peoples of the world, I have tried without incident, and I recommend it to you if you wish to give yourself cramps in punishment for some indiscretion); another one, finally, if we do not already have the seven, in some other absurd position. I do not remember if I have seen Americans seated on the backs of their chairs with their feet on the cushion, but I am sure that I never saw one of them proud of sitting in the natural way.[9]

U.S. informality intrigued Sarmiento. This may be, in part, because the very word "informal" means something quite different in Hispanic civilization than it does in the United States and can, therefore, be a clue to diverging cultural sensibilities. In the United States, informal always signifies something positive. It means someone is easygoing, hospitable, and does not stand on ceremony—in short, an "approachable" person. In Hispanic culture, however, informal means someone lacking in social graces, crude, unreliable—in short, somewhat of a lout. One can thus understand Sarmiento's fascination with behavior that, at home in Argentina, would have been considered deplorable yet is one of the most attractive features of life in the United States. Here is Sarmiento describing the almost oppressive gregariousness of North Americans in the Tremont Hotel:

In the reading rooms, four or five parasites support themselves heavily on your shoulders to read the same tiny bit of print you are reading. If you are going downstairs or want to pass through a doorway, no matter how little traffic there is, the man behind you will push you in order to hang onto something. If you are tranquilly smoking your cigar, a passerby will take it out of your mouth in order to light his own, and if you cannot at that moment take it back, he will personally see to sticking it into your mouth. If you have a book in your hands and close it for a moment to look about, the man next to you will help himself to it and read two chapters. If the buttons on your overcoat have deer, horse, or boars' heads in relief, everyone who spies them will come up to you and go over them one by one, turning you about from left to right to better examine the walking museum. Finally, if in the North you wear a full beard (which means you are a Frenchman or a Pole), at every step you will be surrounded by a circle of men who will look at you with infantile interest, calling to their friends and acquaintances to step up and satisfy their curiosity in person.

All of these liberties, it should be understood, you can take in turn with the other fellow without anyone complaining about it or showing the least sign of disagreeableness.[10]

We should not fail to include Sarmiento's commentaries on the deplorable U.S. eating habits. "The American has two minutes set aside for lunch, five for dinner," Sarmiento writes. "But then," he continues,

What incongruousness, what incest, what promiscuity in their dishes! The Yankee *pur sang* eats all his food, desserts, and fruit from the same plate, one at a time or all together. We saw one fellow from the FAR WEST, an unsettled land like the Phoenicians' Ophir, begin his meal with great quantities of fresh tomato sauce taken straight and scooped up on the tip of his knife! Sweet potatoes with vinegar! We were frozen with horror, and my traveling companion was filled with gastronomical indignation upon seeing these abominations. "And will not heaven rain down fire upon them?" he asked. "The sins of Sodom and Gomorrah must have been minor compared to the ones these Puritans commit every day."[11]

These passages from Sarmiento's discussions of everyday U.S. life reveal a side of his character generally ignored by scholars. This is Sarmiento as a humorist. Every admirer of Sarmiento knows him as South America's renaissance man—as a great president, a great educator, and a great artist—but the passages quoted above reveal a man whose extraordinary accomplishments and tremendous seriousness were often tempered by a light and comic touch. Thus, when we speak about how Sarmiento was the Lincoln or Jefferson of Argentina, its Horace Mann, and, perhaps—as the author of *Facundo*—its Melville, we may now want to add that there are moments when he may have been its Mark Twain as well. Those photographs of Sarmiento in which he never smiles—is it possible that, should we look a little closer, we might discover that, despite that bulldoglike countenance, Sarmiento has his tongue placed, however tentatively, in his cheek?

NOTES

1. Domingo F. Sarmiento, *Sarmiento's Travels in the United States in 1847*, ed. and trans. Michael Aaron Rockland (Princeton: Princeton University Press, 1970), 305.
2. Ibid., 123.
3. Ibid., 152.
4. Ibid., 182.
5. Ibid., 158.
6. Ibid., 183.
7. Ibid., 182.
8. Ibid., 150–151.
9. Ibid., 149–150.
10. Ibid., 148–149.
11. Ibid., 147–148.

Sarmiento and the Narrative of Failure

Nicolas Shumway

In this chapter I will discuss three narratives.[1] The first is taken from *Facundo;* the second is the narrative of Sarmiento as a player in the *Facundo;* and the third is a narrative in which the book *Facundo* is the major player. My definition of narrative is a simple one; as I use the term it is the chain of selected events, episodes, characterizations, and the like that explain a particular conclusion. Narratives are everywhere. If you ask me who I am, I well might tell you where I was born, where I was raised, where and with whom I studied, and so forth. In short, I would answer with a narrative. As Haydn White and others never tire of telling us, history is also narrative. The historian constructs a chain of causes and effects, based on a prior selection of representative conditions, people and episodes. Without this chain, history would be as chaotic as reality with its plethora of phenomena, unconnected except as the human mind perceives and orders them.

In writing *Facundo,* Sarmiento took on himself two tasks, both as daunting as any faced by a novelist or historian: how to make sense of the Argentina of Rosas, and how to change that Argentina in order to produce a different result. Both of these tasks involved narrative, for in explaining contemporary Argentina, Sarmiento sought to link current problems to their causes. Similarly, in prescribing a better future, he sought to change current circumstances to ensure a better outcome. Sarmiento's descriptions and prescriptions helped create what has become an unfortunate genre in Argentine letters: the narrative of failure. We can easily understand why failure obsessed him. During his formative years, Sarmiento witnessed the failure of the several provinces to unite in a single unit; the failure of porteño liberals to provide inclusive leadership; the failure of the masses to elect responsible officials; and the

---

Nicolas Shumway is associate professor of Spanish, Yale University.

failure of high-sounding European theories to effect a constitutional alternative to the rule of the caudillos. It is therefore no surprise that explaining those failures, with a mercilessness that borders on self-defeating negativism, characterizes much of his thought.

In Sarmiento's view, the focal point of failure in Argentina was a specific type—the caudillo—and a specific figure, Juan Manuel de Rosas. As Sarmiento explains, the caudillo is "the mirror which reflects in colossal proportions the beliefs, the necessities, the concerns and customs of a nation at a given moment in history."[2] His rise to power is "destined, inevitable, natural and logical."[3] And it is here that we most clearly see Sarmiento as narrator. Just as novelists must lay out causes that might justify a particular ending, Sarmiento's caudillo must rise as the inevitable consequence of "the beliefs, the necessities, the concerns and customs of . . . [Argentina] at a given moment in history." And what may the preexisting causes be that necessitate the caudillo for Sarmiento? Three main categories spring from Sarmiento's argument: the physical environment; the Spanish tradition; and the mixed-blood poor consisting of gauchos, domestic servants, and common laborers.

Regarding the physical environment, Sarmiento saw the Argentine pampas as a beast to be domesticated. In an argument influenced by Montesquieu's ideas on the relationship between national character and nature in *De l'esprit des Lois,* Sarmiento found in the Argentine landscape a primary source of the country's problems. He writes that "the evil that afflicts the Argentine Republic is its vast emptiness."[4] It is a land where death and uncertainty reign supreme, where mysterious electrical forces excite the human imagination and the land itself militates against European civilization. Like the romantics he read, Sarmiento is fascinated by the horrific power of electrical storms when "a fearful and overwhelming power forces the soul back upon itself, and makes it feel its nothingness in the midst of a raging nature; and makes it sense the presence of God himself in the terrible magnificence of his works."[5] But Sarmiento's is a fascination that does not rejoice; in his view, the mysterious force of the pampas, untempered by forests or cities, is the force of barbarism. Rather than a lost mother to return to, nature must be overcome if Argentina and its peoples are ever to be civilized.

Sarmiento repeatedly laments that even Buenos Aires, despite the European facade carefully sculpted by the Rivadavians, had accepted the barbaric rule of Rosas because "the spirit of the Pampas . . . breathed on her."[6] The caudillos, in Sarmiento's mind, were the incarnation of the "Spirit of the earth."[7] Sarmiento's cause was not then merely a fight against a particular politician, but a monumental struggle that pitted the forces of civilization against the powers of barbarism.

Civilization or barbarism are the choices Sarmiento offers us, and to a degree those terms became the rallying cry of his entire generation.[8]

Unfortunately, lurking behind Sarmiento's view of the land is an implicit determinism that sees Argentina's problems as the result of natural causes rather than human error—a concept guaranteed to deflect accusations of blame. That the country's failure derived from an inherent organic weakness continued to comfort disillusioned intellectuals for generations to come.[9] I mention only one: Ezequiel Martínez Estrada, who repeated Sarmiento's essentialist argument nearly a century later in *Radiografía de la pampa*. Let me insert a short parenthetical here: although Sarmiento surely saw the land as an enemy to progress, he also viewed it as the wellspring of Argentine literature. The empty distances and their gaucho/caudillo inhabitants attracted Sarmiento the romantic just as surely as they repelled Sarmiento the reformer.

If the land in Sarmiento's narrative of failure was the natural cause of Argentina's predicament, Spain was its historical cause. Sarmiento laments that Argentina had not been colonized by a more civilized country that would have left Argentina a better legacy than "the Inquisition and Spanish absolutism." Spain, for Sarmiento, is the "backward daughter of Europe," a country cursed with paradox where democratic impulses are crushed by popular despots, and enlightened religion must regularly submit to Counter-Reformation fanaticism. In Sarmiento's view, from Spain comes "the Spanish American peoples' lack of ability in political and industrial matters which keeps them in constant turmoil, like a ship churning in the ocean, with no port or rest in sight."[10]

Sarmiento's accusations against Spain were reinforced in 1847, two years after he finished *Facundo*. He visited Spain at that time with the "holy purpose of placing Spain on trial" in order to "justify an accusation" that he, Sarmiento, "as a recognized prosecutor," had already made "before the tribunal of American opinion."[11] As Spain in 1847 was at the low point of its history, Sarmiento quickly found much to support the accusations he had made in *Facundo*. In his view, whatever had been great and noble in Spain was now dead. In the intellectual realm, only translations offered the discerning reader anything substantial, because Spanish writers merely clothed their vacuity in "antiquated phrases and outworn, moth-eaten words." Similarly, its historians regularly gave themselves over to "the national bad taste" of violating historical fact in order "to pretend that theirs is an important country."[12] What had been the glory of Spain, Sarmiento finds symbolized in El Escorial, which in Sarmiento's view is "a still fresh cadaver that stinks and inspires disgust." It represents a country that, with the death of Philip II in 1598, also began to die, slowly sinking into the sterility of militarism and monasticism.[13]

Yet, as in his treatment of the Argentine land, the gauchos, and the caudillos, Sarmiento is repelled by Spanish government, culture, and intellectual life but at the same time finds an ambivalent pleasure in its quaint folk traditions and in the violent spectacle of the bullfight, which he considers at once perversely attractive as well as symbolic of "a corrupting government" that entertains the abject masses while giving vent to their worst instincts.[14] In short, Sarmiento's trip to Spain merely confirmed what he already believed: Spain was the cradle of barbarism, a parent to be cast off and replaced.

In berating Spain for Argentina's problems, Sarmiento inserts in his narrative an argument similar to his earlier contention that the land contributes to Argentina's barbarism: both arguments resort to preexisting conditions to explain failure. As this implicit determinism is also a built-in excuse for overlooking human error, failure can always be blamed on the barbarism of the land and the inadequacy of Argentina's Spanish past.

Sarmiento's third cause in his narrative of failure is eugenic: the people themselves are racially unfit for democracy. Following the accepted racialist theories of his time, Sarmiento writes:

> A homogenous whole has resulted from the fusion of the [Spanish, African, and Indian] races. It is typified by love of idleness and incapacity for industry, except when education and the demands of a social position succeed in spurring it out of its customary crawl. To a great extent, this unfortunate outcome results from the incorporation of the native tribes, effected by the process of colonization. The American aborigines live in idleness, and show themselves incapable, even under compulsion, of hard and prolonged labor. From this came the idea of introducing Negroes into America, which has produced such fatal results. But the Spanish race has not shown itself more energetic than the aborigines, when it has been left to its own instincts in the wilds of America.[15]

It is difficult to know exactly what Sarmiento meant by "race." When he speaks of the Spanish race, he obviously uses the term in a cultural sense. When he speaks of Indians and Africans, however, the term takes on eugenic overtones, for the Indians and Africans represented many cultures and were united only by shared physical characteristics. Appearance, though, is not what interests Sarmiento. His narrative makes explicit the supposed connection between race and political failure by deriding the mixed-blood supporters of Rosas as "lomos negros" or "black backs," and even suggests that Rosas's political success was largely due to a "zealous spy network" of black servants from "a savage race" placed "in the breast of every Buenos Aires family."[16] As a result of such support, Sarmiento feels constrained to confess "out of respect for historical truth . . . [that] there was never a government more popular, more desired nor more supported by public opinion" than that of Rosas.[17]

In an odd sense, then, democracy was both the problem and the solution for Sarmiento and his generation. On the one hand, they

subscribed in principle to notions of institutional representative government. On the other, they deeply distrusted the will of the people, since
the masses were solidly behind Rosas and the traditional authoritarian-
ism he represented. Democracy was defined as a government for the
people but not by the people. That the new government would not
include the people in any universal sense was made explicit by Sarmiento:
"When we say people, we understand noteworthy, active, intelligent
people; a governing class. We are decent people, belonging to a patrician
class. For that reason, in our legislature one should not see gauchos,
negros, nor poor people. We are decent people; that is to say, patriotic
people."[18]

Sarmiento's racialism is, of course, another essentialist argument
and also a narrative determiner. Just as the organic structure of the land
produces a specific society, the race or races of that society also give it
specific characteristics, all predetermined and in some sense unalterable.
And in Sarmiento's description of race, we again find ourselves facing a
metaphor of structural organic weakness. When he and his generation
explain failure in terms of the land, the Spanish tradition, and the people,
they suggest that problems are the inescapable result of past, place, and
ethnicity. Consequently, there are no solutions and no one is really
accountable for what goes wrong.

We have seen how Sarmiento defines his terms, attributes causes,
and interprets results. If we accept his premises, his selection of materials,
and his interpretation of motives, we agree with his explanation of
failure. Said differently, we find his narrative compelling and convincing.
But Sarmiento interjects another character into his narrative here—someone to do battle against the causes of Argentina's failure. There is little
doubt that Sarmiento had himself in mind for this task. As a result,
Sarmiento, the narrator who understands the causes of Argentina's
problems, becomes the gnostic who proposes solutions as well as the man
of action who will bring them to pass. In this role, he is no less a character
in his narrative than the Quiroga and Rosas he derides. It is also
noteworthy that the enemy of place, people, and ethnicity Sarmiento
configured for himself is not a straw figure, but an enemy before whom
Sarmiento at the end of his life would admit defeat.

If not audacious in its conception, Sarmiento's program was breath-
taking in its execution. With inexhaustible energy he and his successors
did their best to hammer Argentina into being the civilized country they
dreamed of. To combat the barbarism of empty spaces, they used
gauchos to fight Indians, thus freeing up vast tracts of land that were
then parceled out, fenced with barbed wire, and distributed partly to
settlers but mostly to high bidders from Buenos Aires. To combat the
barbarism of distance, they brought in foreign, mostly British, investors

and engineers to crisscross the country with telegraph lines and build the most extensive railroad system in Latin America. To combat the barbarism of the caudillos, they instituted electoral politics, which allowed for debate and free elections among the elite, and intervened mercilessly when populist sentiment interfered. To combat the barbarism of ignorance, they constructed literally hundreds of public schools staffed by freshly minted normal school graduates who would give Argentina the highest literacy rate in Latin America. (Indeed, as novelist Ernesto Sábato repeatedly points out, those who criticize Sarmiento today probably learned to do so in schools he founded.)

To combat the barbarism of race and culture, they instituted policies that attracted millions of immigrants to Argentine shores. To combat the barbarism of poverty, they greatly expanded the economy by cultivating vast tracts of virgin land with wheat and sorghum while opening their doors to unfettered trade and investment, mostly from Great Britain. (Though the chief beneficiaries of these economic policies were landowners, merchants, traders, and lawyers, common laborers also reached a standard of living higher than that of their counterparts in the rest of Latin America.) To combat the barbarism of personalism, they wrote a constitution and instituted a civil code that followed the latest theories of European jurisprudence. To combat the barbarism of populist armies, they founded military academies to professionalize the armed forces. In all of this, Sarmiento was a major player, a character in his own narrative. Even after his death his words continued to inspire future generations.

Yet, despite all this, Sarmiento's narrative of failure would return to haunt him. At the end of his career, after being rejected for a second term as president and realizing that his time was over, Sarmiento took a hard look at the Argentina of the 1880s and did not like what he saw. Immigration schemes had not attracted northern Europeans as he had planned. Rather, the newcomers were primarily Spanish and Italian, many of them resistant to assimilation and as enamored of authoritarian government as the gauchos Sarmiento deplored. Even worse, the Casa Rosada was now occupied by a new kind of caudillo, the ever resourceful Julio Argentino Roca, who, in Sarmiento's view, corrupted institutional rule through patronage and promises of unlimited prosperity.

As a result of this disillusionment, Sarmiento's last major work, *Conflictos y armonias de las razas en América,* finished in 1883, when Sarmiento was seventy-two years old, is also a narrative of failure. *Conflictos* is a sad book that Sarmiento himself called "a *Facundo* grown old."[19] In *Conflictos* Sarmiento argues that despite an enlightened constitution, a democracy of sorts, prosperity, modern transportation, schools, academies, universities, and all the trappings of progress, Argentine society in 1883, although better dressed and more genteel than under

Rosas, was still plagued by corruption, personalism, and a general disregard for institutional rule. Sarmiento explains this failure as the result of racial inadequacy.

An ambitious attempt to rewrite much of world history from a racial perspective, *Conflictos* provides detailed analyses of English success and Spanish failure in colonization. In each case Sarmiento suggests that the failure of democracy in Spanish America can be explained only by taking into account the inadequacy of Latin peoples, particularly when combined with the barbaric Indians, to govern themselves. Although *Conflictos* may be, as Sarmiento said, "a *Facundo* grown old," there is a crucial figure lacking from its pages. The heroic Sarmiento, the man who in *Facundo* and *Argirópolis* and dozens of other writings would make Argentina a showplace of Western civilization, is nowhere to be found. Because Sarmiento knows his time is over, his narrative does not end with a brilliant success story. Instead the failure he perceived in 1845 when he wrote *Facundo* is, despite his efforts, the failure he dies with. Perhaps as a narrator Sarmiento presented his assumptions too effectively. Perhaps his description of Argentina's ills was too convincing, too compelling. Perhaps, too, Sarmiento met death sensing that the premises of his narrative had eventually engulfed even their creator.

Although the record indicates that Sarmiento did not die in a flood of optimism, I would hate to end on such a pessimistic note. I would therefore point out that although Sarmiento wrote what I have called a narrative of failure, it was hardly a failed narrative. A failed narrative is one that ends in itself, that inspires no discussion, no interpretation, no new reading. Said differently, a failed narrative engenders no new narratives. This hardly describes Sarmiento's *Facundo*. Perhaps more than any other work of Latin American literature, *Facundo* constitutes a remarkable testimony to Argentine (and Latin American) creativity—a creativity that defies European literary and intellectual models at every turn. Gallons of ink have been spent trying to decide if *Facundo* should be catalogued under history, sociology, biography, essay, or some other neat category invented for European letters. Too inaccurate and undocumented for history, too intuitive for sociology, too fictive for biography, and too historical, biographical, and sociological for essay, *Facundo* establishes its own genre.

Nor is labeling the book's ideological orientation any easier: critics, including some of Sarmiento's own generation, still debate whether *Facundo* is fundamentally a romantic work. Although some elements of the work reflect the romantic impulse, *Facundo* is in other ways specifically antiromantic: it finds in the land a source of evil; it distrusts rather than glorifies popular tradition; it converts strongmen into tyrants rather than heroes; and it is specifically international rather than national in its aspirations.

Like much Latin American literature, which from the colonial chronicles onward has stubbornly insisted on its own definitions, *Facundo* demands a new understanding of what constitutes literariness. As a work of literature, *Facundo*, much the same as the mixed-blood peoples its author deplored, gathers like a prism the variegated hues of European influence and New World freshness into a work of enormous originality. In short, *Facundo* would be inconceivable without taking into large account Sarmiento's peculiar genius and the constant intrusion of the New World that eschews representational modes developed in Europe. What irony that a text of such implicit newness in the realm of literary discourse should explicitly denigrate autochthonous Argentina while in essence preaching an imitative submission to foreign cultural templates.

But more than original, *Facundo* is prophetic, for it anticipates the most peculiar aspects of contemporary Latin American fiction. As in Gabriel García Márquez's *Cien años de soledad*, *Facundo* overwhelms the reader with a dizzying abundance of detail through which the author paints in broad strokes a portrait of an entire people. As in Carpentier's *Los pasos perdidos* and *El siglo de las luces*, *Facundo* describes synchronic time frames that coexist in the primitive life of the pampas, the colonial scholasticism of Córdoba, and the ever-trendy pretensions of Buenos Aires, which regularly calls itself the Paris of South America. As in José Eustasio Rivera's *La vorágine* and Juan Rulfo's *Pedro Páramo*, *Facundo* evokes the corrupting and ineluctable presence of untamed nature. As in García Márquez's *El otoño del patriarca*, Carlos Fuentes's *La muerte de Artemio Cruz*, Miguel Ángel Asturias's *El señor presidente*, and Augusto Roa Bastos's *Yo el supremo*, *Facundo* explores the psychology of both caudillos and their followers.[20] Interestingly, each of these works is in some sense also a narrative of failure, anticipated, if not directly inspired, by *Facundo*.

Today's nationalists, who denounce Sarmiento as a facile imitator in thrall to foreign paradigms, read him too literally and fail to appreciate the remarkable contradictions between Sarmiento's avowed sociopolitical intentions and the book he actually wrote: where Sarmiento preaches imitation in economics and government, he writes a book defiant of foreign literary models; where he explicitly wants Argentina to be like the most progressive countries of his time, his book departs significantly from the romantic impulse of his contemporaries; where *Facundo* is today regularly denounced by nationalists as the work of an Argentine sepoy, it foreshadows the most original aspects of contemporary Latin American fiction. While we can ignore neither Sarmiento's intention nor the effect his writing might have on literal readers, *Facundo* remains a work of astounding and prophetic creativity. A narrative of failure, perhaps, but hardly a failed narrative. Indeed, as a narrative able to engender new narratives, *Facundo* is still a work of astonishing fecundity.

NOTES

1. Since it was originally presented at the Sarmiento Symposium held at Harvard University in 1988, portions of this paper have appeared in my *The Invention of Argentina* (Berkeley: University of California Press, 1991).

2. Domingo F. Sarmiento, *Facundo, civilización y barbarie. Vida de Juan Facundo Quiroga*. Foreword and chronological index by Raimundo Lazo (Mexico City: Editorial Porrúa, 1966), 6.

3. Ibid., 4.

4. Ibid., 19.

5. Ibid., 37–38.

6. Ibid., 22.

7. Ibid., 10.

8. Underlying Sarmiento's polarities and the obvious choices they dictate is a complex ambivalence much studied by literary scholars. While Sarmiento, the liberal progressive, wants to eradicate all vestiges of barbarism, Sarmiento, the romantic poet, is attracted to the primitive freedom of the gaucho and the titanic personality of the caudillo. Good studies of this phenomenon are Noé Jitrik's *Muerte y resurrección de Facundo* (Buenos Aires: Centro Editor de América, 1968), which details the ideological ambivalence Sarmiento felt toward the gaucho, and Carlos Alonso's "Facundo y la sabiduría del poder," *Cuadernos Americanos* 5 (January–April 1979): 116–120, which argues that Sarmiento views Rosas as both a barbarian and an instrument of divine power. Though undeniable on a literary level, such ambivalence all but disappeared in Sarmiento's public life where he consistently sought to deracinate gaucho and Indian life, exclude dissenters, and force survivors into his vision of a modern, Europeanized Argentina.

9. Chief exponent of this view in this century is Ezequiel Martínez Estrada whose *Radiografía de la pampa* (Buenos Aires: Editorial Losada, 1961) suggests that, like a sick man with an endemic illness, Argentina is destined to failure.

10. Sarmiento, *Facundo*, 2. Anti-Spanish sentiment was also strongly apparent among some of the Rivadavian liberals. Tomás de Iriarte, a prolific diary keeper who observed nearly a half-century of Argentine history, wrote not long after 1820 that the collapse of the 1816 confederation was caused by the "plebeianism" of "a people educated by Spain." Iriarte, *Memorias*, vol. 3, *Rivadavia, Monroe y la Guerra Argentino-Brasileño* (14 vols., Buenos Aires: Ediciones Argentinas, 1945–1947), 19.

11. Domingo F. Sarmiento, *Viajes en Europa, África i América*. Introduction by Julio Noé. (3 vols., Buenos Aires: Administración Vaccaro, 1922), 2:8.

12. Ibid., 2:45–46.

13. Ibid., 2:49.

14. Ibid., 2:15–37.

15. Sarmiento, *Facundo*, 15.

16. Ibid., 130 and 141. Mármol in *Amalia*, published in 1855, also speaks of the fear Unitarians had of their own servants who in the main supported Rosas. Eduardo in one such instance advises Amalia to fire all her servants from Buenos Aires since "[under Rosas] the doors have been opened to them to threaten

families and fortune under the miserable authority of the lowborn and the *mazorca.*" José Mármol, *Amalia,* ed. Juan Carlos Ghiano (Buenos Aires: Editorial Porrúa, 1971), 18. In another episode in *Amalia,* a maid betrays to the *mazorca* her employer who is trying to escape to Uruguay. Ibid., 48.

17. Sarmiento, *Facundo,* 130.

18. Cited by Pedro de Paoli, *Los motivos del Martín Fierro* (Buenos Aires: Librería Huemel, 1968), 175.

19. Quoted in Allison Williams Bunkley, *The Life of Sarmiento* (Princeton: Princeton University Press, 1952), 503. It has been suggested that *Conflictos* is in fact a series of notes intended to be a book Sarmiento never finished.

20. Roberto González Echevarría has perceptively analyzed the relationship between *Facundo* and the Novels of Dictatorship in "The Dictatorship of Rhetoric/The Rhetoric of Dictatorship: Carpentier, García Márquez, and Roa Bastos," *Latin American Research Review* 15 (1980): 205–228.

Dialogues and Polemics: Sarmiento, Lastarria, and Bello

Efraín Kristal

In *Otras inquisiciones,* Jorge Luis Borges includes his mordant review of a book by the great Spanish philologist and cultural historian Américo Castro. In *La peculiaridad lingüística rioplatense y su sentido histórico,* published in Buenos Aires, Castro deplores the corruption of speech in Latin America, using Argentine speech as a case in point.[1] Castro objects to certain grammatical constructions, to the popular gaucho speech, and even criticizes the vocabulary of Sarmiento, whom he considers Argentina's best writer. Castro's critique of Argentine speech stemmed, as Richard Morse has shown, from his fear that the Spanish language risked plebeian degradation:

> Castro deplored the widespread plebeianization of speech. He attributed it, first, to raw caudillist leadership, which had unleashed the masses and their elemental passions, and second, to diluvial foreign immigration, which had created a welter of appetites rather than collective democratic ties. Scornful of norms or hierarchy, the lower classes had perverted language in anarchic, capricious fashion with their argot, solecisms, and bowdlerization. In backwater Honduras, Castro felt, one would expect the plebeian *vos* form of the second-person pronoun to linger on by inertia; in well-schooled, international Buenos Aires its use was a calculated defiance.[2]

Borges' vehement reaction to Castro's book is not surprising. In his famous essay of 1927, "El idioma de los argentinos," Borges had argued that Argentines should develop a Spanish speech that was neither vulgar nor peninsular and that writers like Esteban Echeverría and Domingo Faustino Sarmiento were pioneers in forging an Argentine language. They were "Argentines with dignity . . . they neither resorted to Spanish

---

Efraín Kristal is associate professor of Spanish, University of California, Los Angeles.

norms nor did they speak a degenerate Spanish."[3] The aim of a cultured Argentine should be the establishment of an authentic Argentine voice just as the Spaniards had their own voice.[4]

Borges' rhetoric is much more aggressive when he reviews Castro's 1941 book. Here Borges points out that in his own travels through Spain, "I have never observed that the Spaniards speak better than us. (They *do*, of course, speak louder than us, with the aplomb of those who have not learned to doubt.)"[5] If anything, Borges intimates that the Spanish spoken in Spain is of a worse quality than that of Argentina. The Spaniards, Borges argues, tend to confuse the dative pronoun with the accusative, are unable to clearly articulate the sounds of words like "Atlántico" or "Madrid," and show a propensity for distasteful cacophony as evinced in the title of Castro's own book: *La peculiaridad lingüística rioplatense y su sentido histórico.*

Borges believes that Castro's arguments are fallacy ridden. Castro assumes, for instance, that the stylized speech of the gaucho and other regional or popular characters as transcribed in literary works represents normal usage. One could make a similar argument against the Spanish spoken in Spain by using the stylized regional speech in Spanish literary works as proof of the deterioration of the Spanish language in the Iberian peninsula.

At stake in this controversy, at least from Borges's point of view, is not the superiority or the inferiority of Argentine Spanish as measured by the parameters of standard Spanish that Américo Castro defends, but something much more serious and profound. Beneath Borges's irony and sarcasm is a rejection of Castro's lifelong intellectual project. Castro was laying the groundwork for a cultural history of Spain that purported to unearth the form of life that underlies the heterogeneity of all the Spanish-speaking peoples. He wanted to understand and celebrate a collective human experience in order to unify rather than divide the Hispanic peoples. To that end, he underscored the importance of language as the vehicle for cultural interaction.

Borges is unfair, and splendidly rhetorical, when he suggests that Castro is driven by a sense of cultural superiority. Borges knows that what is at stake, from Castro's point of view, is not the inferiority or superiority of one brand of Spanish over another, but the fear that linguistic change, beyond certain parameters, would undermine the basis for a common human experience in the Spanish-speaking world. Castro wanted to strike a balance between the heterogeneity of Hispanic culture, which he appreciated, and its essential underlying unity.[6]

Although Borges is well aware of Castro's intellectual project, he is simply not committed to the search for an essential unity between Hispanic-Americans and Spaniards. For Borges, a common language does not necessarily imply a common human experience. The Argentines speak proper Spanish, but do not share a common culture with Spain: "Our discourse is Hispanic, but our verse, our sense of humor, are now from here."[7] Whereas Castro is looking for a link between the form and the content of the Spanish language, Borges suggests that the form of the Spanish language can emancipate itself completely from its Hispanic antecedents. Borges's review essay was a meditated act of defiance against the great Spanish philological tradition. It is therefore not a coincidence that soon after Castro published a second edition of his book on Argentine speech in 1961, Borges published *El lenguaje de Buenos Aires*, a book that reissues both his 1927 essay, "El idioma de los argentinos," the review of Castro's *La peculiaridad lingüística*, and a stylistic defense of *Lunfardo*, or Argentine argot.[8]

In 1842, almost exactly one hundred years before the publication of Américo Castro's book, Pedro Fernández Garfias, a teacher of Latin in Santiago de Chile, wrote a collection of essays that amounts to a language manual designed to correct the misuse of the Spanish language by Chileans.[9] An Argentine exile in Santiago read Garfias's essays and wrote a very critical review of them. The Argentine argued that Garfias had completely missed the point when he criticized Chilean Spanish because linguistic differences reflect cultural differences but not cultural deficiencies. The grammarian, he wrote, "resists the sovereignty of a people in order to conserve routine and tradition. He is the reactionary of speaking society."[10]

The reviewer was none other than the writer we are honoring, Domingo Faustino Sarmiento, and his essay on language was one of the first he published after arriving in the Chilean capital in 1841. Sarmiento did not stop at criticizing Garfias's pedagogical ideas. He published a seventy-page treatise in which he suggested alternative ways to teach Chile's youth how to read. He argued that Chile's pedagogues needed to rethink their language-teaching methodology so that it corresponded to everyday Chilean speech and allowed "children to follow their own instincts" rather than stale and archaic norms.[11]

Sarmiento's critique of Garfias marks the beginning of one of the most important polemics in the history of Latin American culture. This polemic was about the relationship between the Spanish language and the Hispanic heritage, and its major protagonists were Andrés Bello, José Victorino Lastarria, and Domingo Faustino Sarmiento, three major figures of nineteenth-century Latin American literature. To make sense of the polemic we must first say a few words about the unique intellectual climate of Santiago de Chile in the early nineteenth century.

Santiago de Chile in the 1840s was a privileged city. Among its most distinguished citizens were the Venezuelan Andrés Bello, the great Latin American humanist who had returned to South America after a twenty-year stay in London; Simón Rodríguez, Bolivar's mentor; distinguished

Argentine exiles from Juan Manuel de Rosas, Sarmiento and Vicente Fidel López; and a handful of Chileans who were to become key figures in the history of Latin American thought (e.g., José Victorino Lastarria and Francisco Bilbao).

Chile's intellectual world was overwhelmed by the presence of Andrés Bello: he was not only Latin America's greatest poet, but also its most distinguished statesman and philosopher. He was a key adviser to successive Chilean governments; the drafter of several Chilean constitutions; the rector of Chile's first university; and the mentor of a generation of Chilean intellectuals, even of those who later rejected his teachings. Even though Sarmiento disagreed profoundly with Bello's major philosophical positions, his career as a writer was ostensively launched when Bello praised one of his essays on military history, an event that Sarmiento cherished for the rest of his life.[12]

Bello's personal project was to implant an Iberian nation in Hispanic American soil, with or without the aid of Spain. He hoped for a cultural reunification with Spain, even after political independence, on the basis of Hispanic America's Iberian heritage. Not surprisingly, Bello was one of the first intellectuals to study Spanish medieval texts in order to find a common cultural root between Spain and Hispanic America. He was one of the first scholars to study the newly discovered manuscript of *El Cid*, he did some pioneering studies on Spanish versification, and he authored the first contemporary Spanish grammar. It was Elio Antonio de Nebrija who wrote the first vernacular grammar, but as everyone knows, he used the terminology of Latin. Bello was the first grammarian to propose alternative grammatical terms for phenomena in Spanish not found in Latin.

One of Bello's worst enemies in the cultural arena had been one of his best disciples, Lastarria, the man who probably introduced Sarmiento to Chilean cultural life when the latter arrived in Santiago in 1841.[13] A few months after Sarmiento's arrival, Lastarria gave a new dimension to the debate that Sarmiento had prologized with his review of Garfias's essays. Lastarria took on the master himself in an impassioned lecture in which he lashed out at Bello's interest in Spanish culture.[14] Lastarria stated that it was time for Hispanic America to emancipate its literature from that of Spain; that cultural emancipation was the next logical step after political emancipation. Lastarria judged that Bello's enthusiasm for the Spanish classics was dangerous because Spanish culture was undemocratic and hindered the development of the Hispanic American mind.

Lastarria argued that the content of Spanish literature was harmful to Chileans, although one could study certain Spanish authors whose linguistic form is worthy of imitation. He believed that the Spanish language could become a simple and effective instrument of communication for Spanish-Americans if one could separate the burdensome

Spanish culture from the elegant and efficient forms of Spanish speech.

Sarmiento supported Lastarria's position, but his view was even more polemical. He maintained that it was not even necessary to study the form of the Spanish classics because content was relatively independent of form:

> Instead of concerning us with forms, with the purity of the language, . . . with what Cervantes or Friar Luis de Leon wrote, acquire ideas . . . and when your mind awakens, observe your country, . . . and then write with love, . . . and that will be good even though the form may be incorrect.[15]

Sounding like Miguel de Unamuno, but in a different spirit, Sarmiento argues that Hispanic America must break with the Spanish tradition because Spain is unable to express modern ideas.[16] He says that the Spanish inability to break with established norms impeded the artistic development of Hispanic Americans. He points to France as a superior source of ideas and blames Bello's teachings for the intellectual and artistic poverty of Chile. He exhorts Hispanic Americans to open themselves to foreign literatures other than that of Spain. Emir Rodríguez Monegal has summarized Sarmiento's position: "A language is the expression of the ideas of a people and a people must seek its ideas independent of linguistic purity or academic perfection."[17] At the end of one of his most misquoted articles Sarmiento says that if ostracism were a civilized practice, he would call for the ostracism of Bello.[18]

Bello gave a most eloquent response to both Lastarria and Sarmiento in his famous speech at the inaugural ceremonies of the University of Chile in 1843. His views accord, to some extent, with the spirit of Américo Castro's position. Bello said that if one accepts positions like that of Sarmiento, "America will reproduce the confusion of dialects and gibberish, the Babylonian chaos of the Middle Ages; and then people will lose one of their most powerful links, one of their most precious instruments of understanding."[19]

Lastarria responded to Bello's speech with a book in which he rolls up his polemical sleeves. In *Influencia social de la conquista i del sistema colonial de los españoles en Chile*,[20] Lastarria argues that the political break from Spain would not be meaningful unless Hispanic Americans purge their Spanish heritage from their language and culture. He inscribes himself in the tradition of the "black legend," branding the Spanish conquistadors as robbers who came to the New World for gold and enslaved and decimated the indigenous populations, forcing them to live in a world of ignorance and fanaticism. Spanish avarice, he suggests, was masked by a religious discourse that has inhibited true spiritual life in Hispanic America. Lastarria does not seem to differentiate Chileans of European descent like himself from the indigenous populations. He lauds the Araucanian Indians—with the epithets used by Alonso de Ercilla y Zuñiga in his great epic—as the true heroes of Chilean history and suggests that it was these heroes' heritage that was threatened by the Spaniards.[21] In short, Spanish colonization accounts for the fanaticism, intolerance, and hypocrisy that enlightened Hispanic Americans ought to eradicate.

In his essay reviewing the *Influencia social de la conquista*, Sarmiento approves of Lastarria's attack on the Spanish heritage, but he rejects Lastarria's defense of the Indians, past or present:

> When one reads Ercilla and hears today about the purported virtues of Colocolos and Lautaros, one risks believing that the ancient Araucanians were different than the Araucanians we know today; those stupid, drunk, ignorant, and crass Southern savages who lack every feeling of dignity, except the desire for independence, which is inherent in all savage tribes.[22]

Sarmiento praised Spain's military campaign against the Araucanians and argued that Lastarria was missing the point when he attacked the Spaniards for having silenced a civilization he considered worthless. Rather, Spain had to be attacked because it had "stifled all progress and movement towards civilization."[23]

Bello also responded to Lastarria in a series of review essays in which he vindicated the Spanish heritage and dismissed the Indian question on the grounds that pre-Columbian civilization was on the way to extinction. Like Sarmiento, Bello condemns those who accuse Spain of abusing its power during the conquest of the New World. But unlike Sarmiento he argues that the conquest was carried out with respect for the rights and dignity of the indigenous population.

Bello maintains that Spain had undertaken an unprecedented civilizing mission. Its mistake was not the domination of Hispanic America, which it had a natural right to do, but the fact that it did not fully incorporate the Western Hemisphere into Iberian culture as it had promised to do since the middle of the sixteenth century with the Laws of the Indies.

Had Spain united Hispanic America to the crown, there would not be any possible justification for independence. But it had abandoned that project and wanted to make Hispanic America a colony. In doing so, "Spain sacrificed not only the interest of its American territory but also its own interests: in order to maintain America dependent and submissive, Spain became poor and weak."[24] Thus Spain's failure was not a result of its domination of Hispanic America, but a result of the *way* it chose to dominate.

The only justification of independence that Bello supported is one in the name of implanting Spanish culture in Hispanic America when

Spain itself had abandoned that project:

> It is the Iberian element that has allowed us to prevail against the Mother country. Spanish culture has clashed against itself. . . . The veteran captains of the legions of transatlantic Iberia were defeated and humiliated by the caudillos and armies improvised by young Iberia.[25]

As Spain had failed to assimilate the population of the New World to Spanish culture, it was the task of a Hispanic American elite to do so. But that meant affirming rather than denying Spanish language and culture, which must be studied in order to be applied in an authentic way, given the geographical and historical realities of the New World.

The next protagonist in this debate was one of Lastarria's disciples, Francisco Bilbao. In his hyperbolic "Socialibilidad chilena," published in *El Crepúsculo* (a journal edited by Lastarria to which Bello contributed assiduously), Bilbao goes a step further than Lastarria by equating barbarism with Christianity and Christianity with the project of Spanish colonization.[26] He argues that Spanish resistance to modernity and progress has permitted the creation of the *huaso*, an individual of "Catholic and Spanish beliefs" who is an enemy of progress and civilization. The *huaso* is a good hunter and horseman. Because of his bellicose qualities, he is a grave threat to urban life:

> These are men who have descended from the mountains and plains of the south to the voice of those who incited them to fanaticism in promise of a rampage. Here they are! See in action the spirit of the jungle, the spirit of rancor of the ignorant and the savage against all things new and civilized.[27]

The depiction of the *huaso* is so close to Sarmiento's ulterior depiction of the Argentine gaucho that it is obvious that the Argentine exile read Bilbao's essay with great interest. Bello, on the other hand, must have been angered by the heretic and intransigent tone of Bilbao's essay, and he withdrew his collaborations from *El Crepúsculo*. Bello's reaction was mild compared to that of the Chilean conservative elite. Bilbao was tried in a court of law and was convicted of blasphemy and immorality.[28] The journal was abolished by law and Bilbao opted wisely for exile.

Argentine exiles like Sarmiento suffered severely from the Bilbao incident. They were portrayed in public and in private as the instigators of Bilbao's essay. This coincided with the arrival in Chile of a diplomatic delegation sent from Argentina by Rosas and headed by Baldomero García. According to Sarmiento's biographer Ricardo Rojas, García's primary object "was to complain about the political asylum given the Argentines and for the tolerance shown for Sarmiento's writings against a government friendly to the Chilean government."[29]

Sarmiento chose to withdraw from the polemic that could only alienate him further from the elements of Chilean society that might be sympathetic to his political opposition to Rosas's regime. Sarmiento decided to mend his fences with Bello: he translated religious literature for schoolchildren (Bello wrote reviews in praise of Sarmiento's efforts), and was careful, in his writings, to assail barbarism and not the Spanish heritage as the primary cause of the political chaos of the present.[30] In the serial entitled "Civilization and Barbarism" that later became the famous *Facundo*, Sarmiento underscored the dangers of a barbarism that could destroy both Spanish and more modern civilization in Argentina. His efforts did not gain him the widespread support he had hoped for, and he decided to leave Chile. His travels took him to the United States and back to Argentina, where he would have a prominent role in his nation's political history.

The dialogues and polemics in Santiago de Chile in the 1840s informed, to some extent, the rhetorical strategies that Sarmiento adopted in his *Facundo*. More broadly, they set up the terms in which discussions about the cultural emancipation of Hispanic America have been framed ever since: whether to apply the positive elements of Hispanic America's cultural and historical heritage in an original way (which is Bello's project), or to try to make a clean slate of the Hispanic cultural and historical heritage, viewed as a barrier to modernity (which is Sarmiento's position). In his own polemic against Américo Castro on the purity of the Spanish language in Hispanic America, Borges deployed a series of arguments that were charged with a hundred-year-old history, and whose originator was none other than his admired Sarmiento.

NOTES

1. Jorge Luis Borges, "Las alarmas del doctor Américo Castro," in *Otras inquisiciones* (Buenos Aires: Editorial Emecé, 1964), 43–49; Américo Castro, *La peculiaridad lingüística rioplatense y su sentido histórico* (Buenos Aires: Editorial Losada, 1941).

2. Richard M. Morse, *New World Soundings: Culture and Ideology in the Americas* (Baltimore: The Johns Hopkins University Press, 1989), 18. In an illuminating overview of language use in the Western Hemisphere, Morse situates the polemics between Borges and Castro in its wider philosophical, cultural, and historical contexts.

3. Jorge Luis Borges, *El idioma de los argentinos* (Buenos Aires: M. Gleizer, 1928), 177.

4. Ibid., 181–183.

5. Borges, "Las alarmas," 45.

6. For a lucid account of Castro's contributions to the historical foundation of Hispanism, see Francisco Márquez Villanueva, "Américo Castro y la historia," in *Américo Castro, The Impact of His Thought; Essays to Mark the Centenary of his Birth,*

ed. Ronald E. Surtz, Jaime Ferrán, and Daniel P. Testa, (Madison: The Hispanic Seminary of Medieval Studies, 1988), 131. "Heir of the purist European philological tradition, Américo believed that the time also had come to emphasize Spanish history in our thinking. . . . The result of Américo Castro's efforts is a 'disarming' history, which for the first time unites Spaniards under the flag of a common experience, instead of dividing them." [Editor's translation]

7. Quoted in Morse, *New World Soundings,* 18.

8. See Américo Castro, *La peculiaridad lingüística rioplatense y su significado histórico,* 2d rev. ed. (Madrid: Taurus, 1961) and Jorge Luis Borges and José Edmundo Clemente, *El lenguaje de Buenos Aires* (Buenos Aires: Editorial Emecé, 1963).

9. The essays are entitled *Ejercicios populares de la lengua española* and were published in the journal *El Mercurio.* Emir Rodríguez Monegal has underscored the significance of Pedro Fernández Garfias in the polemic between Sarmiento and Bello in *El otro Andrés Bello* (Caracas: Monte Avila Editores, 1969), 260–264. For another pioneering work that considers the Santiago de Chile polemic, see Fernando Alegría, *La poesía chilena; Orígenes y desarrollo del siglo XVI al XIX* (Mexico City: Fondo de Cultura Económica, 1954), 184–222.

10. My English translation is a paraphrase of the following: "Los gramáticos son como el senado conservador, creado para resistir a los embates populares, para conservar la rutina i las tradiciones, . . . Son a nuestro juicio, si nos perdonan la mala palabra, el partido retrógrado, estacionario, de la sociedad habladora" Domingo F. Sarmiento, *Obras de D. F. Sarmiento,* vols. 1–2, *Artículos críticos y literarios, 1841–1842* (53 vols., Santiago de Chile: Imprenta Gutenberg, 1885–1903), 1:209.

11. Domingo F. Sarmiento, *Análisis de las cartillas, silabarios y otros métodos de lectura conocidos y practicados en Chile, por el director de la Escuela normal* (Santiago de Chile: Imprenta del Progreso, 1842), 61. I am grateful to Andrew Chuppe for bringing Sarmiento's pedagogical treatise to my attention.

12. The article on the battle of Chacabuco appeared in *El Mercurio* (11 February 1841). It is included in Sarmiento, *Artículos críticos,* 1:1–7. In *Recuerdos de provincia* Sarmiento recalls his excitement when he learned that Andrés Bello had read it and even praised it. See Domingo Faustino Sarmiento, *Recuerdos de provincia* (Santiago de Chile: Imprenta de Julio de Belín i Cia., 1850), 174–175.

13. In his *Recuerdos literarios* (Santiago de Chile: J. Nuñez, 1878), 95–99, José Victorino Lastarria recalls introducing Sarmiento to Manuel Font, who found employment for the exiled Argentine. In *Recuerdos de provincia* Sarmiento does not acknowledge any assistance he may have received from Lastarria. See the chapter dedicated to Sarmiento's stay in Chile, pp. 174–193.

14. Lastarria, *Recuerdos literarios,* 113–135, reproduces the text of his speech on 3 May 1842 and states that the same text was published as a pamphlet a few days later.

15. Sarmiento, *Artículos críticos,* 1:223.

16. Sarmiento called for a break with Spanish tradition as well as with Spain. Unamuno exhorted Spaniards to break with many aspects of Spanish tradition in order to rejuvenate Spain. It is curious to note that Unamuno interpreted Sarmiento's writings as a rejuvenating force in Hispanic culture:

Whenever I hear Sarmiento's invectives against Spain, I say to myself: "But this man says against Spain what we Spaniards who most love it say! He speaks, true, badly of Spain, but he speaks badly of Spain as only a Spaniard can speak badly of her; he speaks badly of Spain, but he does it in Spanish and in very correct Spanish.

Sarmiento is for me the most correct Spanish writer of the past century, and he kept that correctness because he avoided reading our classics of the sixteenth and seventeenth centuries. Because he never sought to imitate them or write like them, he wrote in the most vigorous and genuinely Spanish manner. [Editor's translation]
Miguel de Unamuno, "Domingo Faustino Sarmiento," in *Obras completas*, vol. 4, *La raza y la lengua* (9 vols., Madrid: Escelicer, 1966–1971), 905.

17. Rodríguez Monegal, *El otro Andrés Bello*, 264.

18. Sarmiento was not calling for the ostracism of Bello, as has so often been misrepresented. He was, however, calling Bello's teaching anachronistic, and used the unhappy counterfactual statement that has been quoted out of context as an affirmation. See Sarmiento, *Artículos críticos*, 1:223–224.

19. Andrés Bello, "Discurso pronunciado por el Rector de la Universidad, Don Andrés Bello, en la instalación de este cuerpo el dia 17 de Setiembre de 1843," *Opúsculos literarios i críticos, publicados en diversos periódicos desde el año 1834 hasta 1849* (Santiago de Chile: Imprenta Chilena, 1850), 97.

20. José Victorino Lastarria, *Influencia social de la conquista i del sistema colonial de los españoles en Chile* (Santiago de Chile: Imprenta del Siglo, 1844).

21. Ibid., 17.

22. Sarmiento, *Artículos críticos*, 2:217. Sarmiento's review essay was first published in *El Progreso*, 27 September 1844.

23. Ibid., 2:217.

24. Andrés Bello, "Investigaciones sobre la influencia de la conquista i del sistema colonial de los españoles," *Opúsculos*, 119.

25. Ibid., 123.

26. Francisco Bilbao, "Sociabilidad chilena," *El Crepúsculo* 2 (1 May 1844):80.

27. Ibid.

28. For details, see Allen L. Woll, "The Philosophy of History in Nineteenth-Century Chile: The Lastarria-Bello Controversy," *History and Theory* 12 (1974): 283–284. Woll's article is an illuminating and informative contribution to the genesis of the philosophical position of Chilean liberals like Lastarria and Bilbao. However, I cannot agree with Woll's suggestion that Bello's primary aim was to diffuse the "potentially incendiary nature" of Lastarria's school in order to maintain his position of institutional power: "As long as government maintained peace, order, and prosperity, and an intellectual climate suitable for work, then Bello was satisfied" (p. 289). Bello's own philosophical position—that it is para-doxical and misguided for Hispanic Americans to dismiss the Iberian heritage wholesale in order to adapt British or French models mechanically—is a legitimate argument against positions like those of Sarmiento, Lastarria, and Bilbao.

29. Ricardo Rojas, *El profeta de la pampa: Vida de Sarmiento* (Buenos Aires: Editorial Losada, 1945), 199.

30. See Bello's review essay, "Vida de Jesucristo con una descripción de la Palestina. Traducida por D. D. F. Sarmiento," Andrés Bello, *Obras completas*, vol. 9, *Temas de crítica literaria* (15 vols., Caracas: Ministerio de Educación, 1951–1956), 441–446.

Sarmiento's Vision

Ricardo Piglia

S armiento's literary ability was first acknowledged by his enemies.[1] Sarmiento himself often told the anecdote that summarizes the history of that recognition. Rosas, to whom someone had sent a copy of *Facundo*, tells his collaborators: "Gentlemen, this is how to attack, let us see if any of you is capable of defending me in the same way." The enemy's reading best grasped, beyond its contents, the book's rhetorical efficacy. (Rosas was clearly impressed with the literary form of *Facundo*. More impressed, we could say, than the Unitarian Valentín Alsina, who noted minutely the inconsistencies and errors in the book's contents.)

The anecdote about Rosas's opinion lays the foundation of a tradition that can be contrasted with the liberal reading of *Facundo* (of which Alsina's notes are the first example). The nationalists have appreciated the unique *form* of Sarmiento's texts. In contrast, the official tradition has canonized the truth of the *contents* and the historical and political lessons of Sarmiento's work. Of course, Sarmiento is much closer, in language and style, to the great nationalist prose writers (e.g., Ignacio B. Anzoátegui, Carlos Ibarguren, Julio Irazusta, Marcelo Sánchez Sorondo, Leonardo Castellani) than to the sad tradition of the liberal essayists who claim to be his disciples (e.g., Eduardo Mallea, Ezequiel Martínez Estrada, José Isaacson, H. A. Murena, Víctor Massuh). Borges, as is well known, has the intonation and boldness of the polemicists of the antiliberal right and he knows how to use the classic abusive emphasis in the style of Sarmiento. (For example: he writes in *El tamaño de mi esperanza*, "Sarmiento, the North Americanized Indian thug, great hater and misinterpreter of the Creole way, Europeanized us with the faith of a man who has recently acquired and who expects miracles from culture."

Ricardo Piglia is professor of Argentine and Spanish American Literature, Universidad Nacional de Buenos Aires.

The best description of Sarmiento's polemical style is in "The Art of Insult," a manual for the rhetoric of verbal war, an antiliberal model of dialogue. (Another example, of course, is "Las alarmas del Doctor Américo Castro," which mimics and exaggerates Sarmiento's polemics with Bello.)

Facundo is a clear case (the clearest, I would say, in all Argentine literature) of a text written with a practical and extraliterary purpose that has gained ground in literature until becoming a classic. The way it is constructed has taken precedence over its political contents and ideological declarations. Through a paradox that is typical in literary history, this pamphleteer and committed writer has become today a writer for writers, and *Facundo* a laboratory of forms and a thesaurus of styles and narrative solutions.

The enemy's reading is a key category in how *Facundo* moved away from politics to literature. (The enemy's reading always sees something else: not the truth in Sarmiento's work but his methods of concealment and fictionalization. To read in opposition to Sarmiento's historical "truths" presupposes analysis of the rhetorical reasons for his effectiveness.) But if Sarmiento's writing transcended political occasion and practical function, it was above all because of its formal extravagance. Beyond its scholarly, historical, academic, political, and pedagogical purposes, Sarmiento's writing always had a strain of formal excess that resisted categorization. I will call that extravagant nucleus, using an expression of Pier Paolo Pasolini, "the will to be a poet" (see his *Empirismo erético*). That will to be a poet, present from the beginning in Sarmiento, should not be understood anachronistically in the sense that one can recognize it in Almafuerte or Lugones. Rather, one should speak of the historical impossibility of carrying out that will. The free and personal use of language is controlled simultaneously by a strong extraliterary requirement (especially the practical efficacy and public function of his writing) and by a condition that we could call preliterary in that literature is neither already existent nor autonomous.

Sarmiento's writing is a megalomaniacal response to that double demand. All the reiterations of "I" and self-references and all the excesses and foolishness that have become part of the Sarmiento legend and anecdotal and semipsychiatric biography are simultaneously a political tactic and an effect of style. (They are a quality of Sarmiento's work in the same sense that dandyism is a quality in Baudelaire's work.) We are dealing with a basic rhetorical nucleus that we could define as the "out-of-place" author. I mean by this that the out-of-place position of the author is simultaneously a key to his style and to his situation in society.

Sarmiento's writing can be summed up under what Elias Canetti (speaking of Schereber in *Masa y poder*) calls *the posture of exaltation:* excessive ambition, the need to be unique, polemical euphoria, excessive confidence. That is, the passionate resort to symbols is precisely intended so as not to lose that extremist exalted posture. Omnipotence defines a type of writing, but that type of writing sustains the omnipotence. (This is why Sarmiento overwrites.) Sarmiento, on the one hand, tends toward confessional and autobiographical writing, to self-reference, to private language, and to the personal letter, to the "idea reader" (*ideolecto*) as an extreme position. On the other hand, he tends to oratory, to pamphleteering, to public polemics, to paranoid propaganda, to conspiracy, and to persecutory mania. The two forms coexist: the author moves from one place to the other, from the private to the public, from the emotional to the political. In that double use of language, Sarmiento defines a new metaphorical field: its basic form is the *ver doble* (double vision), to see a thing as if it were something else. This double link is the central approach of a perception at once pragmatic and antirealist, political, and metaphorical, which we can call *Sarmiento's vision*. Its shape is that of a mirage, an imprecise, distant silhouette of what one wishes to see. The optical illusion builds reality, permitting views of what no one else sees. (Martínez Estrada is the conscious heir of that manner of seeing: an x-ray of the pampas is implicit in Sarmiento's writing and that medical image could be *Facundo's* title.) In fact, visual and scientific metaphors, the laboratory as model, and optical instruments proliferate in Sarmiento's work. We could say that there are continuous references to this matter of seeing, of the counterfeit look, of deciphering the concealed. The trail blazer series ties in with telescopes, maps, and footprints until reaching its culmination in the pseudomagical vision of a Quiroga able to see and to prophesy the future. That line of mirages and optical metaphors comes together in the scene that Sarmiento describes in *Campaña en el ejército grande:* in the midst of an exasperating dream, the author sees reality like in "a picture taken through a kaleidoscope."

Let us consider here one aspect of that "to see as if" series: the use of analogies and equivalencies in *Facundo*. Sarmiento's vision has a magical function: it serves to establish the link between terms that at first sight have no relationship. Everything acquires meaning if it is possible to reconstruct the equivalencies between what one wants to explain and something else that is already agreed upon and written about. For Sarmiento, to know is to decipher the secret of analogies: resemblance is the mysterious form that makes meaning evident. If Sarmiento overdoes his somewhat wild passion for culture, it is because for him to know is to compare. Culture functions above all as a repository of examples that can be used as terms of comparison.

Analogies and equivalencies proliferate in *Facundo* and appear in the text from the beginning, supported explicitly by a French quotation:

"*La pleine lune a l'Orient s'elevait sur un fond bleuatre aux plaines rives de l'Euphrate*" [A full moon was rising in the East from the bluish plains of the Euphrates]: And, really, there is something in the Asiatic solitudes, one's spirit finds some analogy between the Pampa and the plains that lie between the Tigris and Euphrates; some bond between a fleet of lonely wagons (*carretas*) crossing our solitudes and the camel caravans going to Baghdad or Smyrna. Our travelling wagons are like a kind of fleet of small vessels.

Here, condensed, is the basic process that the text will develop, combine, and change until transforming it into the foundation of the book.

We have just seen that the context for the equivalencies is almost always cultural: comparison with the Orient (something that was then common) is based upon his reading. "I have always had the notion that Palestine resembles La Rioja." Sarmiento has never been to Palestine, but the epigraph that heads this chapter (Roussel, *Palestine*) explains the origin of this comparison. At the same time, if one compares the known with the unknown (Sarmiento's key technique to which we will return) it is because the unknown (the Orient, Africa, Algiers, etc.) has already been judged and defined by European thought. They are the regions of the world that endure the expansion of colonialism, the regions that liberal ideology has begun to define as barbaric and primitive, the regions that must be civilized. Comparison with Europe is the obverse, in the book, Europe is utopia. Civilization and barbarism each have their own terms of comparison. The Orient or the Middle Ages are the past or backwardness as present in South America: Europe and the United States are the future of Argentina.

Deep down, making analogies is, for Sarmiento, both a method of knowing and a conception of the world. In fact, he finds in it another element to distinguish the civilized person from the barbarous masses. "The masses are unable to clearly compare one epoch with another; for them the present is the only moment at which they look." In the same way, it is remarkable that Pedro de Angelis, a political antagonist of Sarmiento in the opposing ideological camp, had written in 1833: "The field most full of errors is the too common system of comparing peoples with peoples, institutions with institutions, and circumstances with circumstances."

In analogizing, one of the fundamental ideological bases of *Facundo* must be recognized: the logic of equivalencies dissolves differences and magically resolves contradictions. Sarmiento defines and argues by analogy because he builds a system where to compare is already to define and to judge. He compiles a kind of ideological dictionary in which one of the terms of comparison always appears defined and evaluated. In establishing the equivalency, Sarmiento gives us reality already judged. First, reality must accept the analogy (La Rioja is like Palestine); then the analogy proves that what is assumed is known already ("what is good for La Rioja is applicable without change to Santa Fe, San Luis, Mendoza").

Rather than proving what is done, the analogy asserts similarities, and frequently this procedure is broadened and used to make the book move on. In *Facundo*, analogy functions as syntax. "The wagon foreman is a caudillo, just as the leader of the caravans in Asia," Sarmiento writes. From there on, the chain of analogies is internal to the text and completes it. "What I said in the beginning about the wagon foreman is exactly applicable to the rural judge." And a bit further along: "What I said about the rural judge is applicable to the rural commandant." And a hundred pages later: "If the reader remembers what I said about the wagon foreman, he will guess the character, courage and strength of the ox driver." Sarmiento looks for a caravan chief in Asia who acts as an equivalent, and beginning there the analogy expands and proliferates as a system of proof, which is always at risk of tautology.

Sarmiento's writing tends to be exhaustive, he does not want to leave residues: everything has to be explained. "What mysterious links connect all these deeds?" he asks himself at the beginning of the book. This quest is constant and functions as a duty, or better, as an order. "I need to clarify this chaos a little"; "to classify the contradictory elements"; "to explain all." It always involves discovering connections, grouping dispersed facts into vast units of meaning. Reality is subjected to a catalog of forms, ordered by similarities: deep down for Sarmiento, to compare is to classify.

If similarities allow different situations, societies, and distinct eras to be connected and assimilated, it is because a specific relationship sustains the identification. To compare is to establish the order of causes in the disorder of the world. Gauchos are compared with North American Indians, with Bedouin hordes, not only because the similarity involves a value judgment, but because of a will to demonstrate that the existence of something in common makes them what they are. If this is so, the analogy simply deciphers the secret cause. A concept based on geographic and cultural determinism defines the commonality that makes it possible to put the similarities in order. Here, too, the comparisons are presented in a cultural discourse, but in another key that should be called more abstract or more stereotyped. "Many philosophers have also believed that the plains prepared the way for despotism, in the same way that the mountains lend themselves on occasion to resistance, and to liberty." And further on: "Comparative phrenology and anatomy have demonstrated, in effect, the relations that exist between external forms and moral dispositions." There is no need to cite, or rather, a social discourse is cited that is taken as accepted: science, known by all, is the general truth that supports the book's logic.

The order that the book ends by establishing in the chaos of the world is, we now see, an order of the causes. But that order of forms and similarities is, at the same time, always threatened by tautology, abstraction, contradiction, and voids. Let us look at only one example. This is what Sarmiento said about Argentine rustic society: (1) "It is the opposite of the Roman municipality"; (2) "It is similar to ancient Croatia Slovenia"; (3) "[However,] it was agricultural"; (4) "It differs from the nomadic tribe"; (5) "Basically it is something similar to the feudalism of the Middle Ages"; (6) "But what this society presents that is noteworthy with regard to its social aspect is its affinity with ancient life, with Spartan or Roman life"; (7) "On the other hand it did not have a radical dissimilarity." This extravagant syllogism appears in a single paragraph.

The points of comparison can be extended to infinity and can close in on themselves. Everything is similar to everything else, but at the same time everything is different from everything else. Similarities and differences simultaneously chain together and separate analogies and voids; here is what could be called an example of metaphorical reflection. This is the place where Sarmiento's vision is clarified. The mystery and the fascination of the analogies make the text unreal and confine it. The secret of *Facundo's* literary character is in this process, which is the foundation of its ideology.

NOTE

1. This paper was presented in Spanish at the symposium "Domingo F. Sarmiento: Argentine Nation-Builder, 1811-1888," held at The Library of Congress, Washington, D.C., on 11 October 1988. The manuscript was received without footnotes. The translators are Kristine L. Jones and the editor.

Sarmiento, the United States, and Public Education

Georgette Magassy Dorn

D omingo F. Sarmiento knew more about education in the United States than did any other Latin American of his generation.[1] A statesman, essayist, journalist, and educator, he set out to open up Argentina to the outside world during the formative period of the nation-state. Like Alexis de Tocqueville before him, Sarmiento admired the U.S. educational system. He devoted the greater part of his life to improving Argentine public education and tried to model it on the system developed in the United States.

According to Mary Peabody Mann, Sarmiento was "not a man but a nation."[2] Ricardo Rojas posed the intriguing question of whether "a journalist and a schoolteacher, could be considered a genius." There is little doubt that Sarmiento was a whirlwind, a self-made man who, from his earliest years, admired Benjamin Franklin and who accomplished much in several areas of endeavor during his own long and fruitful career. Sarmiento also lived "in perpetual exile . . . the prophet of a promised land which remained in the future."[3] Natalio Botana states that Sarmiento devoted his life to the creation of a democratic republic and a political community in Argentina.[4] Sarmiento knew that to attain true democracy it would be necessary to "educate the sovereign [the people]." Therefore, his principal passion became the improvement of public education. Most of Sarmiento's educational reforms, such as the passage of the law establishing public education (PL 1420), are still relevant to contemporary Argentine life.

Owing to family circumstances, as well as to the lack of educational opportunities in his native Province of San Juan, Sarmiento only attended primary school, but he did receive private tutoring. In a letter to Mary Mann

Georgette Magassy Dorn is a specialist in Hispanic culture, The Hispanic Division, The Library of Congress.

he explained years later that "an uncle of mine who was a priest, taught me Latin, and after being exiled, at the age of fifteen I opened a school in the countryside of San Luis to teach reading and writing."[5] Back in San Juan, Sarmiento rounded out his education by reading the classics and many other books lent to him by friends like Manuel José Quiroga Rosas, a frequent traveler to Buenos Aires. In 1826 Sarmiento taught in a rural school in San Juan while also working in a store.

In 1831 he was forced to flee to Chile for political reasons. As a youth Sarmiento espoused progressive political causes, and consequently most of his early years were spent on the move. Upon returning to San Juan in 1836, he continued his intellectual and political activities and in 1839 established the first high school for girls in San Juan. Sarmiento was the only son in a rather large family of girls. His mother had little formal education herself, but she was a strong, supportive, and thoughtful woman. Her son became a steadfast supporter of women's education, believing women were as capable as men. He outlined his progressive ideas in a booklet entitled *Programa de un colejio de señoritas en San Juan*,[6] in which he maintained that society would benefit if women received the same education as men. As part of his endeavors to promote education, Sarmiento also published the newspaper *El Zonda*, in which he wrote about education, the sorry state of Argentine politics, and the urgent need for agricultural and industrial progress.

> I realized that all of my country's ills were rooted in Barbarism! I had been raised in a family which was sympathetic to the Federalists, but I suddenly rejected that tendency; and two years later I handed in the key to the store, in order to take the sword against Quiroga, the Aldaos and Rosas. In moments of rest I only dreamed of founding schools and teaching the masses to read![7]

Profoundly influenced by European ideas and by the writings of Juan B. Alberdi, Esteban Echeverría, and others, Sarmiento was a product of the romantic era. During his second exile in Chile in the 1840s, he quickly earned the admiration and friendship of Andrés Bello, José Victorino Lastarria, and other intellectuals. He began writing for *El Mercurio* in Santiago de Chile.[8] His articles attracted the attention of Manuel Montt, the minister of justice and public education, and later president of Chile. Encouraged by Montt, Sarmiento returned to his favorite calling—teaching. He established a normal school in Santiago de Chile, the Escuela Normal de Preceptores, the first in Latin America. Embarking wholeheartedly on radical reforms, the budding educator recommended creating many primary schools, printing modern textbooks, and preparing school programs and curricula. Sarmiento also wanted to simplify Spanish orthography, to base it completely on phonetics, and he presented his arguments in *Memoria sobre ortografía americana*. Bello endorsed many of Sarmiento's ideas, and the University of Chile accepted some of his innovations.

In recognition of his contributions, Sarmiento was appointed to the Faculty of Philosophy and Humanities at the University of Chile. And he formed a lifelong friendship with Manuel Montt, a political conservative who held progressive ideas about education and the improvement of social conditions.[9] In a short period of time, Sarmiento, a foreigner, had established himself in the intellectual circles of Chile and was writing for the major newspaper in a capital where he had arrived knowing no one and without a university education.

Sarmiento the writer was very productive during the 1840s. During that time he wrote his major works: *Facundo, Recuerdos de provincia, Viajes en Europa, Africa i América,* and *De la educación popular.* At the same time he was being hounded by a special diplomatic Argentine mission headed by Baldomero García and Bernardo de Irigoyen, who had been sent by Rosas to secure his extradition. Sarmiento was able to elude his pursuers when Minister Montt sent him to Europe and the United States to study the most advanced educational systems and to recommend ways of improving the Chilean one. Sarmiento's travels in Europe proved somewhat of a disappointment. He felt that the European countries were characterized by great inequalities of opportunity and could not offer an innovative development model for South America. He found France particularly shocking, for despite its art treasures it was "still in a state of barbarism."[10]

Although he had run out of money after completing the European and African portions of his journey, he determined, with the help of a Chilean friend, Santiago Arcos, to proceed to England and the United States. In England Sarmiento read by chance Horace Mann's *Seventh Report of the Secretary of the Massachusetts Board of Education.* It made as profound an impression on him as it had made on the British educational establishment. He determined to meet Mann at any cost, and remembered years later that "when that important report came to my hands, I then had a fixed point where to go in the United States."[11] His good fortune continued, for aboard ship he met George Bliss, a politician from Massachusetts, who gave him a letter of introduction to Mann.

Like Alexander de Tocqueville before him, Sarmiento set out to chronicle the success of the young republic. He exulted that

> [It is] the only country in the world where the ability to read is universal, where writing is practiced by all in their daily lives, . . . Is there any country in the world which can compare with it in these respects? . . . In the United States, every man has a natural right to a role in political affairs, and he exercises it.[12]

While Sarmiento expressed his admiration for North America, he did not want to transform South Americans into Yankees; he only wished to bring the benefits of universal literacy, representative democracy, equality, and progress to his own country and its neighbors. He perceived a communality of experience between the former colonies in North America and South America and foresaw the possibilities for change that could be attempted in the New World.[13]

In Boston, Sarmiento visited Horace and Mary Peabody Mann.[14] Horace took him to the normal school he had founded in West Newton, Massachusetts. Sarmiento also visited several other schools in the Boston area, and he marveled at the fact that 3,500 schools in Massachusetts had approximately 7,000 teachers, "a greater number than there were soldiers in Chile."[15] In these schools he saw men and women studying together; women were being trained in the sciences and in physical education. Through Mary Mann he met other prominent New Englanders, among them Ralph Waldo Emerson, George Ticknor, Henry W. Longfellow, Louis Agassiz, Wendell Phillips, and Benjamin A. Gould. For those who fault Sarmiento for not criticizing the existence of slavery in the United States, it should be pointed out that the Argentine visitor chiefly met the flower of New England's progressive intelligentsia, most of whom favored abolition. He also traveled more extensively in the North than in the slave-holding South.

Upon his return to Chile, Sarmiento wrote *De la educación popular,* setting out his ideas for educational reforms, most of which coincided with those of Horace Mann. Sarmiento also wrote approvingly about financing schools through taxes, school inspections, curricula, public schools, the education of women, and Spanish orthography. He proposed "civilizing barbarism" through education.[16] This work contained all his basic ideas on education, and it provided the framework and essence for his later writings on the subject, such as *Educación común* and *Las escuelas: base de la prosperidad i de la república en los Estados Unidos.* Like Horace Mann, Sarmiento believed that society has the duty to raise the educational level of the people, that people who have not developed their minds are not complete, and that ignorance should be considered almost a crime.[17] Sarmiento found in Mann a kindred spirit, and he saw in the educational system of the United States a model that could be emulated by other young countries. Sarmiento thought of himself as the Argentine Horace Mann. He wrote to Mann's widow: "You have had the great satisfaction of having been able to nurture and aid [two] pioneers [in education] at both ends of the American continent, now that your name is associated with mine to honor him [Horace] even more.[18]

After Rosas's defeat in 1852, Sarmiento returned to Argentina, and lived in Buenos Aires for the first time in his life. He became the director of the Department of Education of the State of Buenos Aires, editor of the newspaper *El Nacional* (to which he contributed articles on education and politics), and the founder of the journal *Anales de la educación común.*

Sarmiento's plans to establish coeducational schools and to train women teachers to staff them met with the unbending opposition of the entrenched Sociedad de Beneficencia, which had been charged from the days of Bernardino Rivadavia with the education of women. Despite opposition from several quarters, Sarmiento was able to accomplish major educational reforms. He also served successively as a congressman in the State of Buenos Aires, as a senator, and as governor of his native Province of San Juan.

Between 1856 and 1861 Sarmiento founded thirty-six new schools in Buenos Aires and ordered the preparation of new textbooks and the translation of some foreign texts.[19] As governor of San Juan during the chaotic years 1862 to 1864, he seized the opportunity to implement some of his ideas. He was especially interested in undertaking the building of public libraries and schools. He stated:

> Let us establish schools, fellow citizens. Let us educate the new generation; let us seize fully the opportunity in these revolutionary times since we have already wasted so many years. Education offered to the greatest number will result in greater productivity. Our province is poor; let us increase the number of those who could attain wealth.[20]

He also endeavored to introduce economic reforms in agriculture and mining. Several people, among them the caudillo Ángel "Chacho" Peñaloza, opposed his proposals, such as the one for land reform, and Sarmiento had to resign in the midst of an untenable situation.[21]

President Bartolomé Mitre, aware of Sarmiento's frustrations as governor of San Juan and his unhappiness with the Chacho affair, appointed him minister plenipotentiary to Chile, Peru, and the United States in 1864. Sarmiento set out for the United States as soon as he assembled a small legation staff. Upon his arrival, he marveled at how much progress had been made in spite of the Civil War in the nearly two decades since his first visit. He saw the incipient triumph of the Industrial Revolution and the early days of Reconstruction.

After reading a notice that a Horace Mann statue was being erected in front of the State House in Boston (Mann had died in 1859), Sarmiento wrote Mrs. Mann to describe the many reforms he had carried out in South America that were partly inspired by the Manns. He also expressed an interest in translating a biography of Horace Mann into Spanish.[22] Through assiduous correspondence Mrs. Mann became Sarmiento's friend and adviser. Although they only met about three times during his entire sojourn in the United States, there developed an enduring epistolary interchange between the two. She called him "Mr. Sarmy," and translated into English his epoch-making essay *Facundo* and selections from his *Recuerdos de provincia*.[23]

Sarmiento set up his residence in New York, where he found greater opportunities to observe the educational and business establishments. He continued to study the educational innovations being introduced. In letters to Mrs. Mann he expressed his fondest dream of establishing in San Juan a U.S. type of university that would teach the latest scientific advances in agriculture and mining. He rued that it took so long for the knowledge of any improvement to travel from the Argentine coast to the country's heartland.[24]

Mary Mann helped Sarmiento to reacquaint himself with the people he had met in 1847 and introduced him to other influential figures. He met educators Henry Barnard, Kate Newall Doggett, and James Pyle Wickersham. He also participated in congresses on education, saying in a letter, "I leave for Washington where I have been invited to address a congress of School Superintendents about the necessity to require that in order to qualify as a citizen one must know how to read and write."[25] He tried to acquaint North Americans with Argentina and addressed the Rhode Island Historical Association about "North and South America."[26] As his English was less than fluent, Sarmiento relied on the help of Bartolomé Mitre, son of the president, who spoke it well. Young Mitre was indispensable, as well, in the legation's day-to-day business.

In New York, Sarmiento founded *Ambos mundos,* a journal devoted to educational and cultural affairs. Only five issues appeared. His main project, however, was to recruit U.S. schoolteachers for Argentina. Sarmiento wanted to introduce more advanced teaching techniques, coeducational schools, and foreign languages there. He promised his North American contacts that the teachers would have an opportunity to "mingle with the best families" in the provinces and that they would be in good hands.[27] He wanted to send the first group of teachers to the Province of San Juan. They would travel by sea from New York to Buenos Aires, where they could rest, and then proceed by stage coach "traveling ten days, well protected, secure, and cared for." Sarmiento pioneered the novel idea of native speakers teaching English in Argentine public schools. Mary Mann, Kate Doggett, Wickersham, and Barnard all looked for suitable and willing candidates in places as diverse as Massachusetts, New York, Illinois, Minnesota, and Wisconsin. Meanwhile, Sarmiento discussed his plans for school programs and curricula with Commissioner of Education Henry Barnard. The latter had invited Sarmiento to the Congress of the American Institute of Education and kept him informed about developments in education.[28] "Travel, study, and honors satisfied his curiosity and vanity."[29] Before returning to Buenos Aires, Sarmiento was persuaded by young Mitre to attend a commencement at the University of Michigan in Ann Arbor. To his complete and utter surprise, he was awarded an honorary doctorate, which meant a great deal to the self-made statesman and educator.[30]

Sarmiento was anxious to implement in Argentina many of the new things he had observed. When his ship docked in Brazil, he learned that he had been elected president of Argentina. Once Sarmiento took office he did many of the things he had always wanted to do. He ordered the taking of the first national census, introduced improvements in agriculture, encouraged immigration, built the National Observatory in Córdoba (the first in South America), built many schools and libraries, and substantially reformed Argentine educational practices. He introduced the white uniform worn by students today. In 1869 Congress created a national normal school network.[31]

The first North American teachers, the New Englanders Samuel Storrow Higginson and Foster Thayer, arrived in 1867, while Sarmiento was still in the United States. Governor Valentín Alsina of Buenos Aires was unwilling to help them find work; shunned, they left for Montevideo and, after an uprising there, promptly returned to the United States. For the plan of bringing foreign teachers to Argentine schools to succeed, high-level support was indispensable. As president, Sarmiento was able to overrule the opposition to using foreign teachers.[32]

The first teacher to arrive during Sarmiento's administration was Mary Elizabeth Gorman from Wisconsin. Unfortunately, members of the English-speaking community in the city of Buenos Aires advised her against undertaking what they perceived as a dangerous stagecoach trip to the Province of San Juan. Persuaded, she decided to remain and teach in the capital and she later married the man who dissuaded her from traveling to the Andes. The next three teachers, Anne and Elizabeth Dudley and Fanny Wood, also preferred to remain in the capital city and to teach kindergarten instead of setting out for the more primitive provinces, especially after they lived through an experience with yellow fever.[33] Sarmiento greatly lamented his failure to secure teachers for the remote provinces.[34]

Despite these early difficulties, additional teachers began to arrive. They all had received a progressive education; many had learned Latin, French, and Italian; and, owing to that preparation, they quickly became proficient in Spanish. They were also trained in practical domestic education.

The first U.S. teachers went to provincial posts in 1870. Sarmiento chose George Albert Stearns to establish a model normal school in Paraná, Entre Ríos. He arrived with his wife Julia and Lucy Wade, Nyra Kimball, and Sarah Armstrong. A few years later George Lane Roberts took over as principal. The school withstood many adversities, such as the revolutions led by the caudillo Ricardo López Jordán and economic difficulties. When his wife died in an epidemic, and his contract had expired, Stearns returned to the United States. He left behind a primary school that had been created as an annex to the normal school and where the students practiced teaching. Foreign languages were part of the normal school curriculum, along with modern sciences and gymnastics.

Stearns (and Sarmiento) fought for updated textbooks in Spanish, and if they were not available, used foreign textbooks. By 1874 the first translations of English and French textbooks into Spanish appeared. During the eight years that the normal school functioned, 526 teachers received diplomas and 18,281 students attended the primary school attached to it. The normal school of Paraná also became a training ground for newly arrived teachers from the United States. Here, they perfected their knowledge of Spanish and learned the customs of the land.[35]

Since the *colegios* and universities were closed to women, the Ministry of Education criticized Stearns for not training a larger number of teachers. In some areas a few religious elements raised objections to Protestants and foreigners teaching in the public schools, but in Paraná this did not present a major problem. As long as the school received the support of President Sarmiento and later President Nicolas Avellaneda, it was able to survive. It had to close in 1878 because the teachers were not being paid due to the economic depression (soldiers guarding the frontiers were not receiving their salaries either). The school reopened in 1880 with Argentine teachers and is known today as the Escuela Normal José María Torres. Stearns had written to his family in the United States that if someone had visited his school, he or she would not have been able to distinguish it from a U.S. school except for the language.[36] John William Stearns, George's brother, along with Lucy Wade and Mary Conway founded the normal school of Tucumán. Conway was one of the seven among the sixty-five teachers who were Roman Catholics.

Sarah Armstrong, a native of Buffalo who had taught in Winona, Minnesota, was perhaps the U.S. teacher who left the most lasting legacy. Arriving during Avellaneda's administration, she founded the normal school in the city of Catamarca in 1878 and was its director. It still bears her name. She feared no one and allowed nothing to frighten her. Ten years later, leaving the school in the hands of Argentine teachers, she went on to administer the normal school of San Nicolás de los Arroyos, then to a school in Buenos Aires, and finally to Rosario.[37] Sarah Chamberlin Eccleston, another pioneer, was known as "the grandmother of the kindergartens in Argentina," just as Elizabeth Peabody, sister of Mary Mann, is remembered as the founder of the first pre-schools in the United States. A young widow, Eccleston arrived with her fourteen-year-old daughter and worked with Argentine preschoolers for thirty years. She founded four public kindergartens, the first of which was attached to the primary school at the normal school in Paraná, and two private kindergartens. She taught several generations of students.[38]

A dream of Sarmiento became reality when Mary Olstine Graham arrived in San Juan in 1879 to establish and direct a normal school. Sarmiento had chosen her personally for "his San Juan." She was probably the North American teacher remembered with the most affection for the eight years she spent administering the school. From there she transferred to La Plata, where she built a school complex and taught until her death in 1906. Many of her former students established the "Mary O. Graham Center" with a library for the study of the sciences and culture.[39]

Another fondly remembered teacher was Jennie Howard of Massachusetts, who arrived in 1883 with a group of twenty-three teachers, two from Boston and the others from the Midwest. In her book *Distant Climes and Other Years*, Howard describes the experiences of many of the teachers in Argentina. She died in 1933, having taught and administered schools in Corrientes, Córdoba, and San Nicolás until she lost her voice in 1903. Upon her retirement, she was given a grand farewell in San Nicolás. Many of her former students kept in touch with her for almost thirty years. In 1928, on the feast of St. John (her "namesake" and patron saint), more than a hundred former students organized a celebration in her honor. Many came from afar, and when learning that teachers' pensions had been reduced, they organized a petition to secure additional funds for her.[40]

The teachers from the United States generally were received with admiration and affection and, when they completed their contracts, were asked to recommend their successors.[41] Usually, they left the schools in able Argentine hands. The only one to have an unpleasant experience was Francis Armstrong in Córdoba, a center with strong colonial Catholic traditions. Here, the governor objected to the program of physical education for the girls and to "heretic" Protestant teachers. To avoid a confrontation, Armstrong and her assistant finally left Córdoba for other positions. The North American teachers earned somewhat more in Argentina than they would have in the United States, but their salaries gradually were reduced with the recurring economic crises. They all taught in Spanish. In some of the remote areas they faced special hardships.[42]

Between 1871 and 1888 the North Americans founded thirty normal schools in Paraná (1871, 1883), Tucumán, Mendoza, Catamarca, San Juan, Rosario, Corrientes, Córdoba, Esquina, Concepción del Uruguay, Jujuy, La Rioja, Goya, La Plata, San Nicolás, Mercedes, and Buenos Aires. Approximately seventy teachers (Luiggi identified sixty-five) went to Argentina, only four of them were men. About half were from New England or New York, and the other half from the upper Midwest. Of the sixty-five studied by Luiggi, thirty-six taught an average of thirteen years, sixteen left the classroom after fulfilling their first contract, two married before completing their contracts, twenty married after finishing their contracts, and twelve died while teaching during the epidemics.[43] The idea of inviting teachers from another country and culture was ahead of its time, a nineteenth-century Peace Corps. The schools these teachers established became the basis of Argentina's teacher colleges.

Jennie Howard summed up the teachers' overall assessment when she said that they all felt freer to pursue more vigorous intellectual activities in a new environment. Wherever they went, they enlivened the society's social life. Many of them founded women's clubs and encouraged civic activities. They never stopped expressing their gratitude, not only for the kindness, friendship, and generosity of their students' parents, but also for the warm recognition and affection they received from their pupils.[44] Although the North American teachers came from several states, they all shared the philosophy of Horace Mann, rooted in positivism and the firm belief in forming and improving the whole person. They were earnest and dedicated and they earned the respect of the communities in which they lived and worked.

Sarmiento understood that his country had to reach out to other countries to become part of the international community. His legacy is still alive today in Argentina with the law that established public schools and the system of normal school networks that he created. Understanding the United States better than his contemporaries, Sarmiento found a kindred spirit for his educational theories in Horace Mann. Sarmiento saw clearly that to achieve true democracy and train the citizens, the country had to create a universal system of public schools. Such a system should be financed through taxes. To complement schools and to promote the formation of an informed citizenry, he encouraged the creation of public libraries. He believed that to attain freedom, a community had to be composed of rational, literate, and informed individuals. He wanted public schools governed by local communities, as he had observed in New England.

At the beginning of Sarmiento's administration there were thirty thousand school children in Argentina. When his term ended six years later, there were more than a hundred thousand. His lifelong ambition had been "to make the whole Republic a school." In his mind "schools are [the basis for] democracy."[45] Among his many accomplishments as an essayist, journalist, and political leader, his greatest achievements remain those in the field of education. Thanks to his efforts, Argentina was able to boast one of the most advanced school systems of the Americas. However, the country failed to become a democracy and to accord full participatory citizenship to its population until the second decade of the twentieth century.

NOTES

1. This paper was originally presented at the Sarmiento Centennial Symposium held at the University of Ottawa, Canada, 13 October 1988.

2. Domingo F. Sarmiento, *Sarmiento's Travels in the United States in 1847*,

ed. and trans. Michael Aaron Rockland (Princeton: Princeton University Press, 1970), 5.

3. Ricardo Rojas, *El profeta de la pampa; Vida de Sarmiento* (Buenos Aires: Editorial Losada, 1945), 721, 724; Enrique Anderson Imbert, *Genio y figura de Sarmiento* (Buenos Aires: Editorial Universitaria de Buenos Aires, 1967), 11. All translations are my own unless otherwise indicated.

4. Natalio R. Botana, *La tradición republicana* (Buenos Aires: Editorial Sudamericana, 1984), 483–484.

5. Domingo F. Sarmiento, Oscawana Lake, Peekskill, New York, to Mary Mann, 15 June 1866, *Boletín de la Academia Argentina de Letras* 4 (1936): 312. Hereafter cited as *BAAL*. Mary Mann will be cited as M. Mann.

6. We will follow Sarmiento's spelling when quoting him. See Manuel Antonio Ponce, *Sarmiento i sus doctrinas pedagójicas* (Valparaiso: Imp. i Lib. Americana de F. T. Lathrop, 1890), 29–31; *El Mercurio* (Santiago de Chile), 20 August 1841; Domingo F. Sarmiento, *Obras completas*, vol. 3, *Recuerdos de provincia. Biografías* (53 vols., Buenos Aires: Editorial Luz del Día, 1948–1956), 5–6, 69–71, 180–181; ibid., vol. 12, *Educación común*, 196; ibid., vol. 28, *Ideas pedagógicas*, 323–334.

7. Sarmiento, *Obras completas*, vol. 22, *Discursos populares*, 244–245.

8. Paul Verdevoye, *Domingo Faustino Sarmiento, éducateur et publiciste entre 1839 et 1852* (Paris: n.p., 1963), 217–223.

9. Rojas, *Profeta*, 189–190; Verdevoye, *Sarmiento*, 230–232.

10. Sarmiento, *Sarmiento's Travels*, 176 and 183–184.

11. Sarmiento, *Obras completas*, vol. 11, *De la educación popular*, 25; Sarmiento, New York, 8 July 1865, to M. Mann, in *Las escuelas: Base de la prosperidad i de la república en los Estados Unidos. Informe al ministro de instrucción pública de la República arjentina. Pasado por D. F. Sarmiento* (New York: n.p., 1870), 51.

12. Sarmiento, *Sarmiento's Travels*, 152.

13. Alison Williams Bunkley, *The Life of Sarmiento* (New York: Greenwood Press, 1969), 279–280; Anderson Imbert, *Genio*, 81–82. An important source, especially for the U.S. schoolteachers, is Alice Houston Luiggi, *Sesenta y cinco valientes; Sarmiento y las maestras norteamericanas*. Foreword by Alberto Palcos (Buenos Aires: Editorial Agora, 1959), 23–25.

14. Mary Tyler Peabody Mann was the sister of Sophia Peabody, founder of kindergartens in the United States, and of Elizabeth Peabody, wife of Nathaniel Hawthorne. She was an educator and became an adviser to Sarmiento throughout a thirteen-year correspondence. See Louise Hall Tharp, *The Peabody Sisters of Salem* (Boston: Little, Brown, 1950).

15. Sarmiento, *Las escuelas*, 50–51.

16. Sarmiento, *De la educación popular*, 14–17 and 87–88; Domingo F. Sarmiento, *Viajes. Estados Unidos* (Buenos Aires: Vaccaaro, 1922), 125.

17. Domingo F. Sarmiento, *Anales de la educación común* 1 (1859): 298ff.

18. Sarmiento, New York, 20 May 1866, to M. Mann, *BAAL*, IV (1936): 297.

19. Bunkley, *Sarmiento*, 378–379; Sarmiento, *Obras completas*, vol. 26, *El camino del lacio*, 16–45, 97, and 305.

20. Domingo F. Sarmiento, *Los discursos populares de D. F. Sarmiento, 1839–1883. (Arreglados por A. Belín Sarmiento)* (Buenos Aires: Impr. Europea, 1883), cited in Aníbal Ponce, *Sarmiento, constructor de la nueva Argentina* (Buenos Aires: Espasa-Calpe, 1932), 150.

21. Sarmiento, *Obras completas*, vol. 7, *Quiroga. Aldao. El Chacho, 1845–1863*, 336–337.

22. Anderson Imbert, *Genio*, 7; Sarmiento, New York, to M. Mann, 8 July

1866, in *Las escuelas,* 50–51. Sarmiento's translation of the life of Horace Mann appears in *Las escuelas,* 79–119.

23. M. Mann, Concord, to Sarmiento, 13 July 1865, Library of Congress, Manuscript Division. Hereafter cited as LC/MSS. See also M. Mann, Cambridge, Massachusetts, to Henry Barbard, 23 December 1867, LC/MSS.

24. Sarmiento, New York, to M. Mann, 23 January 1866, *BAAL* IV (1936): 84–85.

25. Sarmiento, New York, to M. Mann, 5 February 1866, ibid.: 89.

26. [Domingo F. Sarmiento], *North and South America. A Discourse Delivered Before the Rhode-Island Historical Society, December 27, 1865. By His Excellency, Domingo Faustino Sarmiento, Argentine Minister to the United States* (Providence: Knowles, Anthony & Co., 1866).

27. Sarmiento, New York, to M. Mann, 13 April 1866, *BAAL* IV (1936): 97–98.

28. Sarmiento, New York, to H. Barnard, 12 January 1866, LC/MSS; *Sarmiento's Travels,* 58–59.

29. Rojas, *Profeta,* 492.

30. Sarmiento, New York, to M. Mann, 9 May 1868, and M. Mann, Cambridge, to H. Barnard, 10 April 1867, LC/MSS.

31. Sarmiento, Buenos Aires, to M. Mann, 30 December 1870, LC/MSS, describes the difficulties he was experiencing in establishing the observatory, in bringing the North American Benjamin Gould to Córdoba, and in raising transportation funds for the U.S. teachers coming to Argentina.

32. Juana Manso, Buenos Aires, to M. Mann, 12 July 1871, LC/MSS.

33. Sarmiento, Buenos Aires, to M. Mann, 12 July 1871, LC/MSS, talks about the epidemic for which the capital was unprepared and in which Miss Wood died after having bravely assisted the sick. Miss Wood had even offered to pay the cost of her passage, but Sarmiento refused to accept it. Luiggi, *Sesenta y cinco,* 76–89.

34. Sarmiento, Buenos Aires, to M. Mann, 14 July 1870, LC/MSS.

35. Luiggi, *Sesenta y cinco,* 90–97. In 1872 Julia Stearns was the first Protestant to die in Paraná, and there was confusion as to whether she could be buried in a Catholic cemetery. While he was waiting for the decision of the church, Stearns stood by the coffin overnight in order to prevent predatory animals from getting into it. Jennie E. Howard, one of the teachers who taught in the normal schools, wrote her memoirs, *In Distant Climes and Other Years* (Buenos Aires: The American Press, 1931). Here I use the Spanish translation of Eduardo Rípodas, *En otros años y climas distantes* (Buenos Aires: Raigal, 1951).

36. Luiggi, *Sesenta y cinco,* 99. See also Tristán Enrique Guevara, *Las maestras norteamericanas que trajo Sarmiento. Conferencia pronunciada en el salón de actos del Servicio Cultural e Informativo de la Estados Unidos de América, en Buenos Aires, como adhesión al Día del Maestro, el 10 de setiembre de 1954* (Buenos Aires: Servicio Cultural e Informativo de los Estados Unidos de América, 1954).

37. *Conmemoración del 80 aniversario de la fundación de la escuela normal Clara F. Armstrong* (Buenos Aires: n.p., 1958), 5–6; Guevara, *Maestras,* 16. Some ladies from Catamarca complained about the Protestant headmistress Armstrong to Friar Mamerto Esquiú. The learned Franciscan responded that he was satisfied with the atmosphere of morality and religious tolerance that he saw in the school. Howard, *Otros,* 104–105; Luiggi, *Sesenta y cinco,* 127–131.

38. Ibid. Luiggi, 170–171.

39. Guevara, *Maestras,* 16–17; Luiggi, *Sesenta y cinco,* 234–240.

40. Ibid. Luiggi, 169–200; Howard, *Otros,* 14 and 108.

41. Ibid. Howard, 137.

42. Luiggi, *Sesenta y cinco,* 122–123; Howard, *Otros,* 61–71.

43. Sarmiento, *Sarmiento's Travels,* 67–68; Luiggi, *Sesenta y cinco,* 68–72. A listing of the North American teachers is in Howard, *Otros,* 137–140.

44. Ibid., 107–108 and 113.

45. Quoted in Sarmiento, *Sarmiento's Travels,* 67.

"Woman" in Sarmiento

Laura V. Monti

I have always compared Domingo Faustino Sarmiento to the hot and violent wind of his native land, called Zonda. Even on austere winter days, Zonda subdues everything with its heat and violence as it blows through the mountains to the neighboring towns of San Luis and Mendoza, leaving even in the most hidden corners of the Andean provinces and cities a film of dust and sand. Sarmiento fought all the established ideas with the same passion and violence, depositing the seed of his new ideas, on all topics, in all places, from the small villages of his province to the great cities of Europe and the United States, where he is honored and where monuments are erected in his memory.

His ideas are sometimes full of contradictions, but they are always sincere; his actions, most often impetuous but always well informed, resulted in the creation of public and vocational schools, museums and libraries, printing presses, roads, and railroads. Before and during his presidency (1868–1874), he founded the Academy of Sciences, the Observatory of Astronomy of Córdoba, and the naval and army academies. He established the national bank, introduced the telegraph, secured passage of the civil legal code, ordered the first national census, and took so many other steps that his government was and still is considered the most progressive in Argentine history.

For the immensity of the measures he took, Sarmiento was either criticized or admired. But neither the criticism nor the admiration stopped him from thinking of new actions and implementing them as fast as he could, as if the time left was too short to accomplish the multitude of things he had in his creative mind. If we add to all his practical deeds the fifty-three volumes of his written works—books, letters, articles, speeches, reports, etc.—we have to agree that his was the

Laura V. Monti is keeper of rare books, Boston Public Library.

labor of a giant in a land torn between tyranny, internal dissensions, and personal envies.[1] But the source of his inspiration was deeper than the circumstances surrounding him. It was in his own life, his readings, and his numerous trips to foreign lands where he observed and learned.

Sarmiento envisioned an Argentina that occupied a position of leadership in South America and that was on an equal footing with the other great nations of the civilized world. As a means of arriving at that leadership role, he placed education above all other considerations. He saw education as a right of every citizen to have and a duty of every citizen to acquire.[2] His innovative idea was to place women in the top posts in education and to make them the most powerful instrument in spreading education.

If we follow Sarmiento through his *Recuerdos de provincia,*[3] we can see very clearly how he got that vision of female power, a very new concept at the time. He saw the dignity and pride of his impoverished aunt arriving from her properties in Angaco, "dragging a bad looking hack crowned with two saddlebags filled with legumes and chickens for sale hanging on each side of its bony back."[4] He saw the image of a perfect mother in Paula de Oro, the wife of his uncle Ignacio Sarmiento. She had a "character as soft as a dove, severe and affectionate as a queen."[5] Sarmiento witnessed the great moral courage of his own mother. Her dignified independence allowed her to support the household, while her dreamer of a husband got involved in impractical enterprises, which required long trips to the other provinces, and helped out only occasionally. Sarmiento saw his mother's physical strength when she crossed the rugged mountains of the Andes to see him in exile for the last time. He sensed his mother's soul and understood that she was a profound and dedicated believer in God, but far removed from the practices of organized religion.[6] He saw his sisters breathing new ideas of beauty, good taste, and comfort as a legacy of the nineteenth-century revolution, introducing in their traditional homes elements of renewal, personal improvement, and certain elements of impiety that had lingered on since that era.[7]

He saw women fighting like lions against the *montoneras,* whose orgies of crimes and devastations illuminated the horizon of the countryside with burning roofs and grass.[8] Undoubtedly, it was life itself that allowed him to see, to give value, and to discover the infinite possibilities and capacities of women. The inspiration Sarmiento received from these observations gave him the great idea of regarding women as persons with their own virtues and defects, their own needs and capabilities, not only as companions of men, as wives, as mothers, or as decorative elements in the home, but as important participants in the task of civilization. His trips taught him that in other countries women had already begun to exercise a more active role in society and their voices were being heard.

He discovered that in the United States references were made specifically to man and woman as separate entities, taking woman out of the general term "man."

In Lima, Sarmiento saw that women daily enjoyed two hours of freedom, when, married or single, they left their homes wearing a long skirt, their heads covered with a shawl, and only their naughty and picturesque eyes uncovered. From this moment, unrecognized, all social restrictions disappear, public criticism does not reach them, and the timid and reserved young women become provocative and playful. When the *"tapadas"* (as they were called) returned home, they resumed their ordinary lives or their role of housewives.[9] Sarmiento saw this, approved of it, and enjoyed it, for he understood it was a way for women to assert their own independence. All these things that he witnessed and the emotions he had felt since his childhood formed in him a very modern image of women and their role in society. To be successful in this new role, a woman should be educated. In his speech before the students of the Model School of the North Cathedral on 18 July 1860, Sarmiento proclaimed proudly that Buenos Aires was the only state in South America where women received an education in the same proportion as men.[10] This was the goal Sarmiento achieved after fighting all his life for the education of women. When he was twenty-seven years old, he established in his native province the Boarding School for Girls (*Pensionado de Niñas*), also called the School of Saint Rose of America, with the cooperation of a distinguished lady, Transito de Oro. This school, which was meant for young girls only, was the first of its kind in South America. In the prospectus announcing its establishment, the two ideas that would govern Sarmiento's future plans appear very clearly: solve social problems by creating more schools, where more people can be educated, and incorporate women as essential elements.

Later, in his *De la educación popular,* Sarmiento dedicated an entire chapter to the subject of female education.[11] The indifference and lack of importance given to female education during the colonial period was due to the Spanish view that education was only an ornament for women. At the beginning of the nineteenth century there were no schools where women could learn to read and write. In Argentina, Sarmiento noted, it was many years after independence that some interest arose in raising women's cultural level, and it was President Bernardino Rivadavia (1826–1827) who established equal education for both sexes. Spain had not progressed, Sarmiento observed, for it still viewed education as a simple ornament for women of the wealthy classes.

Sarmiento clearly laid down here his reasons for saying that women should be educated. The fate of the state depends on them. Civilization stops at the doors of the homes if a home is not prepared to receive its benefits. In her role as mother, wife, or domestic servant, a woman can destroy the standing of the home. She perpetuates habits, good or bad, and prejudices and concerns, and the ways of society cannot be altered without first changing her ideas and habits. That is why Sarmiento admired the accessibility to education that women had in the United States and Europe. There, the same teachers, at the same schools, taught the same subjects to both sexes, separately or together. For Sarmiento, it made no sense to educate the man and not the woman, the brother and not the sister, the father-to-be and not the mother-to-be. Why, he asked, perpetuate the barbarism in one that one wishes to destroy in the other. Why do the opposite of what nature itself advises, which is to educate the one who, because of her matrimonial union, is destined to be the base of a new family, a mother and a teacher of her children, carrying with her into the house the seed of civilization.[12] For this task, and because of her moral aptitudes, Sarmiento also considered women totally superior to men when it comes to educating children. He stressed this point because French and Italian law placed education in female hands.

In the United States women had begun to participate intensively in public education.[13] This fact amazed Sarmiento. For him the change had come very rapidly, as it was only in 1808 that the first school for girls was opened in Essex, Massachusetts, and only in 1845 that women were admitted to higher education.[14] In Argentina, if women were educated and prepared, they could be the best instrument to spread to the far corners of the country not only their knowledge but also a multitude of small manual industries, such as crafts, design, embroidery, gardening, and so forth, providing people with new means of subsistence.

During the celebration of the one-hundredth anniversary of the independence of the United States that was held in the home of Minister Osborn, Sarmiento made reference in his toast to the transfigurations that women had undergone under the influence of U.S. institutions and the public schools, something he had fought for all his life in Argentina.[15] From 1845, when the first normal school was opened in the United States, to 1866, millions of women had received an education, and the influence of this education was beginning to affect social relations. He felt that these changes, because of the thousands who received an education, gave to the faces of U.S. women something that was lacking in the beauty and pride of upper-class women in other countries: the feeling of self-sufficiency. This feeling led women to modify their attitude toward others—the women, poor but educated, with a skill and a job, felt free and dignified.[16] It is this picture of the U.S. woman that Sarmiento had in mind in 1883 when he told the graduating class at the Normal School for Women (*Escuela Normal de Mujeres*) of Montevideo: "You are going to teach, and teaching to civilize society in mass, in public schools, opening to other women the road that leads to independence."[17]

This, then, is Sarmiento's image of women: cultivated, in control of herself and of her destiny, mother but mother leading civilization. This is a complimentary vision of women, according to Sarmiento the man, the human. Lugones notes that among our hero's qualities was an inexhaustible love for women: "starry guides of his rough existence, smoothing with delicate sensuality the velvet lining of his clutches in order to conquer them or to deserve them."[18] In spite of Sarmiento's rugged ugliness, his large mouth, his heavy lips, his weather-beaten pallor, and his greenish gray eyes when calm, but dusky and somber when angry, he attracted high-caliber women who supported and maintained him during the numerous and profound crises in his life.[19]

Besides his adored mother, the second woman in his life was Benita Martínez, born in San Juan and married in Chile to Domingo Castro y Calvo. Sarmiento was immediately attracted to this passionate and brilliant woman, and she to him. When Castro died, Sarmiento and Benita were married. Intelligent and understanding as she was, her passionate and jealous temperament undermined his love. He wrote about her "insatiable volcano of insatiable passion . . . her love was a venom which ate the vase that contained it."[20] So, the separation came.

During this period, Sarmiento found consolation in various intelligent women. Mary Mann, Horace Mann's wife, who knew the most important people of the day, gave him the satisfaction of introducing him to them at the same time that she translated his *Facundo*. Juana Manso, not a very attractive woman, but of great intelligence, embraced his cause with passion. Educator and writer, she edited the *Anales de la Educación común*, a journal founded by Sarmiento. Manso became the symbol of his fight for female participation in the educational process.

But, above all others, the most influential woman in Sarmiento's life was Amelia Vélez Sársfield. Born into a refined and cultured family, elegant, intellectually brilliant, and full of social graces, Amelia could discuss ideas with the most distinguished personalities of the moment. She was Sarmiento's dream of the totally complete woman. Married very young, unsuccessfully, to a cousin, she met Sarmiento and the friendship that grew between them evolved into a profound love that lasted unchanged and unfulfilled through many years. Both separated from their partners, both followed roads apart according to the proper behavior required by the times. But, she remained until the end Sarmiento's only truthful friend and inspiration.

Tired and sick, she sought a more peaceful life in Paraguay. Sarmiento and Amelia exchanged several letters. He became anxious to see her before his death, begging her several times to visit him. He sat for hours in front of the window waiting, but when she finally decided to come, she arrived too late. Sarmiento was dead. Today, Sarmiento should be remembered for what he was—a pioneer in the fight for women's rights.

NOTES

1. Domingo F. Sarmiento, *Obras de D. F. Sarmiento* (53 vols., Santiago de Chile: Imprenta Gutenberg, 1885–1903).

2. Domingo F. Sarmiento, *De la educación popular* (Santiago de Chile: J. Belín i Cia., 1849), 56.

3. Domingo F. Sarmiento, *Recuerdos de provincia* (Buenos Aires: Editorial Universitaria de Buenos Aires, 1960).

4. Ibid., 37–38.

5. Ibid., 53.

6. Ibid., 81 and 95.

7. Ibid., 98–99.

8. Domingo F. Sarmiento, *Facundo; Civilización y barbarie* (Buenos Aires: Editorial Universitaria, [1961]), 97.

9. Domingo F. Sarmiento, "Discurso de Recepción en el Instituto histórico de Francia—San Martín y Bolivar, Paris, Julio 1, 1847," in *Los discursos populares de D. F. Sarmiento, 1839–1883. (Arreglados por A. Belín Sarmiento)* (Buenos Aires: Imprenta Europea, 1883), 18–19.

10. "Inauguración de la Escuela modelo de la Catedral al Norte. Julio 18 de 1860," in ibid., 88–96.

11. Sarmiento, "De la educación de las mujeres," Sarmiento, *De la educación popular,* 129–195.

12. Sarmiento, "Manifestación de las Escuelas de Buenos Aires á la llegada del Presidente electo. Setiembre 1868," in *Discursos populares,* 202–209.

13. Ibid.

14. Ibid.

15. "Centenario de la Independencia de los Estados Unidos— Brindis en casa del Ministro Jeneral Osborn, 4 de Julio de 1876," in ibid., 315–322.

16. "Manifestación de las Escuelas," in ibid., 202–209.

17. "Escuela Normal de Mujeres. Febrero de 1883. Montevideo," in ibid., 439–451.

18. Leopoldo Lugones, *Historia de Sarmiento* (Buenos Aires: Editorial Universitaria de Buenos Aires, 1960, 21.

19. Ibid., 25.

20. Domingo Faustino Sarmiento, *Antología total de Sarmiento.* Edited by Germán Berdiales (2 vols. Buenos Aires, Ediciones Culturales Argentina, Ministerio de Educación y Justicia, Dirección General de Cultura, 1962), 2:89.

10

Sarmiento and Rosas: Argentines in Search of a Nation, 1810–1852

Joseph T. Criscenti

In the prologue to his edition of *Recuerdos de provincia,* Enrique Anderson Imbert observes that Domingo F. Sarmiento did not belong to a particular philosophical school.[1] Sarmiento certainly was not a methodical or reflective thinker, but he had a tremendous memory and held steadfast to some basic convictions. One belief was that the Province of San Juan, where he was born in 1811, was his fatherland, *su patria.* Sarmiento was a provincial nationalist, and for many years San Juan's welfare was his primary concern. He and his contemporaries were influenced by their patriotic feeling for their native provinces. "Local affections," he once wrote, "are part of our existence."[2]

Located at the foot of the Andes, Sarmiento's San Juan faced Chile and the Pacific rather than Buenos Aires and the Atlantic Ocean. It and the neighboring provinces were little frequented and little known by the outside world, including Buenos Aires, as late as the 1830s. San Juan, primarily an agricultural province, until it was included in the Viceroyalty of the Río de la Plata in 1776, had been part of the Captaincy General of Chile. For this reason, many of its inhabitants, including Sarmiento, had relatives in Chile and felt at home on either side of the Andes. Prior to the outbreak of the independence movement, Spain was the mother country (*madre patria*).

The outbreak of the revolutionary movement had no effect on the primary loyalty of the people to the native province, but South America replaced Spain as the mother country. When José de Oro taught Sarmiento "to love liberty and the fatherland," the provinces were already emerging as small military republics, anxious to form a federation, and loyalty to a new entity, South America, was being superimposed on provincial loyalty.[3] The people were calling themselves South Ameri-

Joseph T. Criscenti is professor emeritus of history, Boston College.

cans rather than Spanish Americans, Governor Estanislao López of Santa Fe began his correspondence with "South American Confederation," and provincial constitutions, like the *Estatuto Provisional* of Santa Fe (26 August 1819), granted citizenship to all Americans.[4] San Martín summarized the new outlook when he spoke of the "Americans or United Provinces."[5] Juan C. Lafinur went further: "America, my dear, will become the common fatherland of all nations, and the asylum of *all liberties.*"[6]

Within the anticipated larger political conglomerate of independent provinces or states, there were short-lived efforts to unite those with similar or supporting economic interests into one republic or confederation. General Francisco Ramírez of Entre Ríos united Entre Ríos and Corrientes into his Republic of Entre Ríos (1820–1821), which had its own customhouses, but he never succeeded in bringing Paraguay into it. José Artigas, anxious to develop the port of Montevideo, formed a loose confederation with his Provincia Oriental del Uruguay, Entre Ríos, Corrientes, Santa Fe, and Córdoba (1815–1820), and hoped to include Paraguay and Rio Grande do Sul. Bernabé Aráoz of Tucumán organized the Federal Republic of Tucumán with Tucumán, Catamarca, and Santiago del Estero (1820–1821). The government of Buenos Aires appointed José de San Martín to govern the Intendancy of Cuyo, and renamed it the Province of Cuyo (Mendoza, San Juan, and San Luis).

The idea of a new *madre patria* (mother country) excited the imagination of Sarmiento's father, who himself was nicknamed "Madre Patria." Sarmiento's father enlisted in the Army of the Andes, or Army of the Fatherland, and fought at Chacabuco (12 February 1817). He undoubtedly was pleased when the Congress of Tucumán declared the independence of the legal but formless federation called the United Provinces in South America (*Provincias Unidas en Sud América*) in 1816. The Congress essentially declared the "independence of South America."[7]

At the same time, conservative leaders in Buenos Aires started looking abroad for a prince to rule "South America."[8] He would rule the *patria grande* (great fatherland), that is, a confederation which would include the Viceroyalty of the Río de la Plata, Chile, and Peru. In 1819 Buenos Aires made an effort to provide a constitution for the United Provinces in South America, but the document was rejected by the other provinces. Entre Ríos and Santa Fe rebelled, and in the Treaty of Pilar (23 February 1820), they forced the city of Buenos Aires to relinquish its position as the capital of the viceroyalty and to revert to its old status and boundaries as a province. A few years later, San Martín and Simón Bolivar formed an alliance, the Confederation of the Towns of South America, but few South Americans joined it.[9]

The idea of South America as the mother country persisted in the interior provinces until 1825 or 1828, and the provincial *cabildos* regarded themselves from the beginning of the independence movement as the capital of separate republics. As a French observer noted, each village, each hamlet wanted to be a *patrie* and to participate in a federation.[10] Sarmiento summarized the situation succinctly. Whether they called themselves "Province, canton, state or Republic," he said, they were sovereign independent states.[11] Some of these provinces combined to form a military federation, like the one San Martín tried to create with the Republic of Cuyo (formerly the Province of Cuyo).[12] Some political leaders, among them Artigas, looked forward to the formation of "a confederation of states similar to that of the United States."[13] The provinces in the former Viceroyalty of the Río de la Plata, officially or unofficially, were recognized as independent states and conducted diplomatic relations with their neighbors. Those provinces that authorized the State of Buenos Aires to represent them in international negotiations reserved the right to ratify any treaty and to confirm the appointment of diplomats. The State of Buenos Aires was itself officially recognized by Brazil in 1821.[14] Porteño leaders still cherished the notion of a unified continent. Their representatives at the Córdoba Congress of 1821, called to "form a State or Nation with those which until now have belonged to the Union,"[15] were instructed to ask "all the free Governments, and Municipalities of the Continent to form . . . a respectable Nation by a federation that subordinated to its united representation the direction and administration" all matters of "common interest to the States, including those of Chile, and these Provinces." Congress also was to seek "the recognition of the Independence of this America." For the Junta de Representantes, the provincial governing body, the Province of Buenos Aires was a "nascent republic," part of a larger federation, and the prevalent view was that its people were citizens of "South America."[16]

As the dream of a continental nation or a confederation of the Argentine provinces, Chile and Peru, the *patria grande*, began to fade in the 1820s, some porteños substituted for the *patria grande* the *común madre patria* (the common mother country), the Viceroyalty of the Río de la Plata and Chile. How long the two concepts coexisted is not clear, but the ability of San Martín to bring Peru within the Buenos Aires orbit was already in doubt by mid-1821. The concept of *común madre patria* lasted a little longer, for there were still echoes of it among Argentine exiles in the 1840s. As the expectation that Chile would join the Argentine provinces in forming one nation dwindled, probably by 1823, there emerged another concept, the *patria común* (common fatherland), the Viceroyalty of the Río de la Plata without Chile. Reconstituting the viceroyalty meant asking Brazil to return the Cisplatine province (the Banda Oriental del Uruguay), persuading Paraguay to abandon its isolation, and stopping the advance of Bolívar into Bolivia. The *patria común* also would give Buenos Aires the monopoly of navigation on the Río de la Plata and the entrance to Meridional America.

The centerpiece of the new state would be the Cisplatine province of the Banda Oriental del Uruguay, "considered the richest in the whole viceroyalty of Buenos Ayres; it not only provided the best pasture and arable land, but the port of Monte Video was the most promising harbour on that part of the coast."[17]

Bernardino Rivadavia, minister of government in the administration of Buenos Aires (1821–1824), who symbolized "civilization and progress," concentrated on putting together the *patria común*. First, he negotiated an offensive and defensive alliance with Corrientes, Entre Ríos, and Santa Fe—the Pact of the Quadrilateral—on 25 January 1822. He then invited the provinces, including Upper Peru, to a congress that would "reunite all the provinces of the territory that from emancipation formed the Viceroyalty of Buenos Aires or Río de la Plata . . . in a Nation" with one government.[18] On 23 January 1825 this congress passed and the provinces approved a fundamental law for the Republic of the United Provinces of the Río de la Plata. The Department of Foreign Relations for the republic, administered by the Province of Buenos Aires, negotiated a treaty of friendship, trade, and navigation with Great Britain (2 February 1825). Later that year war broke out between Buenos Aires and Brazil over possession of the Provincia Oriental del Uruguay, whose port of Montevideo was the key to the Río de la Plata.

In 1826 the Rivadavian majority in the congress, *titulado nacional*, unwilling to wait for the Argentine provinces to act, first elected Rivadavia president of the "Argentine Republic," and then, after listening to Sir Woodbine Parish, approved a constitution for the nonexistent state.[19] The provinces failed to endorse the constitution because, as Fructuoso Rivera, the Oriental leader, put it, they lacked a "national spirit."[20] Instead, eleven provinces, including the Cisplatine province of the Banda Oriental, formed a military alliance (17 May 1827) to resist the constitution. The alliance treaty declared that five ports on the Paraná and Uruguay rivers—Santa Fe, Paraná, Arroyo del China, Gualeguay, and Gualeguaychú—were free ports open to all the provinces, and that export and import duties collected in them belonged to all the eleven provinces. The treaty also called for a congress to meet outside of Buenos Aires. Córdoba withdrew its congressional representatives, notified foreign governments of its action, asked Bolivar for his protection, and declared that there was no republic or nation. Rivadavia was forced to resign in July 1827 because the peace treaty negotiated with Brazil provided for Uruguayan independence. Now, the "nation was dissolved," and with it the "old Argentine Republic," the *patria común*.[21]

Manuel Dorrego, the new governor of the Province of Buenos Aires (there was no longer any "national authority," war-weary Buenos Aires now called itself "the Republic"[22]) quickly concluded treaties with

CHILI, LA PLATA,
AND
BOLIVIA OR UPPER PERU

BY BASIL HALL.

Corrientes, Córdoba, Entre Ríos, and Santa Fe. He arranged for the representatives of the United Provinces of the Río de la Plata, the confederation formed in 1825, to meet in the city of Santa Fe to discuss peace with Brazil. Not all of the provinces were represented at the so-called national convention when it authorized Dorrego to negotiate a peace treaty. Both Dorrego and Juan Antonio Lavalleja, the Uruguayan leader who had begun the war to free the Provincia Oriental from Brazil, saw in a reconstituted viceroyalty the *patria común*. Neither of them favored the "absolute independence" of the Provincia Oriental del Uruguay (since 1829 the República Oriental del Uruguay). Nevertheless Dorrego, in the interest of peace and economic recuperation on both sides of the Río de la Plata, accepted the preliminary peace convention, which did not grant Uruguayan independence.

Rivadavia and veterans of the struggle for independence and the recent war with Brazil felt differently. Anxious to defend "the honor of the Republic," the Province of Buenos Aires, they persuaded General Juan Lavalle, a provincial nationalist, to overthrow and assassinate Dorrego. He did this on 1 December 1828 and then marched on the national convention.[23] There was need for action, for Governor Estanislao López of Santa Fe had closed all roads to the interior provinces and the neighboring republics and the city of Buenos Aires was struck by an epidemic and a famine. The national convention was quick to respond. It appointed López director of war, peace, and foreign relations and commander of the *Ejército Confederado*, authorized him to overthrow the Lavalle military dictatorship, and declared that the Province of Buenos Aires lacked "national character." López and Juan Manuel de Rosas, who had joined him after the assassination of Dorrego and commanded the army of Buenos Aires, defeated Lavalle at the Puente de Márquez (28 April 1829). Peace within the province, something everybody wanted, was reestablished, and as Lavalle and Rosas had agreed, Rosas, a provincial nationalist, took office as governor of Buenos Aires on 1 December 1829.[24]

Rosas's first concern was to restore the prosperity of the Province of Buenos Aires and to protect its independence. At the time, Buenos Aires and many of the interior provinces were reeling from the severe effects of a drought that had begun earlier in the year and was to last for three years. Buenos Aires turned into "an arid desert," with cattle and horses dying from thirst and dust, and people abandoning many areas of the country. Economic activity dwindled, foreign and domestic credit disappeared, war veterans were unemployed, and the bankruptcy of the government was anticipated. Rosas opened new land for settlement on the southern borders of the province, annually sent the Indians the government gifts he had promised them, and promptly paid the militiamen who had served under him.[25]

To the north, Rosas faced the threat of a war with General José María Paz, Lavalle's minister of war, who had fled after the assassination of Dorrego with part of the rebellious "national army" to his native province, Córdoba. There, Paz organized nine provinces into a military league, the League of the Interior, appointed a minister of foreign affairs, and prepared for a war with Rosas, even while signing a pact with Buenos Aires on 27 October 1829 to invite, with the concurrence of Santa Fe, all the provinces to a national body (*cuerpo nacional*) in order to organize and form the republic. The following July the five provinces that Paz dominated—Catamarca, Córdoba, San Luis, Mendoza, and La Rioja—sent their diplomatic agents to Córdoba to sign an alliance treaty and to ask Buenos Aires and Santa Fe to call a meeting to discuss the "Constitution of the State and the organization of the republic." The diplomatic agents of these provinces later met with their counterparts from Salta, San Juan, Tucumán, and Santiago del Estero to designate Paz, on behalf of the "United Argentine Provinces," their supreme military commander, and "to form themselves into a single family."[26] Their ostensible aim was to form a republic that was not dominated by the littoral provinces.[27]

Rosas, who had no intention of forming a separate nation, was unwilling to participate in a meeting dominated by Córdoba and the interior provinces or to recognize their governments, but he was willing, as the British minister had suggested, to approve a general treaty with them. He was warned that they, in desperate economic straits and fearing anarchy, were seeking mutual support; that the unemployed veteran army officers were influencing public opinion; and that acceptance of the idea popular in the interior provinces of a congress attended by Buenos Aires and the littoral provinces could "end the appearances that now support this fantasy Republic." Instead he prepared the defenses of the province, provided Governor López of Santa Fe, Governor Juan Facundo Quiroga of La Rioja, and their Indian allies with financial subsidies so that they could fight Paz, and he concluded the Treaty of the Littoral (4 January 1831) with the provinces of Corrientes, Entre Ríos, and Santa Fe. Santa Fe, the second city after Buenos Aires, was to block any invasion of Buenos Aires from the interior provinces; Entre Ríos was to help restock the Buenos Aires army with horses and protect the roads to Uruguay; and Corrientes was to guard the borders with Rio Grande do Sul. Under the treaty, a "Representative Commission of the Governments of the Littoral Provinces of the Argentine Republic" was responsible for the conduct of foreign relations and could declare war. Only when it withdrew its representative from the commission did Buenos Aires receive authority to conduct the foreign relations of the provinces.[28]

The war ended when Paz unexpectedly was captured by Governor López in May 1831. Paz was sent to Buenos Aires, and while he was a prisoner of Rosas, he wrote his followers in the "rebellious army," including Sarmiento, that they were all Argentines, with the same *patria*, the *patria* Argentina, and that they should surrender in the interest of the *patria común*.[29] López negotiated the surrender of the Paz army, and for having ended the war with "glory for the Republic," the people of Buenos Aires called him the "Liberator" (*Libertador*).[30] A new danger arose with Quiroga's victory over Paz's forces in Mendoza, San Juan, San Luis, and La Rioja, for Quiroga now was in a position to threaten Buenos Aires.[31]

A new era was beginning. The political landscape had changed, and the "fantasy Republic" had disappeared even before the capture of Paz. Now attempts to create new territorial states within the former viceroyalty gathered momentum. After he had signed the López-inspired Treaty of the Littoral, Rosas observed that the "provinces have become real states, different and if a method of fusing them other than the one used until now is not found they will never unite."[32] The treaty itself implicitly had recognized Buenos Aires as an independent and sovereign state, a fact that is confirmed in the draft of a constitution written for Buenos Aires in 1833.[33] The provinces, sovereign and independent states, were already withdrawing from Buenos Aires the authorization to conduct their foreign affairs.[34] In 1831 Quiroga and the Unitarians—those who would base the organization of the future state on the constitution of 1826—offered Bolivia the provinces of Jujuy and Salta in exchange for aid against Rosas. Governor Juan Ignacio Gorriti of Salta was especially anxious to unite his province with Bolivia or to form a new state. The Province of Cuyo opened diplomatic negotiations to become part of Chile in 1835.[35] Some provinces began or resumed coining their own currencies, often importing the minting equipment through Buenos Aires.

Rosas and Governor López believed in the *patria común*, the Argentine Republic envisaged at the Congress of 1826, but to counteract the growing isolation of Buenos Aires from the other provinces—the drought contributed to a physical isolation—Rosas proposed to unite the provinces politically in a confederation.[36] This was to be the new *patria*. It would consist of the provinces that adhered to the Treaty of the Littoral, "a confederation of the provinces belonging to the same nation," and by the end of 1832 all thirteen had.[37] "The holy cause of the Confederation," said General Pinto, "is the cause of the people [*pueblos*], and with it is identified the existence of the *Patria*."[38] The idea of a confederation appealed to López and Quiroga. It also appealed to Córdoba and the interior provinces, where there was still considerable support for San Martín's *patria grande*, the union of the old viceroyalty, Chile and Peru. This explains why the provinces renewed their authorization for the government of Buenos Aires to conduct their foreign affairs.[39] Aside from a month-long conference between Rosas and López, and an exchange of views between Rosas, Quiroga, and Felipe Ibarra, there was no serious discussion of national organization for the next twenty years. The Treaty of the Littoral (1831) became, Rosas's partisans said, the constitutional basis of the Argentine Republic.[40]

Concurrently, two words acquired new geographical dimensions. "Argentina" now included the Province of Buenos Aires and the area beyond its northern border of the Arroyo del Medio. The inhabitants in the *provincias adentro* (Córdoba to the Andes) started to call themselves Argentines, just as Chileans were beginning to call themselves Chileans, not Europeans.[41] "Provinciano" now meant those outside of Buenos Aires and not simply those living between Córdoba and Jujuy. For the porteño Esteban Echeverría, the *patria* Argentina was the area between the Río de la Plata and the Río Paraná and the Andes.[42] His Argentine Republic, unlike that of Rosas, did not include the mesopotamian provinces—the Río Paraná was known as the Río Paraguay or Río de la Plata, but its Indian name of Río Paraná gradually became its only name during the Rosas years—and was not based on land but on the ideas of Liberty, Fraternity, and Equality. One became an Argentine not by being a native of Buenos Aires or seeing it, but simply by accepting the ideas that Rivadavia represented, that is, European civilization and trade or civilization and progress. This *patria* had no fixed territorial boundaries.[43]

Meanwhile, Rosas endeavored to further the economic interests of his *patria*, the Province of Buenos Aires, and to bring the *patria común* into being. When his term as governor ended on 5 December 1832, Rosas undertook, in cooperation with Mendoza and La Rioja, a campaign to push the provincial borders further into Indian territory and to provide for their security. At the same time, he maintained close contact with the leaders of the Republic of Rio Grande do Sul, as he reportedly expected to unite it eventually with Buenos Aires. During Rosas's absence, Buenos Aires passed a law stating that "the Province will not meet as a nation except in a federated form, in accord with the treaties it has with the brother provinces."[44] Rosas was reelected governor on 7 March 1835. One of his first concerns was to restore Corrientes, which had broken away, to the confederation in the interest of "the continental equilibrium of these States and the peace of America."[45] His conduct of foreign affairs was severely tested when France, anxious to defend its citizens, established a blockade of the Buenos Aires coast in 1838. Writing in exile from Chile, Sarmiento suggested that Buenos Aires could minimize the effects of the blockade and obtain European and Asian goods and access to American markets on the Pacific coast if it united with Chile.[46] Rosas successfully defended his *patria*, the Province of Buenos Aires, from foreign intervention, and he extended the province's borders to the south without encroaching on the other provinces, two achievements that engendered strong feelings for the "great Argentine Confederation" and the "great Argentine family."[47]

Building on Argentine nationalistic feeling, Rosas created an administrative structure for his pseudolegal federation. Starting in May 1835, all official acts and correspondence began with the rubric "Argentine Confederation." Florencio Varela, "citizen of Buenos Aires," in a work addressed to the "American Republics," advised them that the "Confederation" did not exist.[48] Foreign diplomats agreed, as the Brazilian reference to the "provinces that claim they are confederated" indicates.[49] Sardinia recognized the "Argentine Confederation as a Sovereign State," but its agent was accepted, Rosas said, by "this Republic." Actually, there was no Argentine Republic, and Rosas could not sign any treaty for it.[50]

The republic of Rosas was simply the Province of Buenos Aires. The Buenos Aires government had its own minister of foreign relations, and the provinces that had authorized it to conduct their foreign affairs addressed the governor as "Director of the Foreign Relations of the Republic."[51] This was diplomatic correspondence within the confederation.[52] Diplomatic correspondence with governments outside the confederation was handled by the "Minister of Foreign Relations of the Government of Buenos Aires, in charge of directing those that belong to the Argentine Confederation."[53] The title experienced several subtle changes. Sarmiento criticized one version, "Director of the Supreme Direction of the National Affairs of the Argentine Confederation." Another version stated that the director was the president of the Argentine Republic and could make peace and war.[54]

The addition of the war- and peace-making functions led seven provinces in 1839 to withdraw the authorization they had given to Buenos Aires to conduct their foreign affairs and led the northern provinces to renew their direct treaty negotiations with Bolivia.[55] Rosas probably viewed these developments as a temporary impediment to his plans. A French observer thought Rosas was capable of realizing the destiny of the Argentine Republic. He further thought that Brazil would encounter difficulties when its southern provinces sought their independence, and later when "a federation of all these small republics, of which Buenos Aires would be the center," would be formed and be in South America what the United States was in North America.[56] Buenos Aires was already issuing passports to those going abroad or to another province, and provincial officials, including ministers of government, were arriving in Buenos Aires on diplomatic passports.[57]

In Montevideo—the influential newspaper *Gaceta Mercantil* of Buenos Aires reported—Juan B. Alberdi, who spoke for one faction among the Argentine exiles, was urging the "porteño or Argentine" exiles to accept French help to establish in Buenos Aires a government compatible with current European ideas of the "Great Nation."[58] "We, the South Americans," said the son of Mariquita Sánchez, hostess of a famed salon in Buenos Aires during the Rivadavian years, "can accept French aid because France is the center of modern civilization." However, another faction, the so-called rosistas, objected to French aid and to identification with President Rivera of Uruguay, who, at French insistence, had declared war on Rosas. This was true of Lavalle.

Anxious to conquer his *patria*, the Province of Buenos Aires, and hating Rosas for personal reasons, Lavalle launched a campaign against Buenos Aires in September 1839 with the financial backing of General Martín Rodríguez, his aide-de-camp. But Lavalle met with little support in Entre Ríos, was not confronted by an assembled army in Buenos Aires, and, unable to obtain recruits, proceeded to the interior provinces. He was expected, the *Gaceta Mercantil* later reported, to dominate the area on the right bank of the Río Paraná, the "Banda Oriental del Río Paraná," and to form a new state, the "Republic of South America."[59] Lavalle unsuccessfully sought an alliance with Rio Grande do Sul, but did form one with the Coalition of the North (Catamarca, Jujuy, La Rioja, Salta, Tucumán), provinces that had withdrawn from Buenos Aires the right to represent them in foreign affairs. However, he was defeated by the Uruguayan General Manuel Oribe, whom Rosas had sent in his pursuit. Declining a French offer of a generalship, a pension, and safe passage out of the region, Lavalle continued fighting until he was killed on 8 October 1841. By then he had lost the military prestige he had acquired during the war of independence, and with it, the support of the Argentine exiles. Meanwhile, the French blockade of Buenos Aires had ended (29 October 1840).

When Rosas was reelected governor in April 1840, the Río de la Plata region was suffering economically. Since 1836 Buenos Aires had only 64.5 days of rain per year; 1841 would be no better, and the locusts came in 1842 and 1844.[60] Buenos Aires had yet to reap benefits from its fertile soil and size, and the "vast and rich countries which formerly constituted the viceroyalty of Buenos Aires" consisted of numerous "distinct and independent states."[61] That both the riverine and interior provinces would benefit from free navigation on the Paraná and Uruguay rivers was becoming clearer as British and French surveys made them and their hinterlands better known and sparked a "golden vision of trade with South America" in which England and France wanted to participate.[62] Looking to the future, Rosas, the "American," unsuccessfully tried to divert the trade of the provinces to Buenos Aires and away from Montevideo and other Uruguayan ports. His blockades of Montevideo, one aspect of the war between "two small states," as Robert Pell described it, were ineffectual, while the Indians successfully hampered Buenos

Aires's communications with the interior provinces.[63]

At the same time, Rosas attempted to breathe life into his creation, the Argentine Confederation, which was viewed abroad as, de facto, only the Province of Buenos Aires. Rosas's vigorous propaganda defense of the confederation suggests he wanted to reconstruct the viceroyalty, for he never recognized the independence of Paraguay or Uruguay. This partially explains why he persistently supported Manuel Oribe, the second president of Uruguay, who was overthrown by his predecessor, Fructuoso Rivera. Oribe retreated to Buenos Aires, was appointed a brigadier in the Army of the Argentine Confederation by Rosas, and then was backed by Rosas in his war to return to power in Uruguay, the Guerra Grande, Oribe's long siege of Montevideo from 1843 to 1851.[64] As Rio Grande do Sul depended on the port of Montevideo, Rosas perhaps thought of including an independent Rio Grande do Sul in his confederation.

To achieve his objectives, Rosas had to overcome many obstacles. Viewing the Río Paraná as "the great road to civilization," foreigners and the "debris of the factions" opposing Rosas thought of establishing foreign protectorates in the region.[65] Montevideo was a de facto French protectorate during the French blockade of Buenos Aires (1838–1840), and afterwards it first sought British, then Brazilian protection. Brazil rejected its offer of disputed territory in return for an alliance and money. Basically, neither the European powers nor Brazil wanted Buenos Aires to acquire Montevideo.

Rosas also faced international competition for dominance in the mesopotamian provinces. Rivera, aware of existing trading patterns, would combine Uruguay, Entre Ríos, Corrientes, Paraguay, and Rio Grande do Sul, and establish a rival to the Buenos Aires–centered confederation of Rosas. In October 1842 Rivera proposed to the governors of Corrientes and Santa Fe that together they form a confederation that would include Entre Ríos. But Paz, director of their war against Rosas, an avowed enemy of Rivera, opposed the idea, quarreled with Governor Pedro Ferré of Corrientes, and resigned. Paz, a provincial nationalist, anxious to form his own party, said Pedro Pablo Seguí, was planning to move on to Córdoba, build a state there with Tucumán, San Juan, and Mendoza, and then make peace with Rosas. He already was in touch with Ángel Peñaloza of La Rioja. Without Santa Fe, his proposed state would be landlocked. One group of Argentine exiles in Montevideo regarded Paz and other Unitarian warriors as "savage unitarians," reported the *Gaceta Mercantil,* and to separate themselves from the military wing of their party, they no longer called themselves the "European Party" but the "Party of the American Revolution."[66]

In 1843 Brazil reportedly decided to ask Chile for a representative to observe its conduct once it placed Uruguay, Paraguay, Corrientes, and other provinces under its protection.[67] The Unitarian press in Montevideo mentioned a possible Brazilian annexation of Uruguay and a Brazilian protectorate over Corrientes and Paraguay. *El Nacional* of Montevideo proposed a confederation of Brazil and the Río de la Plata. This speculation had some foundation, for it coincided with a bid by the Montevideo government for an alliance with Brazil, and with an agreement between Entre Ríos and Corrientes to allow citizens of the "La Plata Republic" to trade freely across their borders. There also was a plan to unite Paraguay, Corrientes, and Rio Grande do Sul. This perhaps is what Paz had in mind when he returned to Corrientes in 1843 with English and Brazilian support to organize an army of foreign mercenaries and Indians. He, as director of the war, and Corrientes signed an alliance with Paraguay on 11 November 1845. Rosas redoubled his efforts to keep Corrientes within the confederation in the interest of "the continental equilibrium of the States and the peace of America."[68] Paz's project collapsed when Governor Justo José de Urquiza of Entre Ríos, a provincial nationalist, at war with Corrientes with the support of Rosas, captured the brother of the governor of Corrientes, Joaquín Madariaga, at Laguna Limpia (4 February 1845). Unpopular, Paz first fled to Paraguay and then to Rio de Janeiro, where he received an unofficial Brazilian pension. At a meeting held at Alcaraz, Entre Ríos, in 1846, one encouraged by British agents, the governors of Entre Ríos, Corrientes, and Santa Fe reportedly considered uniting their provinces in a confederation. Brazil preferred combining only Entre Ríos and Corrientes, as it did not want only one state to control navigation on the rivers.[69]

Exiles from Buenos Aires and other provinces then living in Chile closely followed events in the Río de la Plata. Among the exiles was Sarmiento. He was intensely interested in the economic and intellectual progress of his *patria*, San Juan, and the interior provinces, and these concerns soon made him the exiles' leading publicist in Chile, and by his writings, in the Río de la Plata. His ideas on nation building were based on those of San Martín, who was admired in San Juan and the interior provinces. This meant adapting the best features of the old colonial order, of the new *madre patria* born of the independence movement, with the *patria común* of postindependence. It was the Buenos Aires of Rivadavia that enthralled him, that was his intellectual *patria*, for Buenos Aires was the "republic par excellence," the "cradle of liberal ideas and the center from which the intellectual revolution spread to a large part of America."[70]

For Sarmiento, Buenos Aires, where the "American Revolution" of 1810 began on May 25, had a merchant population that was "active, semi-educated, entrepreneurial, and alert," and was the "most democratic" and the "most intellectually developed" among the Spanish-American colonies. It was born to greatness. This is why he annually celebrated May 25, had a portrait of San Martín in his home, and distributed portraits of San Martín. After the overthrow of Rosas, Sarmiento defended San Martín in the Buenos Aires press, criticized the porteños for calling Ayacucho Bolivar's victory, and persuaded the city to acquire its first statue of his hero in 1862. In the 1840s Sarmiento, exiled from San Juan, found a substitute for Buenos Aires in Chile, the "most cultural and most respected republic of America," the "republic that serves as a model for Spanish America," the "fatherland that he did not find" in his own country.[71]

Chile then was engaged in a press war with Buenos Aires. It reflected a dispute between the two governments over the Strait of Magellan, the treatment of Chilean citizens, property and diplomats in two provinces of Cuyo (San Juan and Mendoza), and the right to freedom of trade and transit between the Province of Cuyo and Chile. Sarmiento, as his articles in *El Mercurio* and *El Progreso* reveal, wanted to improve the economies of the two provinces. Mendoza had not recovered from the earthquake of 1824, San Juan from the devastating flood of 1833, and both from the effects of Paz's destructive rule in the 1830s and the increased direct trade around Cape Horn to Valparaiso. The two provinces needed to strengthen their already close economic ties with Chile. At the same time, Sarmiento never forgot the Argentine Republic, the *patria común*.

Sarmiento had both patriotic and intellectual reasons, not only political ones, for participating in the Chile–Buenos Aires press war by publishing parts of *Civilización i barbarie*, or *Facundo*, first in *El Progreso*, then in *El Mercurio*, and finally in book form in Santiago de Chile in 1845. He was aware that the Argentine provinces were declining in commercial importance, and that Great Britain and France intended to intervene in the Río de la Plata to defend their commercial interests. With a view to bolstering its weak trade with Buenos Aires, he urged Chile to participate in their deliberations in its own interests.[72] Rosas understood and paid tribute to the effectiveness of the attack on him in *Facundo*, when, according to Sarmiento, he praised it to his collaborators. It has never been established, but in keeping with the practices of the period, the Chilean government may have subsidized *Facundo*.

Sarmiento's strident anti-Rosas, pro-Chile newspaper articles and *Facundo* alarmed some Chileans who feared a war with Rosas. Sarmiento believed a war was impossible, but his friend, Minister Manuel Montt, decided to send Sarmiento on a government-sponsored trip to Europe and North America. Sarmiento was gone from October 1845 to early 1848. In France he met the leading politicians, intellectuals, and publicists and established an influential base among the anti-Rosas elements there.[73] On his way back to Chile, he stopped in Montevideo and saw that the second European blockade of Buenos Aires was still in progress, learned

that Urquiza would not relinquish command of his *entrerriano* troops to
Paz in a war with Rosas, and discovered that Buenos Aires and Chile had
not settled their differences. In fact, Rosas's agents were encouraging the
Indians in southern Chile to attack the government, and the economies
of the provinces of Cuyo, as well as Chilean trade with them, were in
ruins. Disturbed, Sarmiento resumed his press attacks on Rosas. He was
confident that Rosas, weakened by the French-supported military efforts
of Paz and Lavalle to overthrow him, would not overcome a third,
possibly French, attempt. To prepare himself for a prominent role in the
Argentine Republic or Confederation of the post-Rosas era, he studied
the historical background and laws of the Río de la Plata, the interprovincial pacts, and the relevant international treaties.[74]

In March 1850 Sarmiento published *Argirópolis, ó la capital de los
Estados Confederados del Río de la Plata* in Santiago de Chile. The work was
dedicated to Urquiza. It was based on treaties and agreements between
the "federal governments of the Republic or Argentine Confederation."
According to Sarmiento, over two thousand copies were distributed.
Among others, they went to the provincial governors, General Manuel
Oribe, and the French representatives in Montevideo. Besides the confederated governments of the Argentine provinces, Sarmiento wanted
to reach the French government. He expected to be heard because in
1849 he had published the first volume of *Viajes en Europa, África i
América,* an account of his experiences and observations in Europe. He
had sent copies of it and *Facundo* to France in the hope that it would
publicize his name and influence the European powers to turn to him
for help in solving their problems in the Río de la Plata.[75]

In 1851 Belín, Sarmiento's son-in-law, printed a French edition of
Argirópolis in Paris, but withheld its distribution until the French legislature began to debate government policies in the Río de la Plata and the
legal status of the Paraná and Uruguay rivers. *Argirópolis* was expected
to inform the French deputies about Argentine laws and the importance
of the rivers to the riverine and interior provinces.[76] With the *patria
común* in mind, Sarmiento's basic thesis was that the riverine and interior
provinces would never enjoy economic development and trade without
unhampered navigation of the Paraná and Uruguay rivers.

When Sarmiento wrote *Argirópolis,* the French government was
supporting the Montevideo government and French marines occupied
an island that Sarmiento had never seen, the island of Martín García. For
Sarmiento, this meant that France had a moral obligation to reestablish
peace among "children" by surrendering the island of Martín García to
a general congress meeting there that would write a constitution for the
Argentine Confederation and the former United Provinces of the Río de
la Plata. Once the congress was called, the temporary authority that the
confederated provinces had given to the Province of Buenos Aires to

conduct their foreign affairs would cease. Buenos Aires would no longer represent the provisional Argentine Confederation abroad as the Argentine Republic, and the congress could organize the *"reyertas,"* as Sarmiento referred to the provinces, into a new nation, the "Great State," a federation called the "United States of South America." This new conglomeration of provinces and confederated states would consist of the Argentine Republic, Paraguay, and Uruguay. Territorially, the Argentine Republic or Argentine Confederation would include all the area between the Atlantic and the Andes, and the Strait of Magellan to Brazil and Bolivia—the *patria común.* Within the new state, all the allied provinces would be treated equally and would be subject to the same laws.[77]

The capital of the new nation of confederated states would be located on Martín García, which would be independent of any province. Martín García would be the administrative and trade center of the new state and contain the common customhouse, which would collect all import and export duties. The capital alone would regulate navigation on the rivers in the general interest of the federation, and guarantee commercial freedom to all the confederated states. Buenos Aires would be unable, as now, to close that part of the Río Paraná that flowed along its borders, and Corrientes, Entre Ríos, and Santa Fe would be free to develop their own ports and trade. No port would receive special treatment. Montevideo would continue as the natural entrepôt between Europe and the riverine provinces and Paraguay, and it and Buenos Aires would receive European goods for and exports from the interior provinces. European goods bound for the interior provinces would first pass through the common customhouse.

The congress of the confederated states would strive to improve communications between the interior provinces and the ports that served them, and between Córdoba, "center of the Republic," and the other provinces, Chile, and Peru. (This is an echo of the *común madre patria* concept.) Little is known about the "country in which we live," Sarmiento noted, but the congress would finance explorations of the rivers and direct immigrants to the most remote areas of the country. Congress also would eliminate the internal customhouses and collect and distribute the general revenues. Finally, the Province of Buenos Aires, a member of the confederated states and an example of progress, would concentrate on its own development.[78] Its source of wealth was within its own boundaries and its contact with foreign trade, which is why it had shown no interest in the prosperity of the interior provinces.

Argirópolis was directed at the riverine provinces. Sarmiento later expanded on his concept in newspaper articles urging the interior provinces to follow the riverine example, and in their own economic self-interest, to withdraw from Buenos Aires the authority to conduct their foreign relations. As Entre Ríos and Corrientes already had opened the rivers to their ports and Paraguay, civilization and trade, he argued, would penetrate South America by way of the Río Paraná.[79] Entre Ríos would supply Brazil, England, and Paraguay with grain. The colonial world was passing, and if the interior provinces failed to act, the "towns" on the eastern side of the Río de la Plata and Paraguay would form a new nation composed of Entre Ríos, Corrientes, Montevideo, and Paraguay; Rosas would continue to obstruct trade with Chile; and the Indian invasions and internal customhouses would make trade with Buenos Aires unprofitable.[80] The trade of the interior provinces with the Pacific had been closed since 1846, and Indian attacks had already depopulated the area through which the old road to Buenos Aires had passed, forcing merchants and travelers to abandon it by 1845 for one going to Rosario. The interior provinces thus would benefit from the establishment of free navigation on the rivers.

What Sarmiento advocated was a first step toward the creation of a homogeneous republic: the upriver and interior provinces would meet in a general federation congress (*un congreso general federativo*) to organize a federal administrative system that would not affect their sovereignty, liberty, or independence. The federation would be divided into three territorial units (*gobernaciones*), each of which would consist of allied provinces with similar economic interests. One *gobernación* would be formed by Corrientes, Entre Ríos, Montevideo, and Paraguay. As the independent governments of Corrientes and Entre Ríos had already opened their ports to all foreign flags, trade now would bring progress, prosperity, and immigrants to them and Paraguay.[81] A second *gobernación*—Santa Fe, Córdoba, and Santiago del Estero—could participate in the commercial system created by the first, and whenever they found it more economical, use Rosario instead of Buenos Aires. Rosario was a port destined to become "one of the most important commercial centers of the Argentine Republic."[82] Using the old colonial roads leading to Peru and Chile, Córdoba could facilitate the access of Catamarca, La Rioja, and the provinces of Cuyo to the Atlantic. Salta, Tucumán, Jujuy, and Catamarca would form the third *gobernación* and would continue to use the Pacific ports and the markets in Bolivia. The provinces of Cuyo, not economically dependent on the littoral, could exchange their products for European goods in Buenos Aires or Santa Fe or in their traditional Chilean markets and develop markets in California. There was no need for Sarmiento to call attention to what everyone knew. From Buenos Aires to Mendoza the *carretas* took seventy days and the peon guide was paid in gold, whereas it was only four days from Mendoza to San Felipe, Chile, and the trade between Buenos Aires and Chile and Peru was insignificant.[83]

What Sarmiento envisaged was a transitional period leading to the eventual creation of the *patria común* and the economic development of the interior provinces with less dependence on Buenos Aires. The organization of the upriver and interior provinces into three groups of allied provinces would only exist until the general congress called under the Federal Pact of 1831 had abolished the internal customhouses, the provincial tariffs on intraprovincial trade, passports, and tariffs on provincial exports to Chile. Until then, Entre Ríos and Corrientes would retain their maritime customhouses, Jujuy and Salta their land ones with Bolivia, and Mendoza and San Juan would establish one at Uspallata. Eventually, the island of Martín García, the location of Argirópolis, would become a free port, the seat of the customhouse belonging to the customs union (Zolverein) formed by Bolivia, Brazil, Paraguay, Uruguay, and the Argentine Republic.[84]

In the months following the appearance of *Argirópolis,* war by France or Brazil against Rosas became even more likely. The French fleet in the Río de la Plata received reinforcements in April. Urquiza was being urged to weaken Buenos Aires's control of the rivers by forming the Entre Ríos Confederation with Corrientes, Paraguay, and Uruguay.[85] Brazilian intentions became clearer in the closing months of the year, when it broke with Rosas (October) and signed an alliance with Paraguay (December). Believing that the moment he had been anticipating was fast approaching, Sarmiento published *Recuerdos de provincia* in December. This is how he presented his candidacy for president of the republic or confederation that would emerge after the fall of Rosas.

Early in 1851 Brazil reached an accord with Urquiza, who declared war on Rosas in April and signed an alliance with Brazil and Montevideo in May. At the same time, Brazil announced that it was not bent on conquest, that it would respect the independence of its neighbors, and that it would not meddle in their internal affairs.[86] Its only concern was that no single nation controlled access to the Río Uruguay and the Río Paraná.[87] This is why Brazil considered urging Entre Ríos and Corrientes to form a separate state and to join it and Uruguay in an alliance. These developments coincided with the decision of the French government to seek a peaceful solution of its problems with Rosas. For the Argentine exiles, France had lost its importance as a source of support and funds. It was now a question of when Urquiza would "invade the territories of the Argentine Republic and advance to Buenos Ayres."[88]

Sarmiento thought it time for him to establish his credentials with the Argentine emigrés in Montevideo and their allies. He had first met many of them in 1846, when he stopped in Montevideo on his way to Europe, and they had viewed him as a foreigner because he came from San Juan, another province.[89] He completed the second volume of *Viajes en Europa, África i América,* which contained his observations on North America. He also published a revised edition of *Facundo* that was less critical of the old Unitarians and that failed to pay tribute to the now unpopular José María Paz. Both works were dedicated to the prominent porteño nationalist, the "pure and noble" Valentine Alsina, and in the dedicatory remarks that appeared in *Facundo*, Sarmiento identified himself with the porteños by referring to Rosas as the "powerful tyrant of our fatherland."[90] Sarmiento called himself a citizen of the "Argentine Republic," not of Buenos Aires, and of "another of the confederated provinces."[91] With these two publications, he ingratiated himself with the pro–United States, pro-American, pro-French, and pro-European enthusiasts among the Argentine emigrés in Montevideo, São Paulo, and Santa Catalina. At the same time he sent Urquiza a portrait of San Martín along with a copy of *Sud-América*. He expected Urquiza to endorse the principle of federation, to remain aloof from politics, and to form the nation, the *patria común*.

Sarmiento was in Chile when Entre Ríos and Corrientes, in an act he had long anticipated, destroyed the "national character" of the Buenos Aires government by withdrawing their permission for it to handle their foreign relations, and Urquiza ordered that a statue of San Martín be placed in the Plaza of Concepción del Uruguay to honor his struggles for "the Independence of the Fatherland."[92] Sarmiento took the earliest available passage to Montevideo, arriving there on 3 November 1851, and then he went on to Entre Ríos to meet Urquiza. During their meetings, he presented Urquiza with another portrait of San Martín.[93] Sarmiento returned to Montevideo in December, and early in 1852 he sailed up the Río Paraná aboard a Brazilian warship with the printing press that he would use to issue bulletins during the campaign against Rosas.

By then Sarmiento realized that he would have no part as "adviser, collaborator in the grandiose tasks of forming a nation with those so favored countries but so poorly populated and so poorly governed."[94] He still believed in Europe, liberty, free navigation of the rivers and the economic principles he had advocated for ten years, but military leaders, he lamented, encouraged writers but refused to allow them to run a nation.[95] He now had seen two famous rivers for the first time, and was soon to enter a city he only knew because of its history. On February 10 or 11 he arrived in Buenos Aires, a city described by the *New York Times* as the capital of the "sovereign State of Buenos Aires."[96] Unhappy with what he saw, the conflict between the Old Federalists and the emigrés of Buenos Aires, he thought of returning to Valparaiso, but the Brazilian representative in Buenos Aires, Hermeto Carneiro Leão, familiar with Sarmiento's favorable disposition toward Brazil and aware of his plans to launch an attack on Urquiza, persuaded Sarmiento to go to Rio de Janeiro. Carneiro Leão and his secretary, José María da Silva Paranhos, accompanied Sarmiento across to Montevideo where he took a ship for

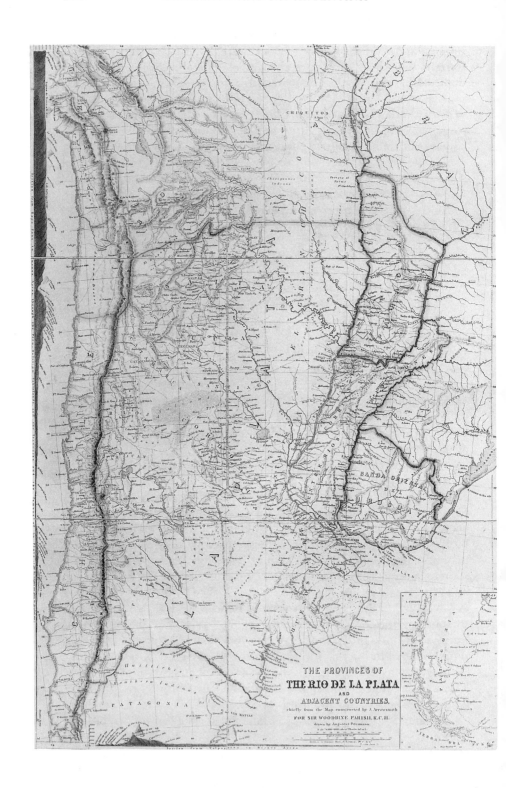

THE PROVINCES OF
THE RIO DE LA PLATA
AND
ADJACENT COUNTRIES,
chiefly from the Map constructed by J. Arrowsmith
FOR SIR WOODBINE PARISH, K.C.H.
drawn by Augustus Petermann.

Rio de Janeiro.

In Rio, Sarmiento spent hours with the young emperor, Pedro II, and his cabinet ministers. From them he learned the terms of the treaties Brazil had negotiated with Uruguay and Urquiza prior to the campaign against Rosas, that Urquiza was advising the Uruguayan government, and that Urquiza had offered to defend Uruguay should it break its treaties with Brazil. The Brazilian officials also told him of their recent awareness that the Argentine Republic, that is, Buenos Aires, had not only military men but also men knowledgeable about political science, constitutions, and the social sciences.[97] Sarmiento does not elaborate further on his conversations with Brazilian officials and says nothing about his conferences with Andrés Lamas. On April 14 the emperor decorated Sarmiento, and later Bartolomé Mitre and Wenceslao Paunero, with the Order of the Rose. They now were entitled to all the deference given to a colonel.[98] Sometime before the ceremony, Sarmiento published locally the first of three segments of *Campaña en el ejército grande de Sud América.*[99] He left for Chile on 18 May 1852.

In *Campaña* Sarmiento started to explain to his contemporaries why he no longer supported Urquiza, but he does not tell the full story. There is no detailed account of the debates and maneuvering that took place among the people who gathered around Urquiza at Palermo. Glimpses of why Sarmiento left Palermo and withdrew his support of Urquiza appear in several essays and letters Sarmiento wrote before completing the third and final segment of *Campaña* near the end of the year. The most significant revelation is that Sarmiento left Palermo because he was unable to help his *patria,* San Juan. "With politics taking tortuous paths unfamiliar to me, my *patria* abandoned to the mercy of the defeated," Sarmiento wrote in October 1852, "I had nothing to say in Palermo."[100] He simply had no decisive voice in policymaking. Another reason was that Urquiza, an admirer of San Martín, was not, as Alsina said, a statesman, though he was striving, in the words of a Correntino newspaper, to create "that great nation that could call itself the Argentine Confederation."[101]

Urquiza simply was unprepared for the world he encountered outside of Entre Ríos, for the world of ideas and different concerns. His conduct in the city of Buenos Aires had simply not been conducive to building the *patria común* that would end the civil wars that "had devoured the population for many years and destroyed the incipient wealth of what is now an uninhabited and forming nation which should have ranked, since its independence, only after the United States on the American continent."[102] He had ignored porteño nationalist feelings and traditions, and his actions tended to confirm rather than dissipate porteño suspicions of a stranger from the hated Province of Entre Ríos. Urquiza also had not paid and released as promised the porteño *pardos* who had refused to fight at Monte Caseros and the returning Buenos Aires troops from the siege of Montevideo, and he had disregarded the provision in the alliance treaty with Brazil to let Buenos Aires freely govern itself. Instead, he had imposed the army's choice for provincial governor, had stationed troops in the city, had taken prisoners, and had disarmed the province. He even had sent troops into the city in a vain attempt to assure the victory of the government list in the elections of 11 April. Finally, he decided that congress should meet outside of Buenos Aires, though Sarmiento had warned him that the provinces should be governed from Buenos Aires, and the porteños "from their own house."[103] These actions destroyed any hope that the constitution would be a real one. Buenos Aires, Sarmiento said, "is not a criminal to be brought in handcuffs to Congress. Buenos Aires is half of the Republic, is its center, its head, its power."[104]

Urquiza also erred, Sarmiento said, in failing to involve the interior provinces, which did not know him, in the overthrow of Rosas and in the organization of the *patria*. (Sarmiento also could have added that Urquiza had failed to realize that the world of the *porteño* began and ended in Buenos Aires.[105]) The interior provinces would have cooperated if Urquiza had shared the Brazilian subsidies with them, and had permitted the people to remove the governors Rosas had appointed. In addition, Urquiza vacillated in his support for a confederation and the free navigation of the rivers. The discussions at Palermo, a participant reported, revealed that neither Buenos Aires nor the interior provinces wanted a *patria común*, but they did want a federation.[106]

There simply were endless disputes, Sarmiento wrote, between "cities which are hardly more than villages, between nations that do not have more population than a department or county."[107] There was no agreement on whether all the provinces, in keeping with the Treaty of the Littoral (1831), should have the same number of deputies in the forthcoming congress. This was the position of Urquiza and Juan Bautista Alberdi, both admirers of the United States. Alsina, Mitre, and Sarmiento instead maintained that each province, irrespective of population changes, should have the same number of representatives it had in the Congress of 1826, and should decide in a free election the type of union it wanted. The previous year Alsina, Mitre, and Sarmiento had decided that in any national organization General Paz should have an important position, for they thought him capable of neutralizing Urquiza militarily. They also wanted Paz to bring his *patria natal*, Córdoba, and the interior provinces into the new confederation, and to become its president. They believed, as Paz did, that the new nation should imitate some Brazilian institutions, though not its monarchy. (Lamas had already conducted a fruitless search for a monarch.) Without Córdoba, they felt, there could be no confederation, but Urquiza did not encourage General Paz to enter

Buenos Aires after Monte Caseros.[108] Without Paz, their plans collapsed. Sarmiento failed to mention in *Campaña* that this setback was only temporary, for the pro-Brazilian faction reportedly received within a few months the financial resources it needed from the empire.

Another failing of Urquiza, Sarmiento noted in *Campaña*, was his demonstrated unreliability as an ally and his anti-Brazilian stance. In the recent campaign against Rosas, Urquiza had shown little respect for the Brazilians and their contributions to the anti-Rosas campaign. Brazil had furnished half the troops at Monte Caseros, yet the Brazilians were not mentioned in the official battle report on Monte Caseros, which Sarmiento and Mitre had written as directed. Sarmiento felt obligated to explain to the Brazilian commander in writing that references to the Brazilians at Monte Caseros in the official battle report had been suppressed.

At Palermo Urquiza and the Brazilian representatives had even exchanged threats of war. Urquiza was then assuring the Uruguayan government of his aid should it break its treaties with Brazil. What Sarmiento failed to mention was that Brazil also was disturbed by talk at Palermo of including Uruguay in the new Argentine confederation. Sarmiento concluded that Urquiza did not appreciate Brazil's importance and power and had abandoned the idea that the Argentine exiles had nurtured of an "alliance of interests" with Brazil. The porteños, however, had extended every courtesy to the Brazilians when they entered the city after Monte Caseros, during their stay there, and when they left. Sarmiento himself had nothing but praise for Pedro II and the Brazilian troops.

Sarmiento was proud of his own connections with Brazil. In *Campaña* Sarmiento reminded his readers and correspondents in the interior provinces that he was highly regarded by all political parties and by the governments of Chile and Brazil and that he maintained "close relations" with Brazil. He had defended the interests of the interior provinces in Buenos Aires and would continue to represent them. He still was popular with some elements in Buenos Aires, especially the resident *estancieros* from San Juan, but his program for a confederation, a *patria común,* and free navigation on the rivers had lost him considerable support by May.[109] Even his friend Vélez Sársfield rejected the idea of a federation. A disappointed Paz said, "What a revolution! What countries these are! Our project for a real confederation is thus ended!"[110] Sarmiento summarized the situation briefly: "The Liberator has replaced the Restorer; Congress the Federation, the unitarians the federalists—liberty, decorum, organization are postponed until later."[111] "Postponed until later," but Sarmiento would not let these ideals be abandoned.

The *patria común,* with the territorial boundaries of the old viceroyalty, for which Sarmiento had struggled and had expected to see organized after Monte Caseros, did not appear. Sarmiento's dream encountered the indifference of the provinces. Rosas also sought to create the *patria común,* but he was forced to concentrate on foreign intervention and the effects of natural calamities and Indian invasions. Neither Sarmiento nor Rosas were able to overcome the strong popular attachment to the *patria,* the suspicion and hostility with which the provinces viewed each other, and the absence of any national feeling. Rosas held the provinces together by bringing together in his confederation the enlightened provincial military leaders. This was the age of the military and not, as Sarmiento and the Argentine exiles wanted it to be, of civilian intellectuals. Both Rosas and Sarmiento, in Sarmiento's words, thought that the city of Buenos Aires, "the richest, most energetic, and the most civilized population of the Republic," should be the capital of the new state.[112] Both favored immigration, economic development, and trade. Sarmiento's dream that the Río Paraná would always be open to world shipping became a reality with the signing of the international treaty guaranteeing it on 10 July 1853. A new *patria común,* one without Paraguay and Uruguay, would emerge after 1880, and with it would come economic progress and trade.

NOTES

1. Domingo F. Sarmiento, *Recuerdos de provincia* Foreword by Enrique Anderson Imbert (Buenos Aires: Editorial de Belgrano, 1981), 18–19. Sarmiento's spelling will be used in citing his works.

2. Domingo F. Sarmiento, *Convención de San-Nicolás de los Arroyos* (Santiago de Chile: Imprenta de Julio Belín i Cía., 1852), 5. How love of *país,* that is, the province, influenced individual behavior and political developments has received little attention from scholars. José Miguel Galán, the porteño commander of the *entrerriano* troops Urquiza had left in Palermo, told his interlocutors during the 11 September 1852 revolution, "I do not wish to fight or surrender; let me withdraw." He did not wish to fight his fatherland or break the military code of honor. Domingo F. Sarmiento, *Obras de D. F. Sarmiento,* vol. 14, *Campaña en el ejército grande* (53 vols., Buenos Aires: Moreno, 1887–1900), 331–334.

3. Domingo F. Sarmiento, *Viaje a Chile del Canónigo Don Juan María Mastai-Ferreti oi sumo pontifice Pio, Papa IX.* Translated from the Italian and with an appendix (Santiago de Chile: Imprenta de la Opinión, 1848), 40; Domingo F. Sarmiento, *Memoria enviada al Instituto Histórico de Francia, sobre la cuestión décima del programa de los trabajos que debe presentar la 1ª clase, "Quelle est la situation actuelle des Républiques du centre et du Sud de l'Amérique"* (Santiago de Chile: Imprenta de Julio Belín i Cía., 1853), 16; Alberto Palcos, *Rivadavia, ejecutor del pensamiento de mayo* (2 vols., La Plata: Universidad de La Plata, 1960), 1:217–218; Aug. de Saint-Hilaire, "Tableau des dernières révolutions du Brésil," *Revue des Deux Mondes,* 1st Ser., Nos. 3–4 (1831): 420.

4. C. A. Rodney to the secretary of state, Washington, 5 November 1819, *Boston Daily Advertiser,* 30 November 1819; Leo W. Hiller Puxeddu, "El

federalismo del litoral en los tiempos de López," *Jornadas Nacionales de Historia del Federalismo, 7 al 11 de octubre de 1986* (Santa Fe: Gobierno de la Provincia de Santa Fe, Secretaría de Planeamiento, 1986), 85.

5. José de San Martín to Tomás Godoy y Cruz, Mendoza, 24 May 1816, Instituto Nacional Sanmartiniano, *Documentos para la historia del Libertador general San Martín* (12 vols., Buenos Aires: Instituto Nacional Sanmartiniano y Museo Histórico Nacional, 1953-), 3:451-459; C. A. Rodney to the secretary of state, Washington, 5 November 1818, *Boston Daily Advertiser,* 30 November 1818; Hiller Puxeddu, "El federalismo del litoral," 85.

6. Juan Crisóstomo Lafinur, *El Nuevo Corresponsal. N° 1° Contestación al papel titulado-Los apostoles del Diablo* (Buenos Aires: Imprenta Nacional, circa 1820), 10. "In this America," he continued, "Buenos Aires will become a powerful and flourishing province" ibid.

7. Joseph T. Criscenti, "Argentine Constitutional History, 1810-1852: A Re-examination," *Hispanic American Historical Review* 41 (August 1961): 381.

8. Mario Belgrano, *La Francia y la monarquía en el Plata (1818-1820)* (Buenos Aires: A. García Santos, 1933), 50-54.

9. Lauro F. Fagalde, "A doscientos años del nacimiento de Bernardo de Monteagudo," *Criterio* 62 (April 1989): 125-130.

10. Saint-Hilaire, "Tableau des dernières révolutions," 420.

11. Domingo F. Sarmiento, *Observaciones con motivo de los artículos suscritos por J. B. A. en el Mercurio de Valparaiso, con el título de CUESTIONES AMERICANAS; i que son un examen de la Constitución del Estado de Buenos-Aires, por Mariano E. de Sarratea, Ciudadano arjentino, del Estado de Buenos-Aires* (Santiago de Chile: Imprenta de Julio Belín i Cia., 1854), 19-20; *Viaje a Chile,* 39-40.

12. San Martín to Vicente Chilavert, Brussels, 1 January 1825, Biblioteca Ayacucho, *San Martín, Su correspondencia (1823-1850),* 3d ed. (Buenos Aires: Museo Histórico Nacional, 1919), 170-172; Alexander Caldcleugh, *Travels in South America, During the Years 1819-20-21; Containing an Account of the Present State of Brazil, Buenos Ayres, and Chile* (2 vols., London: J. Murray, 1825), 1:288-293.

13. "Letters from South America [Buenos Aires, 3 March 1818]," *Nile's Register* 14 (20 June 1818): 288-289.

14. The conduct of foreign relations by the Province of Buenos Aires for the provinces that authorized it to represent them is ably analyzed in Víctor Tau Anzoátegui, *Formación del estado federal argentino (1820-1852): La intervención del gobierno de Buenos Aires en los asuntos nacionales* (Buenos Aires: Editorial Perrot, 1965).

15. Emilio Ravignani, *Historia constitucional de la república argentina* (3 vols., Buenos Aires: Talleres S.A. Casa Jacobo Peuser, Ltda., 1926-1927), 2:140.

16. Ibid., 2:167; Héctor R. Ratto, *Historia del almirante Brown,* 3d ed. (Buenos Aires: Centro Naval, Instituto de Publicaciones Navales, 1985), 128.

17. Nina Louisa Hills, *A Life of Woodbine Parish (1796-1882)* (London: Smith, Elder & Co., 1910), 387, citing Parish's report to the Foreign Office of 25 June 1824. See also Sarmiento, *Viaje a Chile,* 37.

18. Ravignani, *Historia constitucional,* 2: 226. That Buenos Aires was the *patria* of Rivadavia is noted in Benjamin Poucel, *Études. Des intérêts réciproques de l'Europe et de l'Amérique. La France et l'Amerique du Sud* (Paris: Guillaumin et Cie., 1849), 28-29.

19. Without the authorization of the provinces, Buenos Aires would not have signed the treaty. Woodbine Parish to George Canning, Buenos Aires, 24 October 1824, *Britain and the Independence of Latin America, 1812-1830; Select*

Documents from the Foreign Office Archives, ed., C. K. Webster (2 vols., London: Oxford University Press, 1938), 1:116–119; Ratto, *Brown,* 148; Emilio Ravignani, ed., *Asambleas constituyentes argentinas seguidas de los textos constitucionales, legislativos y pactos interprovinciales que organizaron políticamente la nación: fuentes seleccionadas, coordinadas y anotadas en cumplimiento de la ley 11.857* (6 vols., Buenos Aires: Talleres S.A. Casa Jacobo Peuser, Ltda., 1937–1939), 3: part 2, 746. This is the first constitution to contain the title "Constitution of the Argentine Republic." Ibid., 6: part 2, 755–762. The name Unitarian first appeared at this congress and was applied to the followers of Rivadavia. Florencio Varela, *Escritos políticos, económicos y literarios del Doctor D. Florencio Varela, coleccionado por Luis L. Domínguez* (Buenos Aires: Impr. del Orden, 1859), 256. Parish participated in the discussions prior to the adoption of the constitution. Ricardo Piccirilli, *Rivadavia,* [new ed.] (Buenos Aires: Peuser, 1952), 388.

20. Fructuoso Rivera to Julián de Gregorio Espinosa, Belem, 12 November 1828, MSS Archivo General de la Nación, Buenos Aires, *sala* X, *leg.* 2-1-8.

21. Domingo F. Sarmiento, *La guerra constituyente de treinta años. 1829* (n.p., n.d), 8; *Convención de San-Nicolás,* 23–24; *Obras,* vol. 13, *Argirópolis, ó la capital de los Estados Confederados del Río de la Plata,* 52; *Observaciones con motivo de los artículos suscritos por J. B. A.,* 23. By "Argentine Republic" Sarmiento meant the province or, as it was also called, the "Republic of Buenos Aires." See Domingo F. Sarmiento, *Discurso presentado para su recepción en el Instituto Istórico de Francia* (Valparaiso: Imprenta Europea, 1848), 29 and Palcos, *Rivadavia,* 2:108. The terms of the alliance treaty indicate that the provinces did not view Buenos Aires as their only port to the outside world.

22. Domingo F. Sarmiento, *El ciudadano arjentino D. F. Sarmiento electo diputado a la lejislatura del Estado de Buenos-Aires: A sus electores* (Santiago de Chile: Imprenta de Julio Belín y Cia., 1854), 12.

23. Lavalle revealed that he was a provincial nationalist when he called the people of Buenos Aires to a meeting to decide the *"bien de Buenos Aires."* His short announcement read: "Porteños! Todos los somos: hagamos feliz nuestra querida patria—Estos son los deseos de Juan Lavalle." *Bando,* Buenos Aires, 1 December 1828, Library of Congress, fol. 301, no. 26.

24. Hills, *Parish,* 352; Manuel J. García to Juan Manuel de Rosas, Buenos Aires, 13 August 1829, *Correspondencia inédita entre Juan Manuel de Rosas y Manuel José García,* Juan Carlos Nicolau, comp., (Tandil: Departamento de Historia, Instituto de Estudios Históricos-Sociales, Universidad Nacional del Centro de la Provincia de Buenos Aires, [1989]), 62–63; *Gaceta Mercantil* (Buenos Aires) 14 November 1843; Santiago Vázquez, "Confidencias de Don Juan Manuel de Rosas en el día en que se recibió, por la primera vez, del Gobierno de Buenos Aires," *Revista de la Junta de Estudios Históricos de Mendoza,* 2ª ép., 1 (1987): 333–337; Luis C. Alen Lascano, "El federalismo de Santiago del Estero y Estanislao López," *Jornadas Nacionales de Historia del Federalismo,* 133–138. Paz fails to mention in his memoirs that Rosas refused to execute him as the provinces requested, and instead promoted him to general in the army of the Province of Buenos Aires, paid his salary, and provided Paz and his family with lodging in Luján. *British Packet* (Buenos Aires) 3 June 1843. The *Gaceta Mercantil* (Buenos Aires) was Rosas's semiofficial newspaper.

25. *American and Commercial Daily Advertiser* (Baltimore) 22 March 1823; Rosas to Manuel José García, San Nicolás, 11 April 1830, Nicolau, *Rosas,* 31–32; García to Rosas, Buenos Aires, 26 and 27 September 1830, ibid., 65–67.

26. Salvador María del Carril to Juan Lavalle, Buenos Aires, 8 May 1829, Ravignani, *Asambleas constituyentes,* 6: part 2, 189–190 and 197–227; *Gaceta*

Mercantil, (Buenos Aires) 30 October 1843. What Paz meant by "republic" is not clear, but in view of the need for an opening to the sea, the republic probably was to be a new territorial state consisting of Córdoba, Santa Fe, and the interior provinces. The use of diplomatic agents suggests that federation was not synonymous with federalism.

27. Mariano Fragueiro to Juan F. Quiroga, Córdoba, 31 May 1831, *Gaceta Mercantil* (Buenos Aires) 2 August 1831. See also *Gaceta Mercantil* (Buenos Aires) 26 August 1831.

28. Rosas to García, San Antonio de Areco por la noche, 19 June 1830, Nicolau, *Rosas*, 40–42; Rosas to García, Pavón, 21 June 1830, ibid., 42; García to Rosas, Buenos Aires, 25 June and 6 October 1830, ibid., 63–65 and 67–69.

29. *Gaceta Mercantil* (Buenos Aires) 4 May and 9 July 1831; José María Paz to Isidoro Larraya, 13 May 1831, and Paz to Mariano Acha, 13 May 1831, *British Packet* (Buenos Aires) 9 July 1831; José Roque Funes to the governor of Córdoba, 17 July 1831, ibid., 20 August 1831. The brutal rule of Paz in Córdoba is discussed in *Gaceta Mercantil* (Buenos Aires) 31 October 1846. Contemporaries questioned whether the capture of Paz was accidental. By the end of 1830 Paz was no longer able to maintain power, and his partisans were deserting him. At the time of his capture, he was being pursued by an angry Quiroga, whose wife and children Paz had exiled to Chile and whose over seventy-year-old mother Paz had placed in chains. Quiroga had closed Paz's retreat to Chile. *Gaceta Mercantil* (Buenos Aires) 2 August 1831 and *British Packet* (Buenos Aires) 25 April 1831. "Message of the Government to the Provincial Legislature, Córdoba, 4 August 1831," *Gaceta Mercantil* (Buenos Aires) 22 August 1891 reports on the consequences of Paz's rule.

30. Rosas to García, Pavón, 14 July 1831, Nicolau, *Rosas*, 53–54. In August 1831 the drought extended from Arrecifes to the Arroyo del Medio. Rosas to Prudencio Rosas, Pavón, 26 August 1831, in *El sentido común en el poder: Rosas y los problemas de su tiempo*, ed. Lima and Elena Bonura, (Buenos Aires: Impr. Sellarés, 1986), 7880.

31. *American and Commercial Daily Advertiser* (Baltimore) 22 March 1832.

32. Rosas to García, Santa Fe, 28 January 1831, Nicolau, *Rosas*, 50.

33. The Santa Fe constitution of 1841 says it is a "formal state." Ricardo Zorraquín Becú, *El federalismo argentino* (Buenos Aires: Librería y Editorial "La Facultad," Bernabé y Cia., 1953), 199, n. 19. That the Province of Buenos Aires was an independent state is also suggested by the title of Woodbine Parish's famous pro-Rosas book *Buenos Ayres and the Provinces of the Río de la Plata* (London: John Murray, 1839). Andrés Lamas, *Notice sur la république orientale de l'Uruguay. Documents de statistique concernant sa population indigène et exotique et le développement de sa richesse; accompagnés de quelques considérations relatives aux questions politiques et internationales que s'agitent au Río de la Plata* (Paris: n.p., 1851), 9.

34. *Gaceta Mercantil* (Buenos Aires) 5 and 27 January 1831. Rosas noticed Buenos Aires's growing isolation as early as October 1829. Rosas to García, San Miguel del Monte, 27 October 1829, Nicolau, *Rosas*, 24–25; *British Packet* (Buenos Aires) 26 August 1831; Lascano, "El federalismo de Santiago del Estero," 137–138; "La cuestión del Plata," *El Mercurio*, 7, 13, 20, and 28 October 1842 in Sarmiento, *Obras*, vol. 6 *Política argentina, 1842–1851*, 60–63.

35. Ravignani, *Historia constitucional*, 2:264; *British Packet* (Buenos Aires) 10 October 1835; *Gaceta Mercantil* (Buenos Aires) 17 October 1831; Alfonso Crespo [Rodas], *Santa Cruz, el cóndor indio* (Mexico City: Fondo de Cultura Económica, 1944), 119. Domingo de Oro, Sarmiento's relative, was involved in the negoti-

ations with Chile.

36. Rosas to García, [Pavón?], 13 December 1832, Nicolau, *Rosas*, 59; Sarmiento, *Observaciones con motivo de los artículos suscritos por J.B.A.*, 10–12, 21, 31, 37; *British Packet* (Buenos Aires) 5 January 1831; Ravignani, *Historia constitucional*, 2:232.

37. *Gaceta Mercantil* (Buenos Aires) 15 December 1846. The provinces were Buenos Aires, Catamarca, Córdoba, Corrientes, Entre Ríos, Mendoza, La Rioja, Salta, San Juan, San Luis, Santa Fe, Santiago del Estero, and Tucumán. According to Tomás de Iriarte, Bartolomé Mitre thought that Rosas was seeking to build the Argentine Republic. Tomás de Iriarte, *Memorias*, vol. 14, *Luchas de Unitarios, Federales y Mazorqueros en el Río de la Plata* (14 vols., Buenos Aires: Ediciones Argentinas "S.I.A.," 1945–1947), 113.

38. *Gaceta Mercantil* (Buenos Aires) 10 August 1839.

39. Ibid., 7 September 1831.

40. Ibid., 10 August 1839, 7 September 1831, and 26 August 1843.

41. Domingo F. Sarmiento, *Obras de D. F. Sarmiento*, vol. 5, *Viajes por Europa, África i América* (53 vols., Santiago de Chile: Imprenta Gutenberg, 1885–1903), 146.

42. Sarmiento, *Memoria enviada al Instituto Histórico de Francia*, 16; Esteban Echeverría, "Dogma socialista," in *Obras completas de D. Esteban Echeverría* (5 vols., Buenos Aires: C. Casaralle, Impr. y Librería de Mayo, 1870–1874), 4: 4, 57, 79–83, and 201; Bernardino Rivadavia to Julián Segundo de Agüero, August 1835, Palcos, *Rivadavia*, 2:21–22.

43. "La cuestión del Plata," *El Mercurio*, 7, 13, 20, and 28 October 1842 in Sarmiento, *Política arjentina*, 65. The Río Paraná was known to cartographers in the seventeenth century as the "Río Paraguay or de la Plata." Maps published early in the nineteenth century simply referred to the river as the Río Paraguay. When the local inhabitants ceased to think of the river as the Río de la Plata is not clear, but contemporary evidence suggests that the river began to be known only by its Indian name of Río Paraná in the 1830s and 1840s. The entrances to both the Río Paraná and Río Uruguay were first surveyed in the early 1830s. "Le Paragvayr, le Chili, la Terre, et les isles Magellanicques," N. Sanson, *Cartes générales de tovtes les parties dv monde, ov les empires, monarchies, republiques, estats, peuples, &c. de l'Asie, de l'Africve, de l'Evrope, & de l'Amériqve, tan anciens que nouveaux, son exactement remarqués, & distinqués suivant leur estenduë* (Paris: F. Mariette, 1658), No. 96 and W. Faden, *Charts of the coasts of South America* (London: Faden, 1806), Geography and Map Division, Library of Congress; "Map of Brazils, Buenos Ayres & Chile," in Josiah Conder, *Brazil and Buenos Ayres* (2 vols., London: J. Duncan, 1825), I: folding map.

Echeverría, a porteño nationalist who had recently returned from five years in Europe, used the river's Indian name of Río Paraná, and like many of his contemporaries, separated the "continent" of Entre Ríos from mainland Argentina.

44. *Gaceta Mercantil* (Buenos Aires) 15 December 1846; A. D. de P. [Antonio Diodoro de Pascual], *Apuntes para la historia de la República Oriental del Uruguay desde el año 1810 hasta de 1852; basados en documentos auténticos públicos é inéditos y en otros datos originales, extraidos de los archivos y bibliotecas nacionales y particulares de Europa y de la América de origen ibero y robustecidos por la tradición oral de testigos oculares de los hechos* (2 vols., Paris: T. Ducessois, 1864), 2:279–284. Rosas's interest in the "continent" of Rio Grande do Sul is understandable, as it had been part of the Spanish Empire until 1763.

45. *Gaceta Mercantil* (Buenos Aires) 17 November 1843.

46. "La cuestión del Plata," *El Mercurio*, 7, 13, 20, and 28 October 1842 in Sarmiento, *Política arjentina*, 60–83.

47. *Gaceta Mercantil* (Buenos Aires) 15 April 1837.

48. Florencio Varela, *Sobre la convención de 29 de octubre de 1840. Desarrollo y desenlace de la cuestión francesa en el río de la Plata* (Montevideo: Impr. de la Caridad, 1840). A shorter version was published in France: *Considérations sur le traité du 29 Octobre 1840*, trans. Ch. Sergent. Publié par M. A. G. Bellemare (Paris: Impr. de Guiraudet et Jouaust, 1841). See also *Gaceta Mercantil* (Buenos Aires) 15 December 1846.

49. Document no. 19, Visconde de Abrántes to Ferreira Franca, Paris, 6 February 1845, Miguel Calmon du Pin e Almeida Abrántes, *A missão especial do visconde de Abrántes de outubro de 1844 á outubro de 1846* (2 vols. in 1, Rio de Janeiro: Emp. Typ.—Dous de Dezembro—de P. Brito, Impr. da Casa imperial, 1853), 1:53–61.

50. *Gaceta Mercantil* (Buenos Aires) 1 January 1838; [Pedro de Angelis], *Quelques réflexions en réponse à la brochure publiée à Montevideo par d. Florencio Varela, sous le titre–Dévéloppement et dénouement de la question française dans le rio de la Plata* (Buenos-Aires: Impr. de l'É tat, 1841), 4. In a letter to Julián Segundo de Agüero [Rio de Janeiro], August 1835, Bernardino Rivadavia states that he signed the treaty with England for "Buenos Aires or the Argentine Republic." (See Palcos, *Rivadavia*, 2:21–22.) This explains why the British preferred the designation "Republic of Buenos Aires" to the "Argentine Confederation."

51. A legislative act of Buenos Aires refers to Rosas as "Director of the Foreign Relations of All the Argentine Republic." This title simply may be the result of bureaucratic fumbling. *Gaceta Mercantil* (Buenos Aires) 21 May 1838.

52. A dispute between Governor Juan Pablo López of Santa Fe and Rosas led to "the mere suspension of diplomatic intercourse," reported the *British Packet* (Buenos Aires) on 29 January 1842.

53. *Gaceta Mercantil* (Buenos Aires) 13 May 1837.

54. Ibid., 28 February 1838; "El sistema de Rosas," *El Progreso*, 28 May 1845 in Sarmiento, *Política arjentina*, 154–158. After 1843 Rosas's title was captain-general and governor of the Province of Buenos Aires, and Rosas called his government the "Argentine Government." Near the end of the decade Rosas wanted to be called president of the Argentine Republic. On 11 January 1845 San Martín wrote the "Captain- General, President of the Argentine Republic" that illness prevented him from offering his services. *British Packet* (Buenos Aires) 6 June 1846.

55. Varela, *Sobre la convención*, 51; *Gaceta Mercantil* (Buenos Aires) 28 February 1838; "El sistema de Rosas," *El Progreso*, 28 May 1845 in Sarmiento, *Política arjentina*, 154–158.

56. [Cyrille Pierre Théodore] Laplace, *Campagne de circumnavigation de la frégate l'Artémise, pendant les années 1837, 1838, 1839 et 1840, sous le commandement de M. Laplace. Pub. par ordre du roi, sous les auspices du ministre de la marine* (6 vols., Paris: A. Bertrand, 1841–1854), 6:329.

57. The assassination of Quiroga in Córdoba in 1835 raises an interesting question, for he was traveling on a diplomatic passport issued by the government of Buenos Aires. He had received diplomatic clearance to pass through the Province of Santa Fe, but not beyond that point. Governor López of Santa Fe was placed in a difficult position, for his protégé was governor of Córdoba. Why Quiroga did not have diplomatic clearance beyond Santa Fe is not clear.

58. *Gaceta Mercantil* (Buenos Aires) 9 March 1839.

59. Ibid., 4 November 1843. The French navy helped Lavalle cross the Río

Paraná.

60. *British Packet* (Buenos Aires) 8 and 15 January 1842, and 28 December 1844.

61. "The Siege of Monte Video," *Dublin Review* (London) 26 (March 1849): 36–39.

62. "Monte Video and Buenos Ayres—British Interference," *The Economist* (London) 5 (6 November 1847): 1273.

63. *The Times* (London) 16 October 1845; Adolph R. Pfeil, *Resumé des affaires de la Plata* (Paris: Imprimerie Centrale de Napoleón et Cie., 1849), 21–22; Varela, *Escritos,* 175 and 189; Robert Elwes, *A Sketcher's Tour Round the World* (London: Hurst and Blackett, 1854), 111–112; Alfred de Brossard, *Considérations historiques et politiques sur les républiques de La Plata dans leurs rapports avec la France et l'Angleterre* (Paris: Guillaumin et Cie., 1850), 256. The governor of Tucumán called Rosas an American in his message to the House of Representatives on 27 September 1845. *British Packet* (Buenos Aires) 15 November 1845.

64. Both Brazil and Rosas courted the Uruguayan leaders, but not always with success. Brazil awarded Oribe a decoration, but Rosas financed his efforts to return to power. Fructuoso Rivera received a military title from Brazil and Rosas. *British Packet* (Buenos Aires) 9 December 1843.

65. Pfeil, *Resumé,* 20–21; *Gaceta Mercantil* (Buenos Aires) 13 November 1843.

66. *Gaceta Mercantil* (Buenos Aires) 30 October 1843.

67. At the time, both Fructuoso Rivera and Bernardino Rivadavia were in Rio de Janeiro, "the head-quarters of the real and by far the most reputed Chiefs of the Unitarian party, unhappily in exile." *British Packet* (Buenos Aires) 25 May 1844. The sons of Rivadavia and their families were living in Buenos Aires in 1845 and were government employees.

68. *Gaceta Mercantil* (Buenos Aires) 6 and 17 November 1843.

69. Ibid., 2, 12, and 30 October, and 3, 6, and 13 November 1843; "Les deux rives de La Plata, Montevideo—Buenos-Ayres—Rivera—Rosas," *Revue des Deux Mondes* (Paris) 5th Ser., 2 (1843): 26 and 41–45; *British Packet* (Buenos Aires) 26 May and 10 September 1842, 16 September and 4 November 1843, 31 May and 7 June 1845, 18 April 1846, 29 March 1847; Ravignani, *Asambleas constituyentes,* 6: part 2, 254–255; Adolfo Saldias, *Historia de la Confederación Argentina; Rosas y su época,* 2d ed., rev. (5 vols., Buenos Aires: F. Lajouane, 1892), 4: 7–9. Paz left his family in Asunción when he returned to Rio de Janeiro in 1847. Wilfrid Latham, *The States of the River Plate,* 2d ed. (London: Longmans, Green, and Co., 1868), 266, footnote, confirms that the formation of a separate republic composed of Entre Ríos, Corrientes, and Paraguay and its alliance with Uruguay was being considered.

70. Sarmiento, *Discurso presentado,* 29.

71. "El 25 de Mayo," *El Mercurio,* 25 May 1842 and "Interes de Chile en la cuestión del Plata," *El Progreso,* 8 May 1845 in Sarmiento, *Política arjentina,* 48–55 and 151–154; "25 de Mayo de 1849. Convite de Argentinos en Santiago—Reclamo de Estradición de Sarmiento," *La Crónica,* 3 June 1849 in Sarmiento, *Argirópolis,* 273–274; Sarmiento to Bartolomé Mitre, Santiago de Chile, 15 November 1844, Hugo Rodolfo Ramírez de Rivera, "El pensamiento político de Sarmiento y Alberdi a través de 'Facundo o Civilización y Barbarbie en las Pampas Argentinas' y 'Bases y Puntos de Partida para la Organización Política de la República Argentina' (dos obras escritas en Chile)," Academia Nacional de la Historia, Caracas, *Boletín* 63 (July–September 1985): 782–783.

72. *The Times* (London) 16 October 1845; "Conducta de Rosas i sus ajentes con el gobierno de Chile," *El Mercurio,* 19 April 1842 in Sarmiento, *Política*

arjentina, 25–29; "Nuestro derecho de atacar a Rosas," *El Progreso*, 28 April 1845 in ibid., 138–140; "Anuncio de la 'Vida de Quiroga,'" *El Progreso*, 1 May 1845 in ibid., 148–151; "Interes de Chile en la cuestión del Plata," *El Progreso*, 8 May 1845 in ibid., 151–154. Years later Sarmiento returned to the same economic theme in "Lo que Chile debe a Rosas," *La Crónica*, 1 April 1849 in ibid., 175–179, and "El comercio libre por cordillera," *Sud-América*, 17 March 1851 in ibid., 364–373. Sarmiento's interest in free trade between the provinces of Cuyo and Chile, though in another context, appears in his *Campaña*, 343.

73. Sarmiento sought to explain South America to the French in *Discurso presentado para su recepción en el Instituto Istórico de Francia* (Valparaiso: Imprenta Europea, 1848). Allison Williams Bunkley, *The Life of Sarmiento* (Princeton: Princeton University Press, 1952), 278, n. 20, identified another work: *Guerre de l'indépendence dans l'Amérique du sud.*

74. "Anuncio de la 'Vida de Quiroga,'" *El Progreso*, 1 May 1845 in Sarmiento, *Política arjentina*, 148–151; "Lo que Chile debe a Rosas," *La Crónica*, 1 April 1849 in ibid., 175–179; "Rosas en paz con todo el mundo," *La Crónica*, 11 November 1849 in ibid., 213–218; *British Packet* (Buenos Aires) 12 July 1851: Sarmiento, *Campaña*, 342–343.

75. Sarmiento to Johann Moritz Rugendas, Santiago de Chile, November 1849, "Sarmiento y Rugendas," *La Nación* (Buenos Aires) 6 April 1952.

76. "El tratado Leprédour sea no contar con la huéspeda," *Sud-América*, 9 August 1851 in Sarmiento, *Argirópolis*, 238–245.

77. Domingo F. Sarmiento, *Argirópolis*. Introduction by Ernesto Quesada (Buenos Aires: "La Cultura Argentina," 1916), 35, 78–79, 86, 89, 131, 154, and 180.

78. Ibid., 66, 87, 97, 101, 107, 127–129, 165, and 184–186.

79. "Dos políticas," *Sud-América*, 24 August 1851 in Sarmiento, *Argirópolis* [Moreno edition], 230–237.

80. "Las filípicas de los Andes," Santiago de Chile, 24 July 1851 in ibid., 198–200; "Decreto del Gobernador de Salta Alzándose con el Poder," in ibid., 227–228. Sarmiento here referred to the Río Paraná by its old name, the Río Paraguay.

81. *Sud-América*, 1 February and 17 July 1851 in Sarmiento, *Campaña*, 28-39. Sarmiento would not place Entre Ríos and Corrientes, as Varela suggested, *"under the direct auspices of French military colonists."* *British Packet* (Buenos Aires) 5 July 1851.

82. Rosario, 1 January 1852, Sarmiento, *Campaña*, 54–55.

83. Elwes, *Sketcher's Tour*, 111–112, 123–126, and 162; Pfeil, *Resumé*, 21; James R. McCulloch, *Dictionary, Geographical, Statistical, and Historical, of the Various Countries, Places and Principal Natural Objects in the World* (2 vols., New York: Harper, 1843), 1:488; Isaac G. Strain, *Cordillera and Pampa, Mountain and Plain; Sketches of a Journey in Chili, and the Argentine Provinces in 1849* (New York: H. H. Moore, 1853), 18–21, and 157; *El Iris Argentino* (Paraná) 7 August 1851.

84. *Sud-América*, 1 February and 18 July 1851 in Sarmiento, *Campaña*, 31, 39–41, and 94; "Las filípicas de los Andes," Santiago de Chile, 24 July 1851, Sarmiento, *Argirópolis* [Moreno edition], 199–200.

85. "'Un Argentino' [Ángel Elías] to Justo José de Urquiza, Buenos Aires, 12 June 1850" in Leandro Ruiz Moreno, *Centenarios del pronunciamiento y de Monte Caseros* (2 vols., Paraná : Editorial "Nueva Impresora," 1952), 2:66–72.

86. "El tratado Leprédour," *Sud-América*, 9 August 1851 in Sarmiento, *Argirópolis* [Moreno edition], 238–254.

87. The free navigation of the rivers issue was aptly stated by Lord George

Canning in a letter to Lord Viscount Sandon, Foreign Office, 17 August 1844. He said: "So far as the Paraná flows through the territory of Buenos Ayres, it must be considered as composing a part of the domain of that state, and that consequently the Buenos Ayrean Government have the right of regulating its navigation." Quoted in *British Packet* (Buenos Aires) 28 June 1845. As Great Britain had recognized the Republic of Buenos Aires, Lord Canning thought that Buenos Aires controlled both sides of the Río Paraná. Actually, Buenos Aires controlled both banks of the Río Paraná only when it was responsible for the foreign relations of the riverine province.

88. *New York Times,* 7 November 1851.

89. In San Juan a foreigner (*extranjero*) was a person who came from another province. Dean Gregorio Funes felt that he was a foreigner in Buenos Aires. Porteños thought the same of people from another province. Sarmiento, *Recuerdos,* 242–244; Broadside, Gregorio Funes, Buenos Aires, 24 February 1814, University of California Library, Berkeley. The word *extranjero* evidently was also used in describing European and North American immigrants. According to an article of 24 December 1842 in the *British Packet,* Rosas's party did not object to European immigrants, but only to the European mercenaries who—along with the Indians from Corrientes—formed the basis of most Unitarian armies.

90. "Dos políticas," *Sud-América,* 15 August 1851 in Sarmiento, *Argirópolis* [Moreno edition], 230–237; Domingo F. Sarmiento, *Facundo; Edición crítica y documentada.* Foreword by Alberto Palcos (La Plata: Universidad Nacional de La Plata, 1938), 24. In Rosario on 1 January 1852, Sarmiento referred to Rosas in almost similar language. Sarmiento, *Campaña,* 54.

91. Ibid., 19.

92. *El Iris Argentino* (Paraná) 24 July 1851.

93. Sarmiento praised San Martín in the introduction to the first edition of *Facundo.* Palcos, *Facundo,* 21.

94. Sarmiento, *Campaña,* 134. Sarmiento mentions his expectations in a letter to Manuel Montt, Montevideo, 2 December 1851 in *Sarmiento y Urquiza, dos caracteres opuestos, unidos por el amor a la patria; Interesante correspondencia,* ed. Antonio Pedro Castro (Buenos Aires: Museo Histórico Sarmiento, 1954), 59–60. The tone of the letter suggests that Montt, now the Chilean president, had given Sarmiento a mission that is not identified.

95. Sarmiento to [Ange de] Champgobert, Montevideo, 6 December 1851, MSS Archivo del Dr. D. Andrés Lamas, Fondo Documental ex-Archivo y Museo Histórico Nacional, Archivo General de la Nación, Montevideo, *caja* 6, *leg.* 112. I am indebted to Professor Juan E. Pivel Devoto for calling my attention to this collection.

96. *New York Daily Times,* 24 March 1852.

97. Sarmiento, *Convención de San-Nicolás,* 17–18 and *Campaña,* 294–297.

98. Sarmiento to Bartolomé Mitre, Rio de Janeiro, 13 April 1852 in Sarmiento, *Campaña,* 69–71, and 286; A. Deavoize to minister of foreign relations of France, Montevideo, 6 March 1852, "Informes diplomáticos de los representantes de Francia en el Uruguay, 1851–1853," *Revista Histórica* (Montevideo) 2ª ép., 17 (December 1951): 222–225. Brazil awarded both military and aristocratic titles. The provincial governments only awarded military titles. Military titles sometimes were honorary. This was a way to establish a bond.

99. [Domingo F. Sarmiento] to José Posse, Rio de Janeiro, 10 April 1852, [Sarmiento], *Epistolario entre Sarmiento y Posse, 1845–1888.* [Aclaraciones y biografía por Antonio P. Castro] (2 vols., Buenos Aires: Museo Histórico Sarmiento, 1946–1947), 1:28–30.

100. Sarmiento, *Convención de San-Nicolás*, 5.

101. *La Organización Nacional* (Corrientos) 9 July 1851, quoted in *El Iris Argentino* (Paraná) 31 July 1851.

102. Sarmiento, *Campaña*, 230.

103. Sarmiento, *Convención de San-Nicolás*, 13.

104. [Domingo F. Sarmiento], *San-Juan, sus hombres i sus actos en la rejeneración arjentina. Narración de los acontecimientos que han tenido lugar en aquella provincia antes i después de la caí da de Rosas–Restablecimiento de Benavídes, i conducta de sus habitantes en masa con el caudillo restaurado–Tomada de fuentes auténticas i apoyadas en documentos públicos* (Santiago de Chile: Imprenta de Julio Belín i Cia., 1852), 5.

105. Xavier Marmier, *Lettres sur l'Amérique. Canada–Etats Unis–Havane, Rio de la Plata* (2 vols., Paris: A. Bertrand, 1851), 2:228-237.

106. Andrés Somellera to Andrés Lamas, Buenos Aires, 2 August 1852, Archivo Andrés Lamas, *caja* 109, *leg.* 7; Sarmiento, *Memoria enviada*, 16.

107. Sarmiento, *Argirópolis* [Moreno edition], 71.

108. Valentín Alsina to Mitre, [Buenos Aires], 20 June [1852], *Archivo del general Bartolomé Mitre* (28 vols., Buenos Aires: Biblioteca de "La Nación," 1911-1914), 21:138-139; John S. Pendleton to the secretary of state, Buenos Aires, 1 March and 9 July 1852, Department of State, National Archives Microfilm Publications, R69 R9. On 1 October 1852 Paz was reincorporated in the army of the Province of Buenos Aires.

109. Sarmiento to José Posse, Rio de Janeiro, 10 April 1852 in Castro, *Epistolario*, 1:28-30; Luis J. de la Peña to Lamas, Montevideo, 25 May 1852, Archivo Andrés Lamas, *caja* 105, *leg.* 12; Sarmiento to Lamas, Rio de Janeiro, 14 May 1852, Archivo Andrés Lamas, *caja* 112, *leg.* 6; Juan B. Alberdi to Félix Frías, Valparaiso, 4 November 1852 in *Cartas inédita de Juan Bautista Alberdi e Juan María Gutiérrez y a Félix Frías,* ed. Jorge M. Mayer and Ernesto A. Martínez (Buenos Aires: Abeledo-Perrot, 1973), 264-267.

110. The quotation appears in Sarmiento to Lamas, Rio de Janeiro, 11 May 1852, Archivo Andrés Lamas, *caja* 112, *leg.* 6.

111. Sarmiento to Lamas, Rio de Janeiro, 14 May 1852, Archivo Andrés Lamas, *caja* 112, *leg.* 6. Sarmiento's defense of the pro-Brazilian faction (and indirectly of its leadership in the minority-led revolution of September 1852) appears in his letter from Yungay to Urquiza of 13 October 1852. The Brazilian connection with the September revolution is discussed in Luis J. de la Peña to Andrés Lamas, Buen-retiro, 22 March 1855, Archivo Lamas, *caja* 105, *leg.* 13; Pedro de Angelis to Andrés Lamas, Buenos Aires, 31 December 1856, Archivo Lamás, *caja* 89, *leg.* 29; Mariano Baudrix to Justo J. de Urquiza, Montevideo, 14 January 1859, Archivo particular del Sr. Salvador M. del Carril, Archivo General de la Nación, Buenos Aires, *sala* VII, *leg.* 3.2.1.

112. Sarmiento, *El ciudadano arjentino*, 17.

11

Sarmiento and Immigration: Changing Views on the Role of Immigration in the Development of Argentina

Samuel L. Baily

All students of nineteenth-century Argentina are aware that European immigration—along with political reform, education, and material progress—was central to Sarmiento's vision of building a modern civilized country. Few, however, have taken the time to read his extensive writings on the subject, and, therefore, to understand just how, if at all, his ideas evolved over the course of his life.[1] Some have selectively quoted his early writings and proclaimed that he was an unequivocal champion of immigration. Others, such as Ricardo Rojas, have selectively quoted Sarmiento's later work and claimed that he was concerned primarily with the danger of immigration to the formation of an Argentine nationality.[2] In fact, Sarmiento's sometimes ambiguous and apparently contradictory ideas on immigration did evolve in a complex manner as the circumstances around him changed. Although he emphasized certain of his ideas at one time and others at different times, he consistently was both a champion of immigration and concerned about the threat of unassimilated immigrants to the development of Argentine nationality.

In this chapter I review systematically two neglected volumes of Sarmiento's writings on immigration and place the ideas they contain in the changing context of mid-nineteenth-century Argentine society. Statements on immigration can be found scattered throughout the fifty-three volumes of the *Obras completas*, but two volumes—*Inmigración y colonización* and *Condición del extranjero en América*—concentrate exclusively on immigration and contain the bulk of his writing on the subject.[3] In evaluating these works I will focus on three separate periods during which Sarmiento wrote extensively about immigration: (1) the 1840s, when he was in exile in Chile and traveled to Europe and the United States; (2) the late 1850s, when for the first time he lived for an extended period of time in Buenos Aires

---

Samuel L. Baily is professor of history, Rutgers University.

and confronted directly the reality of Argentine immigration; and (3) the 1880s, the last years of his life, during which he became increasingly preoccupied with the unassimilated immigrant.

THE 1840s: THE FORMATION OF
A THEORY OF IMMIGRATION

On 18 November 1840 the twenty-nine-year-old Sarmiento fled the Argentina of Juan Manuel de Rosas and went into exile in Chile. Here he would remain, with the exception of a two-year trip to Europe and the United States, for more than a decade.[4] In Chile he became a close friend and protégé of Manuel Montt, the enlightened minister of justice and public education in the administration of President Manuel Bulnes. Montt was not only interested in public education, but also in populating the empty public lands of southern Chile with European immigrants. Late in 1845, Montt, on behalf of the Chilean government, sent Sarmiento to Europe to study education and the French methods of colonization in Algiers. Sarmiento returned to Chile in 1848 and remained there for several more years.

Between 1841 and 1845, when he left for Europe, Sarmiento, writing for several Chilean newspapers (*El Progreso*, *La Crónica*, *El Mercurio*), set forth his major ideas on immigration: immigration was essential to the development of the South American countries; governments must take a leading role in encouraging immigration; the state must see that immigrants assimilate to the culture of the host society; and the United States was the model for a successful immigration policy.

European immigration, Sarmiento argued, was essential for the development of Chile. The immigrants were important because they would teach "the systems of cultivation adopted in Europe, the application to agriculture of many instruments that facilitate work and that are unknown among us, and most importantly, the combination and succession of seeds and plants, that save time, land and work and increase production." In addition, the government had to take the leadership in fomenting immigration. "The direction of our legislation and our institutions," he explained, "must have, then, for an acknowledged goal, to open all possible roads to European immigration, facilitating its introduction, assuring it the fruit of its work, and leaving to its individuals the full enjoyment of all the rights that liberty assures to all men."[5]

"North America," he proclaimed, "is our model." He wanted to North Americanize South America, to modernize the South American countries through immigration, education, economic development, and political reform. He believed that many of the obstacles to modernization that he saw were due to the Spanish heritage and he wanted to overcome this influence. Spain was the problem and European immigration the solution. "European immigration is one of the elements of American wealth, power and industry," and was essential for the successful growth of the South American countries.[6]

Yet, even in this early period, when his ideas were based on abstract theory rather than specific experience, Sarmiento was concerned about the potential dangers of large numbers of unassimilated immigrants for the host society. In an evaluation of the plans of European companies to colonize lands in southern Chile, Sarmiento made it clear that he rejected the establishment of exclusively European colonies. Some of the land involved in these projects, he insisted, should be reserved for the govern- ment of Chile to distribute to Chileans. It was essential not to form "the new colonies with foreigners alone, which would be perhaps prejudicial to the country, but to mix them with Chileans, in order that they learn our language, and we improve with their example our industry in manufacturing and agriculture."[7]

Sarmiento's trip to Europe on behalf of the Chilean government greatly strengthened his commitment to the idea of attracting European immigrants to South America. He visited France, Spain, and Algiers in 1846, and was especially impressed with the French defeat of the Arab horsemen—whom he compared to the Argentine gauchos—and with the colonization and subsequent economic development of Algiers by the French.[8]

In 1847 Sarmiento visited Italy, Switzerland, Germany, England, and the United States. He was fascinated with Germany and concluded that the Germans were the best people to help develop South America. Germany was the major source of European emigrants at that time, but most German emigrés went to the United States. Sarmiento wanted to attract them to South America. He became friends with Dr. Wappäus, professor of statistics and geography at the University of Gotinga, a man familiar with Spanish history who had written a pamphlet for prospective emigrants to the Río de la Plata area. Sarmiento had the work translated, and in the preface to the Spanish edition he noted that Professor Wappäus had steered many German immigrants to Chile. Sarmiento urged the Chilean government to publish such pamphlets in France, Germany, and Italy as well.[9]

After Germany, Sarmiento went to Paris, London, and finally the United States. This visit reinforced his belief that the United States was the model for civilization and that immigration was an essential cause of its growth and progress. The immigrants in the United States, he noted, were "a precious and scarce element of civilization." Nevertheless, Sarmiento also learned that there were problems associated with incorporating large numbers of immigrants into a more advanced culture. Immigration remained an instrument of transformation, but there were potential dangers. In the United States, he observed, the immigrants became citizens, whereas in Argentina they did not.[10]

When Sarmiento returned to Chile in 1848, he used the information he had gathered on his trip to promote economic and population growth. In a series of articles that appeared in *La Crónica* in 1849, Sarmiento observed that European immigration was directed to the United States, Algiers, and even to Asia, but not to South America. Why not? Because the former Spanish colonies had a bad reputation in Europe. They did not treat foreigners well. He compared the lack of growth of Chilean cities with the dramatic growth of cities in the United States and blamed this stagnation on the lack of traditions of industry and good government. "Only immigration," he explained, "can eradicate time and add capacity."[11]

California, a symbol of success through immigration, was especially fascinating to Sarmiento. "What is California?" he wrote. "Until yesterday no more than a piece of privileged land, that unfortunately had fallen by luck to the Spanish race: ... Today California is something very different. It is the emporium of the Pacific, the port that the United States opens toward the seas to dominate them with its industry."[12]

He developed this idea further in another article entitled "The Yankee Spirit." The United States, Sarmiento argued, had shown a special quality that had led to its greatness, "the ability to colonize, to populate the land, to transform the forest into a city, the empty countryside into a flourishing State, almost without being aware of it, as if by instinct."[13]

Sarmiento recognized that immigration to Chile would not be spontaneous: he therefore supported the initiatives of Montt and others to develop laws to encourage immigration.

> Immigration is the only method of introducing new industries and industrial practices, or increasing population and production, of exploiting the forests, of developing the coast, of cultivating that which is not cultivated. Immigration to Chile cannot be spontaneous, due to distance, to the habit of emigrating to North America, to the higher cost of passage, to being a less well-known country, etc.[14]

He then set forth specific provisions for a law to encourage immigration.

By the end of the 1840s, Sarmiento had clearly articulated his major ideas regarding immigration: immigration was essential for the South American countries if they were to overcome their Spanish heritage and create new and prosperous civilizations; the government had to stimulate immigration and oversee the immigrants' assimilation into the host societies; and the United States was the model of success.

Table 11.1 Immigration to Argentina and Buenos Aires, 1857–1890

Years	Number to Argentina (A)	Number of Buenos Aires (B)	B\A
1853–56	19,000*	5,500*	28.9%
1857–60	20,000	5,938	29.7%
1861–70	159,570	52,558	32.9%
1871–80	260,885	87,066	33.4%
1881–90	841,122	278,508	33.1%

Sources: Dirección de Inmigración, *Resúmen estadística del movimiento migratorio en la República Argentina, 1857–1924* (Buenos Aires: Talleres Gráficos del Ministerio de Agricultura de la Nación, 1925), 24–25; Comisión Directiva del censo, *Censo general de la población, edificación, comercio é industrias de la ciudad de Buenos Aires. Levantado en los dias 17 de agosto, 15 y 30 de setiembre de 1887, . . .* 2 vols. (Buenos Aires: Compañía Sudamericana de Billetes de Banco, 1889); Comisión Directiva del Censo, *Segundo censo de la República Argentina, mayo 10 de 1895*, 3 vols. (Buenos Aires: Taller Tip. de la Penitenciaria Nacional, 1898).
*Estimated.

RESPONDING TO THE IMMIGRANT CITY, BUENOS AIRES, 1855–1861

With the overthrow of Juan Manuel de Rosas in early 1852, Sarmiento was able to go to Buenos Aires, but he soon left and did not return to stay for any period of time until May of 1855. In the meantime, the Argentine Confederation had adopted a constitution that embodied many, but not all of Sarmiento's ideas—as well as ideas of the other members of the Generation of '37—regarding immigration. The constitution stated that foreigners would be fully protected under the law and that no obstacles would be placed in the way of immigrants. It did not mention the role of the government in assimilating the immigrants. Although some immigrants had arrived in Buenos Aires during the last years of Rosas's rule, the numbers increased noticeably during the years immediately following his overthrow. More than a thousand immigrants a year settled in this city of less than one hundred thousand inhabitants during the eight years from 1853 to 1860 (see Table 11.1).

Buenos Aires had changed dramatically during the previous twenty years. In 1836 it had been a city of some 61,000 inhabitants, 24 percent of whom were black or mixed and only 6.5 percent of whom were foreign born. By 1855 it had grown to over 90,000 inhabitants, and most significantly, 35 percent were foreign born. The black and mixed population had dropped to under 4 percent. The city would continue to grow rapidly during the rest of Sarmiento's life, and within a few years the number of foreign born would represent one out of every two people (see Table 11.2).

Table 11.2 Population of Buenos Aires, 1836–1895

Date	Total Population	% Black-Mixed	% Foreign	% Italian	% Spanish
1836	61,379	24.3	6.5		
1855	92,709	3.6	35.3	11.7	5.9
1869	177,787		49.4	23.6	7.9
1887	433,375		52.8	31.9	9.1
1895	663,854		52.0	27.4	12.1

Sources: Comisión Directiva del censo, *Censo general de la población, edificación, comercio é industrias de la ciudad de Buenos Aires. Levantado en los dias 17 de agosto, 15 y 30 de setiembre de 1887,* . . . 2 vols. (Buenos Aires: Compañía Sudamericana de Billetes de Banco, 1889); Alfredo E. Lattes and Paul Poczter, "Muestra del censo de población de la ciudad de Buenos Aires de 1855," in *Documento de Trabajo* (Buenos Aires: Instituto Torcuato Di Tella, 1968), 26–27; Comisión Directiva del Censo, *Segundo censo de la República Argentina, mayo 10 de 1895,* 3 vols. (Buenos Aires: Taller Tip. de la Penitenciaria Nacional, 1898).

In Buenos Aires, Sarmiento became active in public affairs in part because his friends, Valentín Alsina and Bartolomé Mitre, were in control of the government of the Province of Buenos Aires. Sarmiento became chief of the Department of Schools for the Province of Buenos Aires and was elected to the Municipal Council of the city of Buenos Aires in 1856. In 1857 he was elected to the Senate of the Province of Buenos Aires, a position he held until 1861. In addition he wrote extensively for the newspaper *El Nacional,* which was owned by Mitre.

Sarmiento's increasingly specific and concrete ideas on immigration reflected his change in location, but he continued to support the basic ideas he had articulated during the 1840s. Although his focus shifted from Chile to Argentina and Buenos Aires, he still promoted immigration and the necessity of the government to take an active role in fomenting it and in ensuring assimilation. The United States remained his model.

From the columns of *El Nacional* he argued for increased immigration and stressed its importance for the development of the country. "Immigration is still a desire," he explained, "an empty desire if we do not work to attract it," and he pointed to the growth of the United States as an example.[15] He called for action to attract immigrants. The United States, he noted, due to its freedom, peace, high salaries, and cheap available land, had succeeded in attracting European immigrants almost exclusively. But, he continued, Argentina since Rosas had a number of advantages that it must make known to the prospective immigrants and it must remove any obstacles that deter immigration.[16]

One such obstacle, he believed, was the absence of a law to provide public land at reasonable prices for those who wanted to work it, something like the Homestead Law of the United States. "We have shown ourselves almost adverse to the direct protection that many endeavor to give immigration," he complained. "But we insist always on the necessity of placing within reach, at fixed and reasonable prices, land, with the goal that they [the immigrants] can count on its acquisition, by contract sale, as the only means of acquiring it advantageously."[17]

At the same time that he was working to attract immigrants and to induce the government to take a role in this endeavor, Sarmiento raised anew his concern about assimilation and the obstacles that hindered it. In an article on the foreign community in Buenos Aires, Sarmiento lamented that foreigners formed "entities extraneous to our political life, although almost always sympathetic to liberty and progress." He attacked the newspaper *La Comunidad Extranjera* because it encouraged the immigrants to remain foreigners in Argentina.[18]

Similarly, Sarmiento was concerned that the French and English governments were extending citizenship to the children born in Argentina of French and English parents. The intention of the French government, he argued, was to relieve these children of "the duties that the law of the land in which they were born imposes on them," and "to make foreigners of them in their own land." And he attacked *L'Opinion Éxtrangére* as he argued that "there is no common opinion among the French, Basques, English, Germans, Spaniards and Italians."[19]

He poignantly described the pull of the Old World and of the New that made the immigrant a stranger everywhere. "The immigrant to South America," he explained,

> dreams daily of returning to his homeland, which he idealizes in his fantasies. His adopted land seems to be a valley of toil in which he prepares for a better life. . . . And when one out of a thousand at last returns to his birthplace, he finds that the homeland is no longer his homeland. He is a stranger there, yet he has left behind in his adopted country the status, pleasures, and affections that nothing else can provide. . . . He is a citizen of neither of his two countries, and he is unfaithful to both, failing to fulfill the obligations that the fatherland and the new land impose on those who are born and live in them.[20]

Although by the early 1860s Sarmiento was still a proponent of immigration and of a leading government role in fomenting and controlling it, the reality of Buenos Aires had made him increasingly emphasize some of his concerns about the obstacles to the assimilation of the immigrant.

THE 1880s: THE CAMPAIGN AGAINST
UNASSIMILATED IMMIGRANTS

When Sarmiento left Buenos Aires in 1861, its population was approximately 110,000, of which perhaps 40 percent was foreign born. When he returned to assume the presidency of Argentina seven years later, the population of the city had grown to more than 170,000, and nearly half of the inhabitants were foreign born (Table 11.2).

During the six years he was president (1868 to 1874), approximately 175,000 immigrants entered Argentina, and 55,000 of them settled in Buenos Aires (Table 11.1). Clearly, Sarmiento and his friends had been successful in fostering policies to stimulate immigration and in actually attracting substantial numbers of immigrants. Yet the immigrants who were coming to Argentina were primarily Italians and Spaniards, not the Germans whom he favored, and they continued to refuse to assimilate as he believed they must.

Sarmiento never abandoned his ideas regarding immigration, but increasingly during the 1870s and especially during the 1880s he attacked, with an intensity missing during his prepresidency years, those groups who remained apart and who he believed to be especially recalcitrant to assimilation. Although his main targets were the schools of the large and wealthy Italian mutual aid societies, he also was concerned about the Italian press and legislative efforts to grant citizenship to those who had lived in Argentina for some time but who had not sought this citizenship.[21]

Sarmiento's attack on the Italian schools began in earnest early in 1881. From January 6 to 9 of 1881, a number of the Italian mutual aid societies with schools joined together to hold the First Pedagogical Congress. The members of the congress sought to unify scholastic rules and procedures and to stimulate the growth and expansion of Italian schools. They discussed the issues of language and the "national" (Italian) character of their education. In response to previous Argentine criticism, they also decided to add the Spanish language and Argentine history and geography to the curriculum.[22]

Sarmiento responded a few days later with an article in *El Nacional* in which he attacked the Italian schools because they did not teach in the Spanish language or Argentine history. The public schools, he argued, had developed rapidly in the past decade and were superior to those of the Italians. The public schools were for everyone and should be supported by all.[23]

What particularly bothered Sarmiento was the idea of educating the students "Italianly" (*Italianamente*). "What is this then to educate 'Italianly?' To conserve or to foster in the mind of the child the cult of the *patria* that he does not know, that he probably will not know, displacing his natural instincts which compel him to love the land in which he was born?"[24] What seemed to add even greater urgency to the issue was that the Italian government had supported the schools with modest but very real subsidies since 1872.

A few days later, Sarmiento attacked the Italian press, especially *La*

Table 11.3 Primary School Population in Buenos Aires, 1869–1895
(Primary School Population = 6–14 years of age)

Year	School Age Population	Number Attending School	Italians (6–14)	Number in Italian Schools
1869	22,595		4,200[*]	1,200
1881				2,800
1887	68,059	29,704	8,000[*]	2,000
1895	117,388	67,754	12,000	3,000

Sources: Samuel L. Baily, "Las sociedades de ayuda mutua y el desarrollo de una comunidad italiana en Buenos Aires, 1858–1918," *Desarrollo Económico* 21 (January–March 1982): 484–514; Luigi Favero, "Las escuelas de las sociedades italianas en Argentina (1860–1914)," in *La inmigración italiana en la Argentina,* ed. Fernando Devoto and Gianfausto Rosoli (Buenos Aires: Editorial Biblios, 1985), 165–207, esp. 170 and 180–181; Comisión Directiva del censo, *Censo general de la población, edificación, comercio é industrias de la ciudad de Buenos Aires. Levantado en los días 17 de agosto, 15 y 30 de setiembre de 1887,* . . . (2 vols., Buenos Aires: Compañía Sudamericana de Billetes de Banco, 1889), 2:9, 34, 37, 541–544; Comisión Directiva del Censo, *Segundo censo de la República Argentina, mayo 10 de 1895* (3 vols., Buenos Aires: Taller Tip. de la Penitenciaria Nacional, 1898), 2:xci, clxxiv.
[*]Estimates based on data in the city census of 1887, the national census of 1895, and Favero.

Patria, for defending the Italian schools. He noted that in the United States there was no equivalent among the immigrants. There were no English schools for English immigrants seeking to educate students "Anglicanly."[25] The Italian schools were a danger to the development of the Argentine nationality, he believed. "We must eliminate the intention of certain foreign members, who with disagreeable methods wish to cheat the youth of their nationality."[26]

Sarmiento returned to his attacks on the Italian schools in 1888 and 1889, using the same arguments and language. Although it is impossible to determine with precision what percent of Italian children living in Buenos Aires were involved, we do know that no more than three thousand students attended these schools at any one time between 1867 and 1895. These three thousand students, however, represented approximately 25 percent of the primary school-age population of the city's Italian children, a very real obstacle to assimilation (Table 11.3).[27]

During this period Sarmiento also took up the issue of granting citizenship to those who did not solicit it. Again, he turned to the U.S. model and argued that immigrants must first learn about their adopted country and then seek citizenship if it were to have any meaning.[28]

To Sarmiento, the Italian schools and the Italian press were obstacles
to assimilation that had undermined his plans to create a new Argentine
civilization based on immigration. The ideas of immigration and modernization were not the problem, he insisted. Rather, the inadequate
implementation of these ideas by the state had brought about failure.
Buenos Aires "is a city without citizens," Sarmiento lamented shortly
before he died.

> The most industrious and progressive of its 400,000 inhabitants are
> strangers who, the more one recognizes them as the artisans of its
> transformation, themselves remain unchanged . . . we shall build, if we
> have not already built, a Tower of Babel in America, its workmen
> speaking all tongues, not blending them together in the task of construc-
> tion but each persisting in his own, and thus unable to understand the
> other. . . . One does not construct a homeland without patriotism as its
> cement.[29]

CONCLUSION

The at times ambiguous and to some contradictory nature of Sarmiento's
ideas on immigration masked a fundamental continuity of thought that
has eluded most scholars of nineteenth century Argentina. Sarmiento
consistently endorsed immigration as a means of building his new and
prosperous civilization on the pampas, but he also recognized, and
increasingly stressed, the potential threat of these immigrants to the
development of an Argentine cultural and political identity if they
remained unassimilated. Sarmiento's basic ideas about immigration
remained constant throughout his life. Immigration was essential for
economic development and the creation of civilization. The immigrants
were necessary to dilute the Spanish heritage, to stimulate population
growth, and to bring in the necessary ideas and skills for development.
The government had to play a major role in the efforts to stimulate
immigration. It had to pass laws to provide public land at reasonable
prices, help immigrants adjust when they first arrived, and provide them
with the security of a society governed by law. Assimilation of the
immigrant was an essential item that Sarmiento had first mentioned with
reference to the Germans settling in southern Chile in 1848. The
obstacles to such assimilation had to be removed, especially immigrant
institutions such as the Italian schools and press supported by the Italian
government, and the Argentine state had to be strong and active enough
to ensure such assimilation. Finally, it was the United States, which in his
view had successfully attracted and made citizens of the immigrants, that
provided the model of success that was to be emulated.

One can argue that Sarmiento never confronted certain issues that tended to undermine part of his vision. He never acknowledged that citizenship had few tangible advantages for the immigrants while alien status conferred many benefits, nor did he confront the reality that the immigrants were so numerous and so critical in the development of the country that there was a real question as to the nature and strength of the core culture and peoples to which the newcomers were to assimilate. Yet the basic ideas of Sarmiento—his commitment both to immigration and assimilation—were important precedents for subsequent nationalists such as Ricardo Rojas and José María Ramos Mejía who, during the early decades of the twentieth century, emphasized assimilation rather than restrictions on immigration. Unlike the United States, Argentina never enacted immigrant restriction legislation based on literacy and national quotas, a fact which can be explained in considerable part by the enduring influence of Sarmiento's ideas.[30]

NOTES

1. An important exception is the article of Tulio Halperín Donghi, "Para que la inmigración? Ideología y política inmigratoria y aceleración del proceso modernizador: El caso Argentino (1810-1914)," in *Jahrbuch für Geschichte von Staat, Wirtschaft und Gesellschaft Lateinamerikas*, ed. Richard Konetzke and Hermann Kellenbenz (Cologne: 1976), 13:437-489. This path-breaking article greatly enhanced my understanding of the ideas of Sarmiento and the changing context in which they developed.

2. Ricardo Rojas, *El profeta de la pampa; Vida de Sarmiento* (Buenos Aires: Editorial Losada, 1945), 629-643.

3. Domingo F. Sarmiento, *Obras completas*, vol. 23, *Inmigración y colonización* (53 vols., Buenos Aires: Editorial Luz del Día, 1948-1956) and vol. 36, *Condición del extranjero en América*.

4. The information on Sarmiento's life is taken primarily from the biography of Allison Williams Bunkley, *The Life of Sarmiento* (Princeton: Princeton University Press, 1952). Additional works that are helpful in understanding his ideas are: Natalio R. Botana, *La tradición republicana* (Buenos Aires: Editorial Sudamericana, 1984); Hebe Clementi, *El miedo a la inmigración* (Buenos Aires: Editorial Leviatan, 1984); Frances G. Crowley, *Domingo Faustino Sarmiento* (New York: Twayne Publishers, 1972); Torcuato S. Di Tella, "Raices de la controversia educacional argentina," in *Los fragmentos del poder; de la oligarquía a la poliarquía Argentina*, ed. Torcuato S. Di Tella and Tulio Halperín Donghi (Buenos Aires: Editorial Jorge Álvarez, 1969), 289-323; Gladys S. Onega, *La inmigración en la literatura argentina, 1880-1910* (Santa Fe: Universidad Nacional del Litoral, 1965); Leopoldo Lugones, *Historia de Sarmiento* (Buenos Aires: Editorial Universitaria de Buenos Aires, 1960); and Rojas, *El profeta de la pampa*.

5. Sarmiento, *Inmigración*, 144 and 177-180.

6. Bunkley, *Sarmiento*, 184-186; Halperín Donghi, "Para que la inmigración," 446.

7. Sarmiento, *Inmigración*, 188-192.

8. Bunkley, *Sarmiento*, 261-266.

9. Ibid., 276-278; Sarmiento *Inmigración*, 152-156, and 156ff.

10. Di Tella, "Raices de la controversía educacional argentina," 303–305; Bunkley, *Sarmiento*, 291.

11. Sarmiento, *Inmigración*, 60–79.

12. Ibid., 89–90.

13. Ibid., 123–125.

14. Ibid., 144.

15. Ibid., 355.

16. Ibid., 360–361.

17. Ibid., 372; Halperín Donghi, "Para que la inmigración," 451.

18. Sarmiento, *Condición*, 46–49.

19. Ibid., 30–34 and 44.

20. Translation of Sarmiento, *Condición*, 46–49, in José Luis Romero, *A History of Argentine Political Thought*, translated by Thomas F. McGann (Stanford: Stanford University Press, 1963), 175.

21. For a discussion of the Italian mutual aid societies, see Samuel L. Baily, "Las sociedades de ayuda mutua y el desarrollo de una comunidad italiana en Buenos Aires, 1858–1918," *Desarrollo Económico* 21 (January–March 1982): 485–514.

22. Luigi Favero, "Las escuelas de las sociedades italianas en Argentina (1860–1914), in *La inmigración italiana en la Argentina*, ed. Fernando Devoto and Gianfausto Rosoli (Buenos Aires: Editorial Biblos, 1985), 165–207.

23. Sarmiento, *Condición*, 63; Di Tella, "Raices de la controversía educacional argentina," 309.

24. Sarmiento, *Condición*, 66.

25. Ibid., 77–78.

26. Favero, "Escuelas," 179.

27. Sarmiento, *Condición*, 337–341; Favero, "Escuelas," 181.

28. Sarmiento, *Condición*, 151 and 300–301.

29. Romero, *Argentine Political Thought*, 177.

30. John Higham, *Strangers in the Land: Patterns of American Nativism, 1860–1925* (New York: Atheneum, 1973), esp. chaps. 7 and 11; Halperín Donghi, "Para que la inmigración," 482.

12

Artigas in the Writings of Sarmiento

William H. Katra

The historiographic currents that predominate in Argentina and Uruguay offer dramatically contrasting views of the objectives, actions, and historical legacy of José Gervasio Artigas. This is due primarily to the divergent national goals that were already in embryonic form when the independence struggle erupted on both sides of the Río de la Plata. Historical action, from the start, was accompanied by an intense and deliberate interpretation and dissemination of images. Those who would soon be recognized as ideological founders of the two future states recognized the need for writing histories for their respective countries that would clearly signal national and geographical prefigurations. Each group recognized the importance of fabricating a set of images that would define the centralizing tendencies of that enterprise of forging a nation, in order to combat the debilitating forces of dispersion and fragmentation. Those carefully cultivated images would indoctrinate the masses. The images would cultivate in them those customs and attitudes that would enhance their sense of patriotism, and they would condition the masses' obedience and respect for those leaders who had assumed the task of nation building.[1]

Ironically, the two future nations, with similar historical traditions, cultural practices, and productive capacities, demanded two divergent mythologies in the construction of their respective national projects. The complex factors that accounted for the separation of Uruguay from the provinces that were to constitute today's Argentina, can be mentioned only in passing here: the late colonization of the Banda Oriental—literally, the "Left Bank," or present-day República Oriental del Uruguay—and consequently, that region's relative lack of a traditional oligarchy or an

William H. Katra is lecturer, Department of Foreign Languages, University of Wisconsin, Eau Claire.

incipient middle class; Uruguay's buffer location between two potential powers, Argentina and Brazil; the meddling politics of England and France in their pursuit of influence or control over the trade passing through the mouth of the subcontinent's great river, the Río de la Plata; and the idiosyncratic gesture of a people and a leader who resisted the centralizing impetus of an expansive Buenos Aires and its arrogant leaders. Political separation of the two countries had to be justified and ideologically legitimized. Relevant to this latter issue, Abril Trigo's ground-breaking essay examines the political factors in Uruguayan intellectual and political history that accounted for the figure of Artigas ascending to the status of national hero.[2] In the following paragraphs I summarize some of the features of this "benign" perspective of Artigas. Then, I will contrast it with the negative image promulgated by Sarmiento and other Argentine ideologues that was more conducive to their own nation-state project.

The predominant tendency of Uruguayan historiography since the last decades of the past century has been to portray Artigas as the founder of Río de la Plata federalism, with a steadfast dedication to the cause of independence that compares favorably with that of Simón Bolívar and José de San Martín.[3] Like these two continental heroes, Artigas's early success in realizing many of his goals was followed by defeat, disappointment, and a long exile that ended only with his death in 1849.

In 1811 the struggle for independence from Spain in the Río de la Plata entered its second trying year. Buenos Aires's first Ruling Committee, fearful of the social chaos and the threat to privilege and property that the Jacobin independence leaders were inspiring, signed a treaty with the Spanish royalist forces and withdrew its troops from the Banda Oriental. Artigas, head of that region's *blandengues*, or rural police force, refused to obey the armistice negotiated by the elitist groups of the port city and to have his province returned to its Spanish colonial masters. His distrust of porteño priorities would henceforth be decisive in the great majority of his future actions. Artigas's decision to leave the Banda Oriental with his troops for Entre Ríos, just across the Río Uruguay, was spontaneously embraced by nearly sixteen thousand persons—men, women, and children—who preferred to follow their trusted leader into uncertain exile rather than suffer the abuses of renewed Spanish rule. In no other region of the insurgent provinces would the emancipation struggle be waged with such a high degree of popular adhesion.

1815

While the Buenos Aires Unitarian leaders Manuel Sarratea, Manuel Belgrano, and Bernardino Rivadavia crisscrossed Europe looking for a monarch to rule the provinces in the Río de la Plata, Artigas governed over a confederation of provinces that included the areas bathed by the Río Uruguay and Río Paraná and extended to the hills of Córdoba. From his rustic military encampment at Purificación, near present-day Paysandú, Artigas received emissaries and sent out a steady stream of dispatches. His staunch defense of the region's independence against invasions or economic incursions by the Spanish, Portuguese, and the English, and the reciprocal equality he advocated between the provinces, turned the tables on the political schemes of the leaders of Buenos Aires, who labeled him a "traitor to the fatherland." Artigas's brand of popular democracy, in which blacks, mulattos, Indians, and poor gauchos participated in political affairs, and his policy of granting land titles to any one on condition that they farm the land, could not be tolerated by the dictatorial party, which had centralist, promonarchical, and oligarchical orientations. The Federalist league headed by Artigas demanded assemblies and congresses, not kings; protection for local agriculture, industries, and arts, not domination of local and regional markets by European trading companies.[4]

1819

The intractable Artigas continued his struggle against the Portuguese and the Spanish in spite of the lack of arms and the decimation of his fighting ranks. The war had already claimed the lives of half of the region's fifty thousand inhabitants. The meager holdings of those producers who survived continued to bleed from forced contributions of workers and cattle. Artigas's army of illiterate rural peons, blacks, and Indians, having experienced for the first time the intoxicating freedom of *montonera* life, came to be regarded by the cultured groups of the city as the most formidable threat to the region's security. These elites realized the terrible price that an Artigas victory would have for the region: division of property and an end to social and economic privilege.[5]

A generation would pass before Domingo F. Sarmiento wrote and published *Facundo,* in which he referred to the exploits of this exceptional figure in the Río de la Plata and the Latin American independence movement. Foremost in Sarmiento's mind was Argentina's recent history of destructive civil wars and the savage tyranny of Juan Manuel de Rosas, which had undone many of the progressive reforms produced by the May Revolution of 1810 and had impeded the realization of national consolidation according to the plan projected by its leaders. Sarmiento called attention to two distinct societies—"rivals and incompatibles"—that coexisted in the Río de la Plata at that time.[6] Without agreeing with all of his sociological observations, one has to applaud this penetrating insight.

There *were* two distinct societies, each with its particular class strata, that coexisted within the same national space. First, there was the urban society, with a commercial, bureaucratic, and clerical oligarchy; a heterogeneous working class; and a variety of intermediary groups active in commerce, domestic labors, and a tercerary sector. The rural society, on the other hand, consisted of a small landowning class, an autochthonous proletariat—Indians and seminomadic gauchos—and different intermediary groups, all occupied in agrarian, commercial, and primitive artisanal activities.[7]

Contrasts continued with regard to cultural values and institutions. While the urban experience responded to a more advanced economy of incipient capitalism, in the rural sector precapitalist forms of production and class relations predominated. The urban sector was essentially oligarchical, although it had its popular sectors; while the rural sector was basically populist, even though it had its caudillos. Herein lay the decisive paradox of the Río de la Plata revolution. The educated and Europeanized leaders of the city, with aristocratic and oligarchical spirit, embraced liberalism as their guiding doctrine, but this liberalism opposed the radically democratic spirit of the rustic masses of the countryside. This marks the distance separating Rivadavia and—to all intents and purposes—his ideological heir, Sarmiento, from the rural populist, Artigas. Would it be too much of a generalization to explain the radically differing images of Artigas by referring to this schematic view of the competing, coexisting societies? In spite of the dramatic social, productive, and demographic changes since 1810, Uruguayan intellectuals after midcentury found the image of a benevolent Artigas useful for their task of constructing a myth of nationality. In contrast, Sarmiento and other like-minded Argentines continued in the post-Rosas years to value a more negative portrait of Artigas and the other rural leaders in the region's early social conflicts as a necessary component of their own ideological viewpoint.

Committed historians like Sarmiento rarely wrote in the disinterested pursuit of truth. Sarmiento's historiographical writings were largely flavored by his impassioned and partisan ideas. In some instances, he demonstrated a clear and unambiguous consciousness of the need to "doctor" the facts and shape the historical data at his disposal. At other times, however, the available evidence points to his immersion in the ideology of his class and his full and uncritical acceptance of its principal aspects. Sarmiento's interpretation of the Artigas phenomenon was one such example: it was his expansion and elaboration of the image whose contours had already been shaped and determined by the ideologues of the previous generation. In *Facundo* one reads:

> This was the element set in motion by the renowned Artigas. It was a blind tool, but a tool full of life and of instincts hostile to European civilization and to all regular organization; opposed to monarchy as to

republicanism, because both came from the city and possessed already order and reverence for authority. . . . Its essence was individual action; its exclusive weapon, the horse; its stage, the vast pampas. . . . The *montonera*, as it appeared under the command of Artigas in the early days of the Republic, already showed that character of brutal ferocity and the promise of a reign of terror . . . Artigas, the *baqueano* and outlaw, at war with the authorities of the city, but bought over as provincial commandant and chief of equestrian bands, presents a type reproduced with little change in each provincial commandant who came to be a caudillo.[8]

These words reveal a visceral hatred of the legacy of Artigas, which nourished Sarmiento's willingness to merely repeat many of the ideas he had uncritically received from his cultural experience and to repress other, contradictory information. What explanations might be offered to account for this partisan, perhaps skewed, vision of his nation's historical past? The following paragraphs focus on three factors. First, I treat the circumstances relevant to Sarmiento's upbringing and social position that would account for such an orientation. Second, I consider the theoretical field in which Sarmiento formed his most decisive perspectives and ideas; in particular, the functions of a mythified "Reason" and a "philosophy of history" in his historiographical practice. Finally, I focus upon Sarmiento as a member of Argentina's urban intellectual elite, which, as a group, was determined to subordinate the competing rural society to its own prerogatives. In this struggle, Artigas served them well as an early and representative prototype for that society they abhorred. People such as Artigas, Martín Güemes, Ángel Vicente "El Chacho" Peñaloza, Justo José de Urquiza, and Felipe Varela had to be eliminated through decisive historical action. Concurrently, the surviving memory of these rural leaders' populist struggles had to be purged from the public memory in order that their own liberal (and later positivist) vision of the nation's future might be realized.

Many of Sarmiento's fundamental orientations derived from the trying circumstances that he both witnessed and experienced while growing up in the Andean region of Cuyo. At the time of his childhood, the traditional fabric of society was already in crisis throughout the Río de la Plata provinces, especially in his native region.[9] In previous decades the local economy had become progressively destabilized as the free trade policies promoted by "enlightened" colonial and postindependence leaders allowed the circulation of inexpensive English fabrics and foodstuffs that undersold local goods, thereby relegating thousands of local producers to economic marginality. Then, beginning a decade into the new century, this situation was further aggravated by the prolonged drain on local resources in order to finance the languishing war effort against Spanish royalist troops. Sarmiento's writings provide impassioned testimony of San Juan's admirable "prebourgeois" order that flourished during his youth, but which progressively fell under harder times as the new century advanced.[10] This meant that the propertied and cultured elites, which until then had provided a benevolent, progressive leadership for the region, were increasingly challenged by newly ascendant groups. Sarmiento hardly respected the province's new leaders—primarily men with military backgrounds who were singularly unimpressive on account of "their inertia, their neglect of all that is involved in public life."[11] The ascent of this new leadership was only one of several indications of the region's regression in its moral and material development.

Cuyo's social and economic decline was integrally related in Sarmiento's mind with the disappearance of political stability. Writing at a later date, he would vividly remember the tumultuous events of 1820 in his province, which paralleled the outburst of violent insurrections across the country. At issue was a barracks rebellion that resulted in the overthrow and then exile of the provincial governor, Dr. José Ignacio de la Roza, a respected follower of San Martín and the founder of San Juan's first and only school.[12] In the following months coup would follow coup in the ongoing struggle between Unitarians and Federalists, marking the region's entrance into an era of political instability.

Sarmiento's particularized view of the civil war that ravaged the country focused on the rise to prominence of Juan Facundo Quiroga, the Promethean caudillo leader from the neighboring Province of La Rioja, who progressively extended his authority over all the northern provinces. In 1827 Facundo, with some six hundred mounted *montonera* followers entered the city of San Juan, causing an unforgettable impression on the young Sarmiento, then employed as a storekeeper. In *Recuerdos de provincia* (1850), Sarmiento provided the memorable image of this encounter with Facundo's hoard of ghostly horsemen, with "dust-covered faces, with tangled hair and tattered clothing, and almost without bodies . . . like . . . demons that were half-centaurs."[13] Sarmiento's historical consciousness gravitated around such intoxicating literary images. In his writing and thought the fear-inspiring Facundo and his barbarian horsemen would henceforth be linked with the region's fall into chaos and anarchy. This very negative first impression of Facundo impeded Sarmiento's appreciation of the sincere and significant efforts of that caudillo, in the half-decade before his assassination in 1835, to promote the definitive organization of the country under a constitution.[14]

Only a few years later Sarmiento witnessed the brutal and unprovoked terror that accompanied the uprising of the local militia, later joined by "the scum and gaucho society" (*la chusma y el pueblo gaucho*), against the Unitarian provincial government.[15] In his writings Sarmiento highlighted the social aspects of this conflict: no longer was it a clash over political ideas or organizational principles. Instead, it was the result of the pent-up hatred of the lower classes, predominantly rural in origin and of mixed race, against the province's liberal leaders, who were from the region's wealthiest and most prestigious families. Sarmiento, who hailed from an impoverished branch of one of these families, took weapons in hand to defend the beleaguered regional elite. Childhood fantasies about the glories of military conflict were quickly forgotten when he witnessed the killing of several fellow combatants and barely escaped death himself. Prominent citizens were assaulted and their properties ransacked. The uprising of 1830 was finally quelled, but only by means of a bloody confrontation and the execution of several rebel leaders. From all this Sarmiento concluded that society's elites needed to recur to "vigorous methods of repression" in order to contain the rebellious rural masses.[16] Dating from these tragic circumstances, he would henceforth offer impassioned, and at times violent, opposition to any rural leader who opposed the efforts of society's educated elites to "civilize" the region.

Without a doubt the difficult circumstances Sarmiento experienced in his childhood and youth preconditioned him for accepting the interpretation, then current in his circle, that the rural caudillos were primarily to blame for the country's fall from peace and stability, for the undoing of the progressive reforms initiated with the May Revolution, and for the region's entrance into a period of savage civil conflict. Those early experiences in themselves account for certain vital attitudes, but Sarmiento's interpretation of those events followed closely the pattern of other learned, ideological influences in his largely self-guided education. In the following paragraphs I wish to emphasize two such factors that had a bearing on the development of his ideas: the justification for the predominance of reason over passions or instincts, as he learned from religious sources, and his infatuation with the theories associated with the philosophy of history that dominated the discussions of the young Chilean and Argentine intellectuals during Sarmiento's exile in Santiago de Chile in the 1840s.

The fundamental role in Sarmiento's thought of a mythified Reason in its primordial struggle for ascendancy over emotions, passions, and instincts has yet to be treated adequately by the critics.[17] The idea has obvious eighteenth-century origins, which the young Sarmiento, as a precocious and voracious reader, would have gleaned from any number of works of the Enlightenment. But to my knowledge, no previous critic has yet traced the social and historical origins of this idea to Sarmiento's early familiarity with the thoughts of the early Catholic church fathers, most notably John Chrysostom and St. Augustine. Indeed, in the thought of both, the perpetual conflict between the individual's will and desire, or soul and body, receives explicit social treatment. That is, the hierarchy of moral virtues that views the human ability to reason as supreme becomes endowed with social and even historical significance, and is used to justify the imposition of government—that "necessary evil" in the words of St. Augustine—over society. As such, only when people demonstrate their obedience to authority can they enjoy true liberty. Although St. Augustine praised the other church fathers for their tolerance of differences in society, he himself increasingly urged the use of force, when persuasion would not avail, to suppress dissident behavior or insurrection. Fear and coercion were obviously necessary against the enemies of the Catholic church; in addition, they helped guide individuals along the proper channels leading to human salvation. Chrysostom, of similar mind, believed that government, no matter how corrupt, was indispensable:

> If you deprive the city of its rulers, we would have to live a life less rational than that of the animals, biting and devouring one another. . . . For what crossbeams are in houses, rulers are in cities, and just as, if you were to take away the former, the walls, being separated, would fall in upon one another, so, if you were to deprive the world of magistrates and the fear that comes from them, houses, cities, and nations would fall upon one another in unrestrained confusion, there being no one to repress, or repel, or persuade them to be peaceful through the fear of punishment.[18]

As such, St. Augustine and Chrysostom preached the existence of a dualistic world order, divided between the blessed and the fallen, goodness and sin. Consequently, one can well understand their sensed need for a dual pedagogy. They preached free will, liberty, autonomy, and self-government for that small class of iron-willed individuals who could keep strict control over their passions and could elevate their behavior through the exercise of reason. However, for the great masses of humanity, moral—and therefore social—improvement could come only through willed or forced submission of their rebellious natures to a "good governor" who would lead them on the path of self- and social improvement.

Any reader even remotely familiar with Sarmiento's dualistic interpretation of Argentine social reality—divided in his eyes between an urban, rational, technological civilization and a rural, impulse-oriented, primitive barbarism—can see the parallels between it and this early Christian interpretation of moral and social hierarchies. Sarmiento, in his writings, never mentioned having read the works of St. Augustine and Chrysostom during the years of his early religious education, when he studied under the direction of José María de Castro, a local priest. Still, it is apparent that such interpretations of religious, psychological, and social reality constituted an integral part of the world view of almost any member of the social and cultural elite who had survived the Spanish colonial experience.

Although the fervor of Sarmiento's early religious training later was buried underneath the trappings of his liberal calling, the traces of ideas similar to those advocated by St. Augustine and Chrysostom are readily evident in Sarmiento's description of the archenemy of Río de la Plata progress, the gaucho barbarian Artigas. That *montonera* leader, with "brutal ferocity," was "the blind instrument . . . of instincts hostile to European civilization and to all orderly organization."[19] Artigas was the evil incarnation of the forces of barbaric nature against Sarmiento's mythified city, which was, for Sarmiento, a metaphorical province of Reason and a liberal City of God. Artigas and any similar *comandante de campaña* had to be contained in the interest of preserving order and civility. Though a local, regional conflict, the struggle acquired universal, and even cosmic implications in Sarmiento's eyes. This was a total war that would end only with death or extermination. Failure was not a possibility. Sarmiento believed his class of nation builders was justified in using any means at their disposal to wage this providentially inspired battle. Here is one instance where hyperbolic rhetoric seems to have supplanted studied arguments and humanistic orientations.

A historiographical orientation providing a similar justification for the imposition of reason and civility over passions, brutality, and barbarism was the philosophy of history. These liberal and (pre-)positivist ideas, which enjoyed unequaled prestige in European intellectual circles at the time, were enthusiastically embraced by Sarmiento, Vicente Fidel López, José Victoriano Lastarria, and the other young Argentine and Chilean intellectuals who resided in Santiago de Chile in the early 1840s. Lastarria provided an explanation and justification for this brand of historiographical praxis, which was based on the assumption that the facts of a particular situation were of relatively small importance if the historian gave due emphasis to the "necessary" and "inevitable" expansion of the progressive ideas associated with European liberalism. The key here was the historian's evaluation of the development of a given society according to the universal criteria of "liberty" and "progress."[20]

The historical progress of societies, as these intellectuals perceived it, was unilinear and impersonal, and unfolded in step with the newest developments of science and technology. As such, human progress was both teleological and political. On the one hand, the Santiago youths of liberal persuasion believed that Providence, through the unfolding of new scientific discoveries, defined the direction for society's progress that was beyond the understanding or control of any individual. On the other hand—and somewhat in contradiction—they believed that the leader who understood what they took to be the universal science of history and society could take appropriate actions to accelerate or guide that process.

At the time, these ideas were severely and judiciously criticized by Andrés Bello, the Venezuelan intellectual who then resided in Santiago. Bello's major complaint was that Lastarria and the other romantically inspired youths, in their historical writings, sacrificed the pursuit of truth for political objectives. Bello clearly perceived that in their supposed "philosophical" treatment, they mistakenly evaluated the Latin American countries with historical criteria derived from the experiences of the more developed societies, such as France and England. In doing so, these writers failed to take into account the vast differences separating one from the other with respect to the different stages of development in their social, economic, and cultural institutions.[21] One could go a step further and point out the strong ethnocentrism implicit in this historiographical practice: the young historians mistakenly believed that their own urban, Europeanized, and elitist orientations constituted universal categories. With a hubris that approached arrogance, they viewed themselves as a chosen sect exclusively empowered to understand such truths; to them and them alone belonged the responsibility for indicating the providential path of future progress for their continent. The particular emphasis advocated by Sarmiento and his group of activist historians was that their region's liberal transformation required the rural sectors to assimilate the priorities established by the progressive, Europeanized population of the city, even if this caused the elimination of Indians and gauchos as a people.

This explains why Sarmiento and his generation of writers continued the liberal tradition of condemning the legacy of Artigas. In spite of his undisputable contribution to the struggle against Spain a few decades before, Artigas represented values and objectives that were diametrically opposed to their own. While Artigas idealized the primitive rural society, they dreamed of an urban, progressive, and technological future. While the epic struggle of Artigas was waged primarily by and on behalf of Creoles, Indians, and mestizos—the popular and autochthonous groups of the region—the ambition of Sarmiento and his cohorts was to mold the future civilization of the Río de la Plata with a population of white, European immigrants and their descendants.

As such, the philosophical objectives had clear political and social implications in Sarmiento's historiographic pursuits. Indeed, his political and propagandistic reasons for writing *Facundo* are well known. The work, originally a libel, was intended as an ideological "cannon-blast" at the foundations of rosismo. Sarmiento admitted to General José María Paz in a letter of 22 December 1845, that it was "an improvised work, by necessity full of distortions—intentional at times—that has no other importance than becoming one of several instruments for helping to destroy an absurd government and to prepare the path for a new one."[22] Undoubtedly, the parts of that work that describe Artigas, Quiroga, and Rosas—that is, the "barbarian" leaders of the region's primitive rural society—are replete with such "inexactitudes" and creative disfigurations.[23] The intentional distortion of historical material, if performed in the name of progress, was, according to Sarmiento, totally justifiable.

For Sarmiento, the Rosas regime, like those of Artigas and Quiroga, was the incarnation of retrograde ideological and institutional tendencies: a feudal colonial culture centered around demagogic religious practices; a primitive cattle economy based on the labor of rude gaucho horsemen; a political organization linking despotic caudillos to ignorant half-breed masses; the impeded development of educational, commercial, or cultural institutions; and, in general, a network of human relationships that fed upon human passions and impulses and discouraged the cultivation of higher rational faculties. Seen in this light, Sarmiento did not lack philosophical or ideological reasons for opposing either the legacy of Artigas or the regime of Rosas. Given the noble goals he promoted, any form of conspiracy that he could muster against the living traces of barbarism was legitimate and justified.

Sarmiento was hardly alone in the hatred he demonstrated toward Artigas and the ideas and values represented by that intrepid leader of the early independence movement. One can observe a similar orientation in the writings of historians and social commentators from Buenos Aires beginning with the period of Artigas's influence and extending at least to the end of the century. Within this corpus of nineteenth-century liberal writing, Sarmiento's opinions stand out. This is due solely to his memorable style and to the very wide diffusion of his works. Perhaps even more important is the leadership role he assumed, first in opposing Rosas and Urquiza, and then in behalf of the Buenos Aires elites who finally succeeded in unifying the country according to porteño prerogatives. On this account, David Viñas is undoubtedly correct in his assessment that Sarmiento is his country's "major ideologue of the progressive bourgeois romantics."[24]

Indeed, Sarmiento's advocacies at midcentury echo those of his liberal predecessors from Buenos Aires during the struggle for independence. Not only are they representative of those members of his generation who accompanied his rise to national prominence, but they also anticipate the program of Julio A. Roca some forty years later. Sarmiento's damning descriptions of Artigas and other caudillos in the pages of *Facundo* were consonant with several of his most dramatic stances as a national leader after 1852: his adherence to the cause of the propertied and cultured elites of Buenos Aires in opposing Urquiza and the Argentine Confederation; his fervent advocacy of and then leadership in the pacification of the interior provinces; his complicity in the persecution and then brutal killing of Ángel "El Chacho" Peñaloza; his promotion of the War of the Triple Alliance against Paraguay; and, when he was president, his military interventions in Entre Ríos and the Andean provinces.

Sarmiento's skewed characterizations of Artigas and other caudillos imitate similar descriptions written by the enlightened leaders of Buenos

Aires who had violently opposed Artigas and his partisans when they
dominated political life in all the littoral provinces. Historian Adolfo
Saldías identified instances of how widely circulating pamphlets written
about 1815 helped implant in the consciousness of the porteño population and subsequent Unitarian ideologues a very negative image of
Artigas.[25] In short, Sarmiento adopted as his own the perspective of
Belgrano and his followers: for them, Artigas, like Güemes in the north,
was the father of anarchy and his policies were aimed at preserving the
stagnant social and cultural heritage of the Spanish colony.[26] The coincidence in views is seconded by the similarities between Sarmiento's
situation and that of his liberal predecessors, over and above obvious
differences in their respective situations. Specifically, all hailed from the
privileged strata of society, and their values and ideas were all heavily
influenced by urban, culturalist, and European orientations.

Sarmiento, born and raised in the remote Province of San Juan,
became president of his country through sheer force of will and deter-
mination. It might be that many of his enlightened acts and orientations
during his presidency and the radical period of his later years, truly
qualified him as "provincial" in Buenos Aires—as his self-styled campaign
slogan read. But when one impartially considers his early contributions
as an activist statesman and historian of his country, Sarmiento exhibited
a decidedly porteño or Unitarian orientation. (According to Alberdi, "it
is the porteños who use provincials to dominate provincials."[27])

This ideological pact with the porteño historical tradition is clearly
demonstrable upon comparing Sarmiento's treatment of Artigas and the
other past great Argentine caudillos with that offered by the two other
great historians of his generation, Bartolomé Mitre and Vicente Fidel
López. Mitre's view of Artigas hardly differs in substance from that of
Sarmiento: he is "the caudillo of vandalism and of the semi-barbaric
federation" (*el caudillo del vandalaje y de la federación semibárbara*), who
lacked "vital principles" and whose only banner was that of *"personal-
ismo."*[28] One courts redundancy in quoting similar, if not even more
damning passages from the widely disseminated historical writings of
López.[29] López, however, rose above the otherwise partisan practices of
his generation when—as mentioned previously—he portrayed the presence and legacy of Quiroga in a balanced, if not positive, dimension.[30]

One cannot, however, talk about ideological solidarity in the historiographical project of the 1837 generation, for that would ignore the
generally favorable views of Esteban Echeverría, Marco Avellaneda,
Brígido Silva, Marcos Paz, Juan María Gutiérrez, Alberdi, and others
about the efforts of Quiroga and Alejandro Heredia to organize the
nation under a constitution during the 1830s and the contributions of
Gutiérrez and Alberdi to the Argentine Confederation in the 1850s.
Risking dangerous simplification, the one idea that stands out in

Alberdi's writings after 1852 was that Buenos Aires's unlimited resources and disproportionate wealth throughout its history served to inflame the ambitions of its leaders and to corrupt the political relations of that province with the rest of the nation. Inherent in this view was a more generous view of the contributions made by the great caudillos of the interior than what the Unitarian or porteño-leaning members of Alberdi's own generation ever allowed.

In conclusion, the figure of Artigas hardly occupies a central role in the writings of Sarmiento, but Sarmiento's negative treatment of the independence leader is representative of his orientation toward the early history of his nation in general, and of the image of nationhood that he envisioned for its future. This view involved an implicit scheme of racial, social, and regional preferences, which held that white, urbanite, literate people occupied the highest rungs in the development of civilization. It also implied the imperative of rewriting the nation's early history to demonstrate that the country's independence and organization were primarily the accomplishments of the Province of Buenos Aires and its indoctrinated followers in the provinces. To highlight the contributions of the rural masses and their caudillo leaders toward these same objectives would be to undermine his own vision of nationality and, consequently, Sarmiento's own authority.

Sarmiento, like the Buenos Aires leaders before him and of his own generation, possessed a contradictory baggage of liberal goals. While all of them were unswerving supporters of the country's political independence, they distrusted the democratic sentiment of the popular classes. They denounced the excesses of romantically inspired reforms that tended to unleash the energies of the masses and to threaten social stability. Through their partisan historical writing, they supported a democracy based on the exercise of Universal Reason (as expressed in their generational manifesto, the *Dogma Socialista*), because they were repelled by the fact that Artigas, López, Güemes, Quiroga, and Peñaloza, as leaders and heads of broad, popular movements, personified the spontaneous and genuine interests of their barbaric, uneducated, lower-class followers. In a pact that extended across the generations, these elitist historians embraced a concept of a desirable future for the country that could only result from a leadership inspired by Europeanized, urban, educated perspectives.

Sarmiento's politically inspired interpretation of the causes for his country's crisis approaches the view of regional conflict that set the Unitarian leaders against Artigas's federalist movement a generation earlier. In some ways, it was a simplistic analysis: Sarmiento described a dispute between European and nativist culture, between the urban way of life and that of the rural interior. In Sarmiento's thinking, Argentina was engaged in a struggle of epic and universal proportions: a clash pitting reason against the brute force of instincts, civilization, and barbarism. The hatred Sarmiento displayed for the gaucho chieftains of his own day found a similar target in the figure of Artigas. Somewhat schematically, Sarmiento believed that the caudillo-led rural masses, with deep hatred of civilized urban leaders, sought to turn back the clock of history and undo the progress of Europeanized elites. Even those learned observers partial to Sarmiento's world view have called attention to how his limited knowledge of the country's civil strife led him to rely on catchy oppositions and simplifications.[31]

Such distorted generalizations abound whenever Sarmiento addressed the topic of caudillos or gauchos. First, he recurred to a gross and, in several instances, false stereotype when he depicted the impoverished gaucho population as naturally opposed to the ideas of political independence, the interchange of ideas, and democratic association. (The immense sacrifices made by the gaucho followers of San Martín, Artigas, and Güemes during the independence struggle makes a sorry mockery of that idea.) Second, Sarmiento skewed the reader's comprehension when he characterized the caudillos of the country's different regions as barbaric, uneducated, and violent, with instinctive hatred for cities and cultural refinements. (Several of the country's great caudillos—Güemes, Artigas, Juan Felipe Ibarra, Quiroga, and Heredia—hailed from the principle families of their respective regions, and most possessed a respectable level of education.) Third, Sarmiento further distorts our understanding in his automatic association of the caudillo with social anarchy and opposition to national organization. (While it is true that most caudillos of the interior stalwartly opposed the domination of Buenos Aires over the rest of the country, several of them—again, Artigas, Heredia, Güemes, Quiroga, and Urquiza—were devoted proponents of national organization based on the principle of equality among the provinces.) Fourth, Sarmiento perpetuated confusion by comparing the cattle-based economy sustaining *caudillismo* with the "feudal" social institutions that had stubbornly survived from colonial days. (This association hardly took into account the fact that the new latifundium cattle industry in the coastal regions arose and underwent consolidation during the Rosas years, primarily in response to the rising demand in the Caribbean states and Brazil for salted meat.) In general, the likes of Artigas, Quiroga, Peñaloza, and Urquiza were spared little sympathy by this committed propagandist and highly partisan historian. In Sarmiento's pages, all were reduced to the vilified common denominator of highwaymen, assassins, and robbers, who imitated the brutish behavior of the semicivilized hoards they led.

Because these distortions were central to his world view, Sarmiento's writings could hardly offer a rigorous or systematic analysis of the crisis confronting his country. He was first and foremost an ideological combatant who wrote in order to move people to action. His social and political ideas were often forged in the heat of conflict, and, when he expressed them through the press, they tended to resemble simplistic generalizations.

Writing was for this "tutelary publicist in a tumultuous and semi-barbarian country"—in the words of Ricardo Rojas—a tool that he used in his "titanic" and even "holy" crusade against the foes of white, Europeanized, urban civilization.[32] The words Sarmiento wrote about Artigas constitute unambiguous documentation for Alberdi's accusation that the aim of historians like Sarmiento was to bury the positive legacy of the caudillos of the interior provinces in the independence struggle.[33] Yet Sarmiento was firmly convinced of the righteousness of his historic—and historical—mission, so much so that he was little troubled about ethical considerations involving the means utilized for achieving it. As an activist historian, this meant that there was no truth worthy of the name outside of the narrow space of his own writing objectives. If this was an invitation for historiographical license and distortion, then so be it. The stuff of the past, he firmly believed, belonged to the historian who was disposed to transform it into a living discourse that could further the goals held by the providentially inspired nation builder.

NOTES

1. In preparing this paper for publication, I gained valuable insights about desirable images for constructing the state and creating the nation from León Pomer, "Sarmiento, el caudillismo y la escritura histórica," *Cuadernos hispanoamericanos: Los complementarios* 3 (April 1989): 7-37.

2. Abril Trigo, "Fundamentos ideomíticos de la nación-estado uruguayo (1875-1903)," paper presented at the conference on "Gauchos and Nation Builders in the Río de la Plata: Literature and the Arts," University of Wisconsin, La Crosse, 14-18 April 1988.

3. Information for constructing the benevolent image of Artigas is from: Eduardo Azcuy Ameghino, *Artigas en la historia argentina* (Buenos Aires: Ediciones Corregidor, 1986); Óscar H. Bruschera, *Artigas*, 3d ed. (Montevideo: Biblioteca de Marcha: Librosur, 1986); Félix Luna, *Los caudillos* (Buenos Aires: Peña Lillo Editor, 1985), 39-88; John Street, *Artigas and the Emancipation of Uruguay* (Cambridge: Cambridge University Press, 1959), 197-286; and Eduardo Galeano, *Memoria del fuego*, vol. 2, *Las caras y las máscaras* (2 vols., Buenos Aires: Siglo Veintiuno, 1982-1984), 129-130 and 137. L. V. L. [Lucio V. López], "Artigas y el Artiguismo," *El Sud-América*, reprinted in Vicente Fidel López, *Historia de la República Argentina; Su origen, su revolución, su evolución y su desarrollo. Continuada hasta 1910 por Emilio Vera y González, ampliada desde el descubrimiento hasta nuestros días por Enrique de Gandia*, new ed. (8 vols., Buenos Aires: Editorial Sopena Argentina, 1964), 2: App. 5, 633-645, strongly criticizes the incipient gestures of this Uruguayan project of historical revisionism.

4. Leonardo Paso, *Los caudillos y la organización nacional* (Buenos Aires: Editorial Futuro, 1965), 271-272.

5. Hugo D. Barbagelata, *Artigas y la revolución americana*. Foreword by José Enrique Rodó, 2d ed., corr. and enl. (Paris: Éditions Ecelsior, 1930), 180–188.

6. Domingo F. Sarmiento, *Obras completas*, vol. 7, *Quiroga. Aldao. El Chacho, 1845–1863* (53 vols., Buenos Aires: Editorial Luz del Día, 1948–1956), 55.

7. This and the following paragraph draw heavily on the analysis offered by Arturo Ardao, *Estudios latinoamericanos: Historia de las ideas* (Caracas: Monte Avila Editores, 1978), 71–88.

8. Quotation, with slight modifications, is from Domingo F. Sarmiento, *Life in the Argentine Republic in the Days of the Tyrants; Or, Civilization and Barbarism. With a Biographical Sketch of the Author, by Mrs. Horace Mann* (New York: Hafner Press, 1974), 59–62.

9. Tulio Halperín Donghi, *Revolución y guerra; Formación de una élite dirigente en la Argentina criolla* (Buenos Aires: Siglo Veintiuno, 1972), 26ff.

10. Noël Salomón, "El *Facundo* de Domingo Faustino Sarmiento, manifiesto de la Pre-burguesía argentina de las ciudades del interior," *Cuadernos Americanos* 240 (September–October 1980), 121–176.

11. Sarmiento, *Quiroga*, 186.

12. Ricardo Rojas, *El profeta de la pampa; Vida de Sarmiento* (Buenos Aires: Editorial Losada, 1945), 41–42.

13. My translation of "caras más empolvadas aún entre greñas y harapos, y casi sin cuerpo... como... demonios medio centauros." Domingo F. Sarmiento, *Obras completas*, vol. 22, *Discursos populares* (53 vols., Buenos Aires: Editorial Luz del Día, 1948- 1956), 245.

14. López, *República Argentina*, 8:99–102, states that Sarmiento's immortalized treatment of Facundo was "sadly" distorted. "There are moments in which the words of Quiroga appear to be those of Rivadavia.... Quiroga was an Argentine who desired the organization of the country; he was not a traitor to the fatherland.... If Lopéz had supported Quiroga's efforts to organize the country and prevent the fatal actions of Rosas, Argentine history would not have included twenty years of tyranny." [Editor's translation.]

15. A. Belín Sarmiento, *Sarmiento anecdótico (ensayo biográfico)*. Definitive, enlarged and corrected edition (Saint-Cloud: Imprenta Belín, 1929), 20.

16. Sarmiento, *Quiroga*, 52.

17. I treat this issue in relation to Sarmiento's aesthetic thought in *Domingo F. Sarmiento: Public Writer (Between 1839 and 1852)* (Tempe: Center for Latin American Studies, Arizona State University, 1985), 71–97. This is an expanded English translation of my article, "El *Facundo*: Contexto histórico y estética derivada," *Cuadernos Americanos* 236 (May–June 1981): 151–176.

18. Quoted in Elaine Pagels, "The Politics of Paradise," *New York Review of Books* 35 (12 May 1988): 29.

19. Sarmiento, *Life in the Argentine Republic*, 59.

20. José V. Lastarria, *Recuerdos literarios; datos para la historia literaria de la América Española i del progreso intelectual en Chile*, 2d ed. (Santiago: Librería de M. Servat, 1885).

21. Bernardo Subercaseaux S., *Cultura y sociedad liberal en el siglo XIX. Lastarria, ideología y literatura* (Santiago: Editorial Aconcagua, 1981), 68 and 73–78.

22. Quoted in Domingo F. Sarmiento, *Facundo*. Edited by Alberto Palcos. Enlarged reedition of the critical and documented edition published by the Universidad Nacional de La Plata (Buenos Aires: Ediciones Culturales Argentinas, 1962), 438–446.

23. I demonstrate how the idiosyncratic application of historiographic

concepts contributes to Sarmiento's partisan treatment of the caudillo in my *Sarmiento: Public Writer,* chaps. 5 and 6.

24. David Viñas, *Indios, ejército y frontera* (Buenos Aires: Siglo Veintiuno, 1982), 95.

25. Adolfo Saldías, *Historia de la Confederación Argentina* (3 vols., Buenos Aires: Editorial Universataria de Buenos Aires, 1968), 1:121–122. Saldías's work, although reputedly generous in its treatment of the Rosas regime, inserts itself fully into the partisan historiographical tradition of Buenos Aires, as shown by its one-sided and incomplete treatment of non-porteño caudillos such as Artigas, Quiroga, and Heredia.

26. Bernardo Frías, *Historia del General Martín Güemes y de la provincia de Salta, o sea de la independencia argentina,* vol. 4, *Tercera y cuarta invasión realista. El General La Serna. La Revolución federal. El año 20. Gobierno de Güemes.* Foreword by Alilio Cornejo (4 vols., Buenos Aires: Edición Depalma, 1971–1973), 187.

27. Juan Bautista Alberdi, *Grandes y pequeños hombres del Plata* (Buenos Aires: Plus Ultra, 1974), 121.

28. Bartolomé Mitre, *Obras completas,* vol. 7, *Historia de Belgrano y la independencia argentina.* (18 vols., Buenos Aires: Congreso de la Nacíon Argentina, 1938–1960), 260.

29. López, *República Argentina,* 1:337–338, 389–393, 539–558, 623–636; and ibid., 4:375 and 544.

30. See Vicente Fidel López, *Panoramas y retratos históricos.* Foreword by Joaquín V. González (Buenos Aires: W. M. Jackson, 1938), 256–263.

31. This is the opinion the Unitarian ideologue and statesman Valentín Alsina expressed in "Notas de Valentín Alsina al libro 'Civilización y barbarie,'" Sarmiento, *Facundo,* 349–419.

32. Ricardo Rojas, *Historia de la literatura argentina; Ensayo filosófico sobre la evolución de la cultura en el Plata,* vol. 1, *Los proscriptos,* 4th ed. (9 vols., Buenos Aires: Guillermo Kraft, 1957), 332.

33. Juan B. Alberdi, *Las cartas rosistas de Alberdi. Comentarios de Adolfo Saldías* (Buenos Aires: Editorial Politeia, 1970), 119.

13

The Failure of Modernization Theory in Nineteenth-Century Argentina

Noel F. McGinn

A common perspective in social science explains the privileges of the rich and powerful—nations as well as individuals—in terms of their attributes, rather than in terms of the process by which they became dominant over others. By postulating attributes as causes, the apologists for this view claim that others can enjoy the same privileges by taking on the same attributes. Disparities of wealth and power in and between societies are claimed to be the consequence of some (individuals or societies) lacking the qualities required for success. The inference is that poverty is caused by the poor, and not by the rich.

This is the central idea of modernization theory as applied to economic development in the early 1950s.[1] The perspective was questioned by few when it became the official ideology of the development community and wealthy nations. Thirty-five years later, development theorists are more modest, but despite repeated disconfirmations of its fundamental assumptions, modernization theory survives and thrives.

The ideology of modernization is not unique to our times—more than one hundred years ago Domingo Sarmiento of Argentina made essentially the same arguments. And, as in the twentieth century, the results of the application of the ideology in Argentina were not fully successful—Sarmiento himself despaired that his country would never attain the objectives he had wished for it.

A vital element in Sarmiento's development theory, as well as in that of modernization theorists in our time, was the critical role of education as an engine of development. This view is not totally wrong, but expansion of education, despite other benefits, has not been the touchstone of political stability and rapid economic growth. An examination of what, in fact, happened in Argentina can help identify fundamental flaws in

Noel F. McGinn is professor of education, Harvard Graduate School of Education.

the ideology of modernization and in the perspective of Sarmiento.

I will begin by sketching out the modernization hypothesis and comparing it with Sarmiento's thought. I will then review proposals for education made by modernization theorists and relate those to Sarmiento's proposals. Then I will use Argentina as an example of the failure of this perspective and suggest an alternative.

MODERNIZATION THEORY

As applied to economic development, modernization is defined as increased material wealth and welfare. Indicators of modernization in an economy are increased levels of productivity as well as total product, which are associated with higher levels of income and consumption of material goods based on increased organizational complexity, diversification and integration. An industrialized country, for example, is considered more modern than a country of similar wealth that relies on agriculture or extraction of raw materials for its income. Associated with modernization are improvements in conditions of life as measured by such indicators as caloric intake, infant mortality, life expectancy, access to medical services, and access to information and education.

Modernization is considered as a universal phenomenon: that is, although countries might differ on particulars, all are modernizing in the same direction and can, therefore, be compared in terms of their rate and level of modernization. This has three implications. First, the constituent elements of modernization are defined empirically, by seeing which indicators of material growth cluster together. In the 1950s statistical analyses showed that consumption of electrical energy was the best single indicator of modernization, because of its high correlation with all other indicators.

Second, the most modernized country is defined as the one with the highest score on the composite scale of indicators. In the 1950s this was the United States, followed at some distance by the northern European countries outside the socialist bloc. In per capita terms, the United States was considered most modern because it consumed about five times more energy, food, newsprint, and other material goods than its population would predict.

Third, because all nations move toward modernization in the same way, the development history of the more modernized nations can be read as maps for the less-modernized ones. The international development agencies controlled by the United States and Western Europe used (and still use) this principle to justify their intervention in the economies of the so-called late-industrializing nations.[2]

A major concern in the 1950s was to identify those factors that would explain *why* some countries were more modernized than others. A fundamental assumption was that the explanations were internal to the countries in question, rather than found in their environments or relationships with other countries. In other words, a given country's modernization was thought to be determined by its attributes.

Statistical analyses showed that even after equalizing countries with respect to physical resources, there were still large differences in modernization levels. This was interpreted to mean that differences in *human* resources might explain differences in savings and productivity. The search began for different personal attributes that would explain variations in economic growth.[3]

A major theory of the period contrasted differences in productivity of urban and rural areas. Economists considered rural people in general as less productive than urban people and, therefore, less modern. Proponents of this theory argued that to improve the overall modernization of a country, it was necessary to move people out of rural areas into cities, where their levels of productivity would increase.[4]

Psychological research identified the attributes of urban dwellers that distinguish them from rural folk, that is, which define their *modernity* as including greater consciousness of time, openness to change, a more developed concept of self as distinct from community, as well as more favorable attitudes toward intervention in nature (e.g., birth control). Typically, members of the upper and educated middle classes scored higher on these measures of modernity than did members of the working class, and peasants scored lowest. It was possible to show that average modernity scores were higher in the more modernized countries of the world. The conclusion was drawn that development could be stimulated by giving more resources to the upper and educated middle classes, rather than to the poor.[5] Education, understood as schooling, was identified as a major source of modernity. Not only did the United States have the highest levels of schooling in the world, research showed that schooling increases time awareness and inculcates modern attitudes.

FIT WITH SARMIENTO'S MODEL

Although it is unlikely that most modernization theorists were familiar with Sarmiento's work (Gino Germani may have been one major exception),[6] the parallels are striking. Sarmiento's central concept was *civilization*, the opposite of barbarism. He defined civilization in terms of what is found in cities and contrasted it with the backward nature of rural life.

> The city is the center of civilization . . . there are to be found the art studios, the shops, the schools and colleges, the courts of justice, all that

characterizes the cultural countries. The elegance of manners, the advantages of luxury, the European clothes, the dress coat and frock coat . . . there are to be found the laws, the progressive ideas, the means of learning, the municipal organization, the regular government, etc.[7]

It would appear that Sarmiento began with the concept of barbarism as a device to stigmatize the culture of his political enemies in Argentina. The ideal of civilization developed as the alternative to the political system he wished to overthrow. Sarmiento's reading of European philosophers provided a positivist definition of the good or civilized society, and vicarious knowledge of Europe provided concrete indicators. He was much taken with life in the United States in the 1840s and, after visiting first Europe and then the United States, changed his definition of civilization to include characteristics of U.S. society at that time.

Sarmiento argued that country life provides little of the structured challenges that shape and develop the intellectual powers of the individual. The openness of the countryside reduces the need to develop civil associations that transcend individual assertiveness. Rural life is physical and ultimately violent because of the lack of constraints on the "natural" person. Cities, on the other hand, provide both constraints and stimuli to develop people's finer, intellectual abilities. Critical for the development of civilization is the political ascendancy of industrialists and merchants, both for their productivity and for their values of thrift, self-discipline, and openness to modern science. Also important, Sarmiento claimed, is the development of political structures that permit popular participation in decisionmaking without allowing mob rule. Sarmiento was highly impressed with the town meeting governments of New England. For him, civilization was at its peak in Massachusetts.

The determinants of civilization, he said, are internal to society, in the makeup of its people. For some, this is a racist explanation of development, but it is also possible to interpret Sarmiento's negative comments on the Spanish, Indian, and African ancestry of Latin American society in cultural terms. In any event, Latin America's relative barbarism compared with North America was attributed not to imperialism or lack of international trade, but to deficient cultures. The Latin American countries lacked qualities requisite for civilization.

Sarmiento suggested three complementary strategies to overcome these traits. The first was massive immigration to Latin America of persons from civilized countries. (Initially, he recommended simply immigration from European countries, but later he claimed that those immigrants who had come were the most barbaric of the sending countries.) The second strategy was wholesale adoption of the U.S. political structure, beginning with copying its Constitution (with slight adaptations to fit the Argentine context).

EDUCATION AS A PATH TO MODERNIZATION

Sarmiento's third recommendation, for which he is well known, was universal basic education for all. Education was necessary to civilize the immigrants and to create the conditions necessary for stable political democracy. Most important, education was necessary to make the Latin American nations like those that are civilized. He justified this assertion by a careful and detailed empirical comparison of more and less civilized states.

Imagine, Sarmiento suggested, a shop with fourteen clocks all of which keep perfect time, strike the hour in unison, etc., and another shop with fourteen clocks that never keep time. Would you not, he asks rhetorically, want to examine the regulators of the clocks that keep good time to see what it is that makes them such reliable timepieces?

Sarmiento used U.S. census data in an empirical analysis of which any positivist would be proud. He began by comparing the population and agricultural production of the state of Illinois with those of the Latin American countries. Why is it, he asked, that this one state has grown so much faster in population and produces so much more? The data suggested that location or the makeup of the people was the answer.

He then compared Illinois with its neighbor, Missouri. Although better endowed in terms of land and minerals, between 1830 and 1860 Missouri had grown less rapidly in population and productivity than Illinois. Sarmiento attributed the difference to slavery; Missouri was a slave state, Illinois was not. But Latin America had eliminated slavery earlier, so that factor could not be used to explain the region's backwardness. Sarmiento then noted that throughout the U.S. South few white children knew how to read, whereas illiteracy was uncommon in the North.

Among the U.S. states, Sarmiento claimed, the most productive were those of New England, and leading all these was Massachusetts. Not only was Massachusetts a leader in industrial production, it also led all other states in investment in public education. Sarmiento then offered the following non sequitur. "From this we can conclude that the accumulation of wealth, and the annual production of each individual, in Massachusetts grows in proportion with the increase of schools and the spread of teaching."[8]

Education, Sarmiento concluded, was the regulator for the clocks of society. How long, he asked in 1866, had it taken "to realize this utopia of a people universally educated, universally apt for industry, universally prepared for government?"[9] Some forty years earlier there had been general apathy in the United States about public education. In response, the American Institute of Instruction was formed in 1830, and in 1837

Horace Mann was appointed to head a council of public instruction for Massachusetts. In 1839 the first teacher-training institution, or normal school, was opened in Lexington, Massachusetts. From this effort came hundreds of high schools and normal schools, spreading across the United States until by the late 1860s almost all the children in the Northern states were in primary schools.

It is important to note at this point that expansion and improvement of education were also taking place in South America. In 1842, in Chile, Sarmiento opened the second normal school in the New World, without contact with the neighbors to the north. This was only one of the many original contributions Sarmiento made to education in Latin America. Others include the development of a system of orthography that would make Spanish completely phonetic; a syllabic method for teaching reading; basic readers based on the method; designs for curricula for primary and secondary schools that emphasized modern rather than classical sources of knowledge; biographies to be used as teaching texts; plans for a system of adult education linked with the community; and proposals for a national system of compulsory primary education financed by local revenues and administered by local bodies. As a private citizen, superintendent of public instruction for the Province of Buenos Aires, minister of education, and president of Argentina, Sarmiento was unceasing in his efforts to build schools and train teachers for the expansion of primary education.

In fact, Sarmiento's achievements were great, and given the circumstances in which he was placed, more impressive than those of Horace Mann. Sarmiento never finished high school, Mann was a graduate of Yale. Sarmiento was one of a small band who fought for improved education, whereas in the United States a large number of university-educated persons carried out reforms like those of Mann at about the same time. The United States had already begun to generate an impressive economic surplus and could afford to spend large sums on education, while Argentina had not yet entered into its golden age. Sarmiento was active and successful in many fields, while Mann's achievements were confined to education. It would seem reasonable, then, to refer to Mann as the Sarmiento of North America.

THE "FAILURE" OF EDUCATION

Sarmiento died believing that he had failed. Although in a few short years he had succeeded in building more schools than had existed in Argentina prior to his efforts, educational expansion had not brought what he considered civilization. Perhaps Sarmiento's expectations were too high. After all, Buenos Aires now had paved streets and its residents read the latest French novels, dressed in the latest fashion, and were entertained by Parisian opera companies. Energy consumption had tripled, the national railway system had doubled in miles of track, and doubled again, the port had been deepened and improved, and internal production and foreign trade had increased by half.

More, Sarmiento's presidency was the beginning of a golden era. During the twenty-five or so years following his administration, Argentina's economy continued to expand and the country became the wealthiest in Latin America—more prosperous than some of the European countries from which so-called barbaric immigrants continued to arrive.

But the question is not whether Argentina had prospered, but whether expansion of education had been the cause of that prosperity and whether the expansion of education had created conditions for a modern democracy such as that of the United States. In other words, did the effects of increased education conform to the mechanistic predictions of modernization theory?

CRITIQUE OF THE MODERNIZATION HYPOTHESIS

A major flaw in the reasoning of Sarmiento, as with twentieth-century modernization theorists, has been limited attention to *stages* of development. Development is not a process of linear evolution but a series of leaps forward, sometimes slipping backward when wrong choices are made. Forward movement often involves fundamental changes in social structures. As a result, what is effective for a country in one stage may not be effective or even possible for another country in a different stage. Improvements in education affect other sectors in a dialectical rather than in a mechanistic fashion. This dialectic cannot be understood without attention to the changing context in which action is taken.

Sarmiento assumed that the civic values and social structures he saw in the United States in the 1840s were an essential part of civilization and therefore had to be recreated in Argentina. He ignored the conditions under which those values and structure had been created in New England. A fundamental condition there had been an economy in which most landholdings were relatively small and worked by their owners. A large portion of the urban labor force was self-employed or employed in small firms using artisanal means of production in which each worker had control over either all the production process or his or her share in it. High productivity depended on the capacity of individual workers to make independent judgments. In that kind of economy education, especially for problem solving and decisionmaking, was essential. In New England this economy was accompanied by a religious ideology that insisted on equality and a system of political governance that encouraged participation through a parliamentary or republican form of democracy. It was this kind of education that Sarmiento promoted for Argentina.

But this was not the kind of education that contributed to the *later* industrialization of the United States. Following the American Civil War, small-scale farming, small towns, and artisans rapidly diminished in economic importance. With industrialization came routinization and segmentation of the production process, so that workers now performed a limited set of tasks that had been simplified so that their judgments would be reduced to the minimum. Education in the United States now became socialization into the discipline of the factory, which required workers to come on time and to understand and follow instructions. Industrialization also eliminated the political dominance of the small town, the tranquility of which depended on the active participation of informed residents in decisionmaking. Cities require citizens who accept the legitimacy of decisions made by distant persons chosen in ways over which an individual has little influence. In other words, the Mann-Sarmiento version of "education for democracy" was no longer followed in the United States.[10] The initial conditions did not hold for Argentina, which never had the small towns that required education for individualism and decisionmaking.

And whereas the economy of the United States grew by policies that favored industrialization for internal consumption, the conditions for Argentina's economic growth depended on expansion of agricultural production for export. Argentina became the major supplier of beef and wheat for Great Britain and parts of Europe until World War I. Cowboys and ranchers, rather than workers and industrialists, were the major actors in this stage of Argentina's development. It was the crude barbarians who furnished the means by which perfumed elites in Buenos Aires enjoyed their modern life. Growth was produced by those with less education, not those who were best educated and, if we accept Sarmiento's earlier characterization, by the most backward elements of society rather than those with the most modern attitudes. Only after Argentina was already "modernized" did industrial production exceed agriculture as a major source of income.

Necessary to the initial process of modernization were political alliances between commercial and banking elites in Buenos Aires and the kings of cattle and wheat. In the name of free trade Argentina reduced its tariffs on imports from Great Britain and other countries, in return for massive purchases of Argentina's agricultural production. As a consequence, industrial development was slow, industrial production was a relatively minor contributor to Argentina's growth, and both capitalists and workers in industry had relatively little influence on national policies. The cities were productive in the sense that workers there received high income for little labor, but that productivity was the consequence of political (and military) domination of rural producers. Only later was free trade abandoned to protect nascent industries competing against the more modern states of the north.

In the golden era of Argentina's development education grew rapidly in the cities, but that growth was as consumption, rather than production of wealth. The dominant ideology was that of the ranchers and cereal growers, who did not welcome gauchos who read political philosophy and who did not encourage universal education. Argentina built more schools than any other Latin American country because it was richer than any other, not because it needed educated workers for its industrial expansion. The rich had more education than the poor, but that education was the consequence rather than the cause of their privileged position.

Nor did the expansion of education produce the kind of democracy that Sarmiento had admired in the United States. Political participation was and is high in Argentina, perhaps higher than in other Latin American countries, and expansion of education may have contributed to that expression of democracy. But the form of participation has been that of mass parties and movements, rather than grassroots democracy, of plebiscitary rather than parliamentary democracy. Argentina's political history was and has continued to be turbulent, the regulator of schooling did not work. Argentina became a country of "twenty million . . . who know quite a bit, who daily read what is necessary to exercise their reason and public and political passions, . . . who are daily aware of everything that is going on in the world, who debate without end public issues which excite them passionately."[11] This is a description that Sarmiento had written with glowing admiration of the United States in the 1840s, and which no longer applies. In the United States high levels of political consciousness were accompanied by decades of struggle between workers and owners, which were not fully resolved until the 1940s. In Argentina, also, increased education brought new forms of still unresolved social conflict. Argentina today no longer enjoys the distinction of being the best-educated country in Latin America, even though its per capita income is the highest in Latin America. Political (and economic) stability continues to be elusive.

AN ALTERNATIVE EXPLANATION

Education does, of course, make a vital contribution to the development of societies. But the form and content of education is, in turn, a product of the society in which it develops. Consider the differences in education in the Soviet Union, Germany, Japan, and the United States in the late

1930s. South Korea in 1945 had a lower level of education than Egypt or the Philippines. Each country has had a particular kind of development, but can we explain that development in terms of the form and content of education? Do the former *attributes* of these countries explain their current levels of development or modernization? By themselves they cannot. Only by reference to relationships with other countries, and internal choices made along the way, can we begin to account for how countries have developed.

On a number of occasions Sarmiento stepped outside the framework of his theory in an attempt to create outcomes that had not been achieved through application of the theory. As president, for example, he relied heavily on police power to implement decisions that local communities resisted, made alliances with groups that he had earlier branded as the most retrograde of society, and, by suspending constitutional guarantees, denied the ability of educated men and women other than himself to arrive at the truth, thereby contradicting his assertion that an educated people will not elect tyrants.

Although in his writings Sarmiento championed a positivist, mechanistic view of history, his life was dominated by the dialectics of politics and choice. He clearly understood the importance of human agency in the production of history and assigned to men and women, rather than to the forces of history or the workings of the economy, the ability to produce a more just and humane society. Ultimately, he saw education as a means to free us from the cultural blinders of our present society, to dream of a new world to build. I believe that he used the concept of civilization, the theory of modernization, as an instrument of persuasion for others, rather than as a road map for himself. Modernization was, therefore, a false ideology.

NOTES

1. W. Arthur Lewis, *The Theory of Economic Growth* (New York: Allen & Unwin, 1955).

2. Cyril E. Black, *The Dynamics of Modernization, a Study of Comparative History* (New York: Harper & Row, 1966).

3. Frederick H. Harbison, Joan Maruhníc, and Jane B. Resnick, eds., *Quantitative Analysis of Modernization and Development* (Princeton: Princeton University, Industrial Relations Section, 1970).

4. Lewis, *Economic Growth.*

5. Alex Inkeles, *Exploring Individual Modernity* (New York: Columbia University Press, 1983).

6. Gino Germani, *Sociología de la modernización; Estudios teóricos, metodológicos y aplicadas a América Latina* (Buenos Aires: Paidós, 1969).

7. Domingo F. Sarmiento, *Obras completas*, vol. 7, *Quiroga. Aldao. El Chacho, 1845–1963* (53 vols., Buenos Aires: Editorial Luz del Día, 1948–1956), 27, trans.

and quoted in James Omar Pellicer, "A comparative Study of Domingo Sarmiento's Social Thought and His Philosophy of Education" (Ph.D. diss., New York University, 1973).

8. Domingo F. Sarmiento, *North and South America. A Discourse Delivered Before the Rhode-Island Historical Society, December 27, 1865. By His Excellency, Domingo Faustino Sarmiento, Argentine Minister to the United States* (Providence: Knowles, Anthony & Co., 1866), 34.

9. Ibid., 36.

10. Michael B. Katz, *The Irony of Early School Reform: Educational Innovation in Mid-Nineteenth Century Massachusetts* (Cambridge: Harvard University Press, 1968).

11. Domingo F. Sarmiento, *Sarmiento's Travels in the United States in 1847*, ed. and trans. Michael Aaron Rockland (Princeton: Princeton University Press, 1970), 176–177.

Reading Sarmiento: Writing the Myths of National Culture

Diana Sorensen Goodrich

Reading Leopoldo Lugones reading Sarmiento is a bit like catching a glimpse of the discourse on the formation of Argentine culture. His *Historia de Sarmiento* deploys the strategies of institutionalization involved in canon formation. I shall trace this particular episode in the long history of the readings of *Facundo,* probing the ways in which a hegemonic reader like Lugones turns interpretation into power, seeks to canonize Sarmiento's key texts, and, in the process, asserts his own discursive domination. In a broader context, all this is part of a study of the history of the reception of *Facundo* and of the ways in which a text is appropriated and made a part of the canon. *Facundo* represents a very complex instance of this process, because its readers have attempted to legitimize it but also to contest and even subvert it at times. Lugones, for his part, epitomizes the hegemonic intellectual—one whose interpretation marks the intersection between discourse and power.

Lugones made the greatest effort of this century to become a national poet whose voice could sing in praise of every aspect of Argentine reality. His conception of the role of the intellectual is imbued with Homeric overtones: he sets out to propound the view that national poets do not merely express their country's spirit, but actually create its nationality. Lugones's *Historia de Sarmiento* interests me on several counts: it rapidly became one of the most influential book-length studies of Sarmiento, the emerging myth, at the time when the centennial of his birth was being commemorated. It also was a means by which Lugones himself etched a subtle, unstated parallel between the object of study and praise, on the one hand, and himself on the other. Hence, it is an interesting case of discourse that traverses two tracks simultaneously: the

Diana Sorensen Goodrich is associate professor of Spanish American literature, Wesleyan University.

173

one that speaks about Sarmiento and the one that alludes to Lugones, who, as an authorial pole, is always encountered by the reader as a looming presence.

Lugone's effort to become a national poet bore fruit, particularly in the first two-thirds of his life. There are multiple proofs of this, but perhaps none so eloquent as the fact that the Sociedad Argentina de Escritores chose the day of his birth to be the "Day of the Writer," a decision that suggests the extent to which the identification between Lugones and the country had been achieved. In 1974 an *homenaje* was published by the same society to honor the one-hundredth anniversary of his birth, much as national heroes like Sarmiento himself have been celebrated. Lugones managed to fulfill hegemonic roles as the representative of different groups that wielded power in Argentina between the end of the nineteenth century and the first thirty years of the twentieth. This is in itself a remarkable phenomenon in light of the fact that the political road traversed by Lugones was marked by the extreme poles of a socialist beginning and a fascistic conclusion. A matter to ponder, then, is the manner in which his centrality in the nation's cultural and political life was achieved and how it bears upon his reading of Sarmiento's work.

Lugones arrived in Buenos Aires from the provinces as a young poet of great promise. His 1897 *Las montañas del oro* was welcomed in an article by no less a figure than Rubén Darío, whose voice had continental authority and prestige. Its title, "Leopoldo Lugones: Un poeta socialista" is indicative of the relevance of Lugones's political views and of the extent to which they were identified with his writing. Why, we may ask ourselves, was socialism not perceived as a threat that might have blocked his access to prestige and, eventually, power? The answer lies in the circumstances within which it operated and in the kind of socialist Lugones actually was.

This early phase was not an object of intense preoccupation among the powerful of the time, who found little to fear in a socialism that was more utopian and intuitive than doctrinaire. In fact, there are indications that the works of Marx did not play a prominent role in their intellectual and political formation. Thus, although Lugones may have caused some concern as he organized the commemoration of the Paris Commune or the First of May and met with the disapproval of the powerful Catholic church, he may have assuaged it with the nature of his writings for a journal that he codirected with José Ingenieros, *La Montaña*, characterized by a defense of maximum freedom and minimal government. Some of Lugones's positions already revealed inconsistencies within his socialist stance that anticipated the views he was to uphold later. A case in point was an article published in *El Tiempo* on 11 July 1896, in honor of the visit of Prince Louis of Savoy:

Hereditary aristocracy is necessary and respectable. The man of good breeding seldom fails to live up to the heritage of honor which he received from his grandparents. . . . Today science affirms the principle of selection on the basis of race. I believe in science and I have great respect for princes.[1]

While Lugones's words were not well received by his socialist friends, they did not alienate him from them because of his prestige as a gifted poet, and, at the same time, they suggested an alignment with the values of the elites. Another factor that did not make Lugones a worrisome case to the elites was his tendency to prefer the field of culture and the spirit over material forces, so that his explanations of national or historical events did not line up with a categorically socialist position. While Lugones's standing as a poet of national stature was being consolidated with the publication of new works, he became influential in the field of education. In that area he held jobs such as that of general inspector of high school education, and he was instrumental in founding an institution of higher learning that was to become very prestigious: the Instituto Nacional del Profesorado. Lugones traveled to Europe frequently and he was recognized as a Latin American intellectual of stature, particularly in France, where he founded *La Revue Sud-Americaine* in 1914, with the intention of establishing an effective organ to diffuse Latin American culture. While this effort was aborted by the outbreak of World War I, Lugones's standing was not affected, as can be proved by two significant instances: he received an official invitation from the French government to visit the battlegrounds in 1921, and he was nominated by the League of Nations to become a member of its Intellectual Corporation, together with Albert Einstein, in 1924.

As early as 1904, Lugones gave signs of ideological allegiances with antiliberal ideas that upheld the role of the armed forces in stopping the force of the masses from displacing the ruling elites. He veered from his early socialist positions toward an alignment with an authoritarian and militaristic far right—a move that culminated in his support for the September 1930 revolution led by General José Evaristo Uriburu. In the twenty odd years that led up to this radically conservative stance, Lugones had adopted less extreme positions that did not define him so clearly, but, rather, allowed him the remarkable achievement of maintaining his standing as Argentina's foremost poetic voice while being extremely well received by the highest governing elite. As his political leanings became progressively more conservative, even fascistic, his pen became an instrument for their propagation and was no longer exclusively devoted to poetry.

Moreover, Lugones resorted to an interesting form of contact with the people he wanted to reach and influence, one that could only work given his intellectual prestige as a poet and man of letters. This was the public lecture held at large, important theaters in Buenos Aires, which had the peculiarity of being not merely a political event but also an activity in the spheres of the intellectual, the artistic, and the political. Interestingly, it was Lugones's hegemony as a cultural figure that allowed him to cross over these boundaries so fluidly and to be listened to as though he were a Homeric bard addressing the less immediate issues that pertained to the very essence of the national spirit. Equally effective was his use of the newspaper as a means of molding and divulging opinions in both discursive fields. Thus, Lugones's power in Argentine society became firmly grounded in a skillful manipulation of both orality and literacy.

As Lugones's views became more markedly aligned with fascism, he faced strong opposition from students and other intellectuals. Toward the end of his life, after he supported Uriburu's revolution (which was to mark the beginning of what has gone down in history as the "Infamous Decade"), Lugones became a symbol of the extreme right and hence his standing among the intellectuals—most of whom were radically opposed to Uriburu's regime—lost ground. This should not be surprising in light of the fact that his positions included defending Mussolini and praising the Peruvian dictator Augusto B. Leguía for having helped adumbrate "the hour of the sword." However, not until he espoused such markedly reactionary views did Lugones's hegemony decline, and after he committed suicide in February 1938, his politics were sublimated even by the intellectual elites and he again became the national poet par excellence. This is in itself an interesting process that can be explained by the nature of Lugones's poetic production and his role in fashioning, like Ricardo Rojas, a national sense of culture.

Lugones the poet was sensitive to the need for a voice that would sing a totality that could be identified with Argentina, in both its synchronic and diachronic axes. Perhaps the most eloquent example of this kind of enterprise is his 1910 *Odas seculares,* published to commemorate the Revolution of 1810. The driving force to produce a poetic inventory of national elements at times jeopardizes the poetic tone: "Let us claim the relevant amendment / To the Rural Code whose reform / Has its norms in the nobility of agrarian law / and in the equity of the herds."[2] Borges rightly decries "the tedious and encyclopedic tenacity inducing Lugones to put into verse all the disciplines of agriculture and cattle raising." And one cannot help but think of his fiercely satirical treatment of Carlos Argentino Daneri in *El Aleph.*

If it was his poetic ventures that placed Lugones in the center of the Argentine intellectual elite, it is also true that some of his prose works fulfilled the same task of identifying him with the national culture. In *La guerra gaucha* Lugones makes heroes of the gauchos who participated in the wars of independence under the leadership of Martín Güemes, as he rescues from oblivion the patriotic role of obscure fighters. In *El payador*, Argentina is endowed with a national epic equivalent to the *Iliad* as Lugones validates the gaucho poem *Martín Fierro* by placing it in a Homeric context.

The *Historia de Sarmiento* is part of a similar program. Published in 1911 by request of the president of the Consejo Nacional de Educación (José Ramos Mejía) to commemorate the centennial of Sarmiento's birth, it is a work dictated by both immediate circumstances and by Lugones's overall project. Despite its title, it is not a work of historical research, both because it was written in only about five or six months and because it was not within the parameters of historical discourse that Lugones set out to write about Sarmiento. In fact, history is subordinated to the dictates of an authorial vision that places itself beyond the need for validation. Lugones's implicit claim is that he is the privileged mediator between the national hero he is presenting—and helping to build—and his readers. The book is informed by the will to recreate, to fictionalize, to work out a vision that will bring the man and his works back to life. The past becomes a source of archetypes on which to construct a sense of security for an uncertain present—not a subject to be analytically problematized. At times, Lugones's writing even takes on a clearly novelistic stance, as can be seen in the following passage, where Sarmiento's marriage to Benita Martínez Pastoriza is romanticized in nineteenth-century terms: "There, in those gatherings we imagine the elegant widow: if in the salon, amid the rustling of silk between the severity of the corset and the grandiloquence of the flounce below which would peep out the adorable feet crossed in a gesture of abandon."[3]

The presence of Lugones the writer is strongly felt in the frequent passages designed to display his own linguistic abilities. The signifier is at times privileged at the expense of the signified, and we are confronted with a text that may actually be saying very little: "He delights in his own caricature in the newspaper and in the mask. What swarms in it is the robust sensuality of the Rabelaisian laughter, and at the same time the rustic tickle of a faun who laughs off his own ugliness at the fountain."[4]

The will to mythify Sarmiento leads to strategies of aggrandizement that defy the credibility of even the most pliant reader. At one point, Sarmiento is proclaimed to be a saint "due to his valiant self sacrifice which overwhelmed his imperfections," and a parallel is drawn between him and Saint Francis of Assisi on the occasion of Sarmiento's foundation of the Society for the Protection of Animals.[5] Behind these discursive strategies, and helping to account for them, lies the glorification of the man who can manipulate them—the intellectual. In this sense, Lugones's approach to Sarmiento is self-serving in that, on a close perusal of its unstated assumptions, one can detect that it is shot through with praise for the writer above all.[6] Noé Jitrik detected this in his book on Lugones: "Someone else's biography can be an excuse to speak about oneself, with the backing provided by the inevitable comparison. Upon reading *Historia de Sarmiento*, for example, I have had the clear impression that Lugones was speaking about himself."[7] The relationship between Sarmiento and Argentina that Lugones posits as the clue for his heroic status mirrors the one we have identified in Lugones's own case: "He had assumed the responsibility for the nation, looking upon himself as its perpetual representative, with the absorbing fire of a great love."[8]

The key word here is "representative," as it points to the function that Lugones assigned to his writing in the context of his own life. Through Sarmiento, then, he was claiming for himself, the intellectual, the hegemonic standing that he felt he deserved. A similar approach underlies his evaluation of other significant figures in Argentine history. Thus, in Chapter 4, "La doctrina y la lucha," after an account of the accomplishments of Manuel Moreno, Esteban Echeverría, Bartolomé Mitre, and Juan Bautista Alberdi, Lugones concludes: "Above all, literary people." As if uncomfortable with the evidence of his own prejudice, he goes on to add: "(The reader will be kind enough to believe I am not defending my own cause.)"[9] The afterthought does little to dispel the evidence supplied by an abundance of other statements. A case in point is his valuation of Echeverría's political treatise *Dogma socialista* (a book to which Lugones assigns a major founding role) as the product of a rigorous mind trained and refined by the demands of poetic composition, "as is a matter of habit among cultivators of verse when they develop such topics; for nothing leads to precision as effectively as the handling of that tool which subordinates word and idea to the triple mathematical severity of meter, rhythm and rhyme."[10]

Not surprisingly, therefore, *Facundo* is made to play a pivotal role in Sarmiento's achievements as well as in the context of the nation itself: "It constitutes Sarmiento's entire program. His literary ideas, his political propaganda, his plans as an educator, his historical concept, are there. That is our great political novel and our great constitutional study."[11] Together with *Recuerdos de provincia*, *Facundo* epitomizes what we might venture to call the "super-textual" powers of literary works:

> They represent . . . the successful attempt to make Argentine literature, which is to say nation: for above all the nation consists in the formation of a national spirit whose exterior manifestation is language. . . . [Sarmiento] is this eternal and enormous thing: the father of a literature, the representative of a people.[12]

Ironically, despite Lugones's proclaimed admiration for *Facundo*, his reading is, in several significant instances, marked by a refusal to be bound to Sarmiento's statements. Within the discursive territory of the text he is interpreting, Lugones carves out a space in which he puts forth his own theories about the factors that came into play in the configuration of the national forces. This is particularly obvious in Chapter 3, "El medio histórico," in which he focuses on Sarmiento's explanation of the Revolution of 1810. In one sweeping, revealing gesture, Lugones concludes the exposition of his views with an authoritarian comment: "The comprehensive principle of Argentine history is easy and simple. The transcendence and complication which have been attributed to its diverse factors stem from an imitation of the historical study required by the Old World nations."[13]

Significantly, the reading of *Facundo* elicits views that anticipate the Lugones of 1930 in a way that makes us wonder if his veering to the right entailed as dramatic a change as has been assumed. There is a racist slant in his analysis that lends it the mark of racial determinism as a principle of explanation. Thus, the impossibility of establishing a democratic order based on the premise of representation stems from the racial inferiority of the mestizos (people of mixed race, particularly in the case of Argentina of white Europeans and Indians) who make up the majority of the voting population. His conclusion leads to a generalization that is highly revealing: "Political and even social equality can be declared where there already existed racial equality."[14] Indeed, for Lugones the gaucho is quite simply a mestizo, and he is not only inferior but also marked by "the original blot" (*la mancha original*). The caudillos who are the focus of Sarmiento's concern, differed from the gauchos in that the former were light haired and blue eyed; their influence, in Lugones's view, had a great deal to do with this racial difference. Unlike the gauchos, then, the caudillos were "decent men" (*hombres decentes*). The choice of "decent" to refer to a racial characteristic has an eloquence that requires no further elaboration. Sarmiento's book, therefore, works as an unavowed repository for the presentation of Lugones's own ideas.

There are several other instances in which this particular form of appropriation can be seen at work. Of particular interest is Lugones's account of Rosas's tyranny, a central theme in *Facundo*. According to Lugones, Rosas represents the political tendencies of the provinces. Their role, in fact, is explained in a way that differs from Sarmiento's in Chapter 4 of *Facundo*, entitled "Revolución de 1810." In Lugones's view, the provinces did not find in the revolution an outlet for their anarchic tendencies, but, rather, a suppression of their commercial autonomy. According to Lugones, the provinces were unable to export their products along routes that led to the north or the west due to the frontier wars that had been waged for over ten years. Buenos Aires was their only outlet, and if it prevailed, then the provinces' chances of having their share of the political power—the very reason they had participated in the revolutionary wars—would be destroyed. Moreover, the provinces were not merely the seat of unruly forces, as Sarmiento claims ("to withdraw from the authority of the king was agreeable, as it meant withdrawal from authority," we read in *Facundo*), but instead the representatives of the aristocratic elements. Rosas, as anticipated above, is explained by Lugones as "the victory of provincial politics." In fact, Lugones under-scores Rosas's aristocratic background and his clericalism, both hall-marks of provincial politics, as the bastion of an isolationism opposed to centralizing forces and of the social and political stagnation that were the remnants of the colonial rule. To some extent, then, Lugones is un-avowedly reading *Facundo* against the grain by assigning to the provinces both an ideology that transcends the warlike disposition attributed to them by *Facundo* and political consciousness as well.[15]

Lugones's disagreement with Sarmiento becomes explicit when he discusses the opposition civilization-barbarism. He aligns himself with the most articulate of Sarmiento's contemporary enemies, Alberdi, who undermines the opposition by replacing it with a purely geographic one: "The only subdivision admitted by the Spanish American man, is *between the man from the coast and the inland* or the Mediterranean man."[16] Lugones insists on the changing, purely circumstantial nature of this distinction and essentially moots its cognitive value. What Sarmiento posits as the epistemological grounding of his interpretive enterprise is dismounted from its privileged status: "There are no such barbarians nor civilized men. Their differences are merely accidental situations which, upon changing, also change their situation."[17] The only substantial difference Lugones envisages in Argentine reality is the one between the decent man and the "the gaucho-like one" (*el agauchado*), once again relying on a racially oriented distinction. As observed earlier, the Lugones of 1930 is prefigured and anticipated in the author of this book.

There is one discursive strategy that allows Lugones to produce such a critical reading of *Facundo* under the guise of celebration and that subsumes the points of divergence I have observed. It is the claim that underpins Lugones's discussion: the privileged status of the realm of ideas and the spiritual. By placing the discussion in this lofty realm, Lugones again asserts the superiority of the intellectual, who, in his Homeric seat, can articulate the national truths. Not surprisingly, though, the seat accommodates Lugones alone, for Sarmiento is toppled from it after a deceivingly brief tenure. Reading *Facundo*, in Lugones's case as in so many others, enacts the process through which the circula-tion, reception, and contestation of meanings are embedded in relations of power and affiliation. Taking the argument one step further, it traces the effect of these relations in the formation of Argentine culture.

NOTES

1. "La aristocracia de sangre es necesaria y respetable. El hombre de raza desmiente pocas veces la herencia de honor que recibió de sus abuelos. . . . La ciencia afirma hoy día la selección de raza. Yo creo en la ciencia, y tengo el respeto de los príncipes." Quoted by Alfredo Canedo, *Aspectos del pensamiento político de Leopoldo Lugones* (Buenos Aires: Ediciones Marcos, 1974), 47. Unless otherwise indicated, I am the translator of all quotations in this paper.

2. Reclamemos la enmienda pertinente
Del códico rural cuya reforma,
En la nobleza del derecho agrícola
Y en la equidad pecuaria tiene normas.

In "Oda a los ganados y las mieses," quoted by Jorge Luis Borges, *Leopoldo Lugones,* 2d ed. (Buenos Aires: Editorial Pleamar, 1965), 37.

3. "Allá en aquellas reuniones, es donde imaginamos a la elegante viuda: si en el salón, susurrada de seda entre el rigor de la cotilla y la grandilocuencia del falbalá, bajo el cual asomaban los mimosos pies cruzados en postura de abandono." Leopoldo Lugones, *Historia de Sarmiento* (Buenos Aires: Publicaciones de la Comisión Argentina de Fomento Interamericano, 1945), 76.

4. "Regocíjale su propia caricatura en el periódico y en la máscara. Hormiguea en ello la robusta sensualidad de la risa rabelesiana, y a la vez una ingenua cosquilla rústica de fauno que ríe su propia fealdad en la fuente." Ibid., 58.

5. Ibid., 61.

6. It is interesting to note the contrast with Ricardo Rojas's evaluation, which was centered on the person of action at the expense of the person's ideas. In each case what emerges is an image of Sarmiento and his work that is dependent on the reader's interpretive position.

7. "La biografía del otro puede ser pretexto para hablar de uno mismo, con el respaldo que da la inevitable comparación. Al leer la *Historia de Sarmiento,* por ejemplo, he tenido la clara impresión de que Lugones hablaba de sí mismo." Noé Jitrik, *Leopoldo Lugones, mito nacional* (Buenos Aires: Editorial Palestra, 1960), 48.

8. "Había asumido la responsabilidad del país, considerándose un perpetuo representante suyo, con esa fogocidad absorbente de los grandes amores." Lugones, *Sarmiento,* 64.

9. "El lector tendrá la cortesía de creer que no defiendo mi causa." Ibid., 126.

10. "Según es habitual en los cultores del verso cuando desarrollan temas semejantes; pues nada predispone tanto a la precisión como el manejo de ese instrumento que sujeta la idea y la palabra al triple rigor matemático del metro, el ritmo y la rima." Ibid., 127.

11. "Constituye todo el programa de Sarmiento. Sus ideas literarias, su propaganda política, sus planes de educador, su concepto histórico, están ahí. Es aquella nuestra gran novela política y nuestro gran estudio constitucional." Ibid., 165.

12. "Representan . . . la tentativa lograda de hacer literatura argentina, que es decir patria: puesto que la patria consiste ante todo en la formación de un espíritu nacional cuya exterioridad sensible es el idioma. . . . [Sarmiento] es esta cosa eterna y enorme: el padre de una literatura, el representante de un pueblo." Ibid.

13. "Así, pues, el concepto comprensivo de la historia argentina es fácil y sencillo. Toda la trascendencia y complicación que se ha atribuido a sus diversos factores, proviene de una imitación del estudio histórico requerido por las

naciones del viejo mundo." Ibid., 114.

14. Ibid., 98.

15. In *Facundo*, Sarmiento decries the "disposiciones guerreras que se malbarataban en puñaladas y tajos . . . ; aquella desocupación romana . . . ; aquella antipatía a la autoridad." *Facundo: O civilización y barbarie* (Caracas: Biblioteca Ayacucho, 1977), 65–66.

16. Quoted by Lugones, *Sarmiento*, 108. Lugones does not acknowledge his source.

17. "No había tales bárbaros ni tales civilizados. Sus diferencias son meras situaciones accidentales que, al variar, los cambian también de partido." Ibid., 110.

15

The Legacy of Sarmiento's Civilization and Barbarism in Modern Argentina

Kristin H. Ruggiero

First-time visitors to Argentina find the country much shaped by European immigration and are struck by the European origins of much of its population. The majority of these immigrants came to Argentina between the last quarter of the nineteenth century and World War I. In 1869 the Argentine population numbered about two million inhabitants; by 1919, this had been augmented by the addition of two-and-a-half million Europeans.[1] The largest group were Italians, and one-third of Argentina's population today is made up of Italians and their descendants. Domingo Faustino Sarmiento was one of the most important promoters of this immigration, which so shaped his country and which continues to leave its mark on the republic.

Sarmiento, as part of the nineteenth-century Latin American intellectual and political elite, accepted the tenets of European economic and political liberalism and positivism. Thus, he encouraged policies that promoted European immigration so as to increase the size of the labor force, introduce new skills needed for economic development, promote European values and even "whiten" the population, and "civilize" the native population, which was viewed as barbaric and an obstruction to progress.[2] The preferred immigrants were northern Europeans, but it was southern Europeans, Italians and Spaniards, who came in the greatest numbers. In 1914, 40 percent of the foreigners living in Argentina were from Italy and 35 percent were from Spain. Russians ranked a very distant third, 4.1 percent, and were followed by groups such as the French, Germans, and British, who ranked between 1 and 3 percent.[3]

Early in his career, Sarmiento began to fix his attention on the advantages of this immigration to Argentina's development. To

---

Kristin H. Ruggiero is Charles A. Dana assistant professor of history, College of the Holy Cross.

Sarmiento, the European immigrant meant civilization, that is, rational-
ism, progress, and a settled life in cities. He said that Argentines needed
"to mix with the populations of more advanced countries, so they . . .
[might] teach . . . [them] their arts, their industry, their activity and
adeptness at work"; that European immigration "would correct the
indigenous blood with new ideas ending . . . [Argentina's] medievalism."[4]
Positivist thought maintained that the European "races" were superior
to the native American ones and that European immigrants, dedicated
to order and progress, would be able to counteract the Creole elements
in Latin American society.[5]

In contrast to Europeans, native Argentines, to Sarmiento, symbolized
the barbarism of gauchos and caudillos, and even of the pampa itself. He
regretted what he saw as the disadvantages of the Indian characteristics in
the native.[6] The Argentine native population, often but not always a mixture
of Indian and old Spanish immigrant (i.e., Spaniards who had come before
the nineteenth century), was viewed by sociologists of the period as "inher-
ently degenerate physically and morally," and totally incapable of fostering
progress and development. It would take at least three generations of
breeding mestizos and Europeans, calculated the sociologist Lucas
Ayarragaray, "before an individual would emerge capable of 'assimilating
European civilization.'"[7] Such racial theories formed an important part of
the discussion on the reasons for the barbarity of the Argentine countryside.
So did the nature of gaucho life.

The gaucho's way of life was seen as being opposed to Argentina's
national interests in that it was nomadic and the work habits irregular.
In his most famous work, *Facundo: Civilización y barbarie*, Sarmiento
asserted that the famous and infamous nineteenth-century caudillo and
dictator, Juan Manuel de Rosas, was "not an isolated incident, an
aberration, a monstrosity, [but] on the contrary, a social manifestation,
a formula for a people's way of being." It is simply a question, he said,
"of being or not being savages."[8] "The Argentine rustic . . . is a man
independent of every want, under no control, with no notion of government, all regular and systematic order being wholly impossible among
such people, [who are] without public aim, without social interest."[9]

In addition to the inferior racial composition of the native popula-
tion, and the disorderly, unprogressive nature of gaucho life, there was
the peculiar nature of the pampa. "Why can't the pampa . . . be a garden,"
Sarmiento asked, thinking of northern Italy, "instead of a wilderness?"
Then he answered his own question: "Because the people of Buenos
Aires, with all their advantages, are the most barbarous that exist in
America; rude shepherds, . . . who have not yet taken possession of the
land." "In the pampa," he explained, "one must complete the work of
God through skill. The canvas being given, one needs the palette and
paints that will color it."[10] But perhaps the Argentines had "not yet taken

possession of the land" because they did not need to. That is, the very fruitfulness of the pampa may have been a problem for Argentina. "Our pampa makes us lazy," Sarmiento wrote, "the easy food of our pastures reduces us to zero." While in contrast, he went on, "cold climates bring forth industrious men, and tempestuous coasts create daring sailors."[11] With European immigration, Sarmiento envisioned "flourishing cities . . . [rising] where today only brambles are growing" and immigrants living "in abundance with only half the work they do right now to keep from starving to death."[12] Europeans believed the Argentine immigration propaganda. Thus, Sarmiento's appeal fell on receptive ears in the Old World: "If we lack an intelligent population, let the people of Europe . . . feel that there is permanent peace and freedom in our country, and multitudes of emigrants would find their way to a land where success is sure."[13]

Not everyone even in his own country, however, shared Sarmiento's views. Some people considered that immigration would deprive native Argentines of jobs and bring drastic changes to the Argentine way of life. In fact, there was a backlash against European immigration in the late nineteenth and early twentieth centuries, although not against European values, and the once disdained gaucho was elevated, at least his romantic part, to national hero. As intent as Sarmiento had been on civilizing barbarous Argentina by means of immigration, he, too, toward the end of his life in 1888, turned against some of the results of Argentine immigration policy.[14]

In the day-to-day consequences of European immigration, colonization, and assimilation in Argentina, something happened to dampen the early enthusiasm toward immigration and to shake people's confidence in this policy's ability to create the kind of republic that statesmen such as Sarmiento desired. The legacy of this period of ambivalence, which modern Argentines have to live with, especially in the countryside, is a confrontation between foreigner and native, civilization and barbarism. Many of today's descendants of nineteenth- and early twentieth-century immigrants still consider themselves gringos. Though they are third- and fourth-generation Argentines, they see themselves as distinct from Creoles. Creoles, the so-called native population, though they are not the indigenous population, are the distant descendants of the early Spaniards who have been in Argentina long enough to have become, so some believe, as wild and unsettled as the pampas themselves. But others think that they represent the true Argentina. The terms gringo and Creole have both positive and negative connotations in modern Argentina. Regardless of how they are used, however, their definitions and connotations are solidly rooted in the nineteenth-century debate on civilization and barbarism.

So much concerning the social fabric of modern Argentina, especially in the rural areas, hinges on an understanding of these attitudes that emerged from the nineteenth-century milieu of immigration and colonization, that one feels very close to Sarmiento's time. In fact, Argentina is scattered with villages that are literally and figuratively relics of this important period—villages that look like abandoned Hollywood movie sets through which the world passed only briefly but which have been left with a very significant residual of tension between gringo and Creole.[15]

Sarmiento and his peers rarely rested a moment from stressing the preferability of hardworking, progressive-thinking, skillful, future-oriented foreigners to the indolent natives. And this is exactly how the descendants of immigrants still view themselves and their role in Argentine society. Their feeling of superiority over Creoles is expressed in various ways, but perhaps it is best to begin with a joke told by a gringo of Italian descent who lives in one of these pampa villages in the Province of Entre Ríos.

> One day in the Chaco a gringo moved into an estancia next door to a creole. Next day the gringo went to introduce himself. The creole asked him what he was going to do there, and he replied that he was going to grow wheat. The creole declared that nothing would come of it. The gringo couldn't understand this because an agronomist had assured him that wheat would grow there, so he said, "Oh well, I'll grow corn." "Corn doesn't grow here either," said the creole. "Well, I'll grow cotton then," replied the gringo, undaunted. "Cotton doesn't grow here either," said the creole. Exasperated, the gringo despaired, "But I was told if I planted__" "Oh," said the creole with sudden understanding, "if you're going to *plant!*"[16]

The crucial word here obviously is "plant." Gringos still chuckle at the thought of a Creole who expected crops to grow spontaneously, although we must recall Sarmiento's reference to the "easy food of our pastures" and the immigrants' own enthusiasm over "the streets paved with gold" in Argentina. So, then, what makes people laugh at this joke? It is because it is still valid. It is because these stereotypes of gringo and Creole are still operative. It is because the values of hard work and entrepreneurship are still used to differentiate gringo from Creole.

Much of life in the countryside is dominated by old-timers, such as the one who told this story, and their reminiscences that, accurately or not, still shape the Argentine present in many ways. Many of their stories recall the ethic of hard work that helped them get ahead in the New World. As an elderly Italo-Argentine man reminisced:

> I remember how hard my parents worked. . . . They didn't come to live the easy life. They worked hard the whole year just to live, nothing more. If they weren't planting and harvesting, they were making charcoal. . . .

But my family got ahead. Here in Argentina it wasn't hard to eat. Everything was at our fingertips. Argentina was a rich land.[17]

At other times, old-timers recall the locust attacks, the lack of tools and seeds, the desire to return to Italy, and the necessity to hire themselves out as peon day laborers to make ends meet. They maintain that they and their families worked like asses and then admit that they had worked like this in Italy as well but had never gotten anyplace.[18]

Gringos got ahead in Argentina, so they say, because they valued hard work and parsimony and because they were enterprising farmers and entrepreneurs. While acknowledging the unpleasantness of the division between gringos and Creoles, gringos prefer to recall that everyone started on an equal footing, but that Creoles were too naive and uncaring to take advantage of the land and get ahead.[19] In the same spirit of Sarmiento's praise of European immigrants who brought progress and new skills to Argentina, today's descendants attribute Argentina's dairy industry to Italians, maintaining that Creoles never would have developed it because they "did nothing . . . [and] only cared that their bellies were full."[20] "Creoles weren't worried about anything. They worked for *yerba* [the herb from which maté is made] and clothes, nothing more, day to day. They never worried about tomorrow. Some days our peons came to work, other days they never showed up at all."[21] This is precisely the attitude with which Sarmiento had characterized the Creoles.[22] The old-timers are not alone in their confirmation of Sarmiento's criticisms of Creoles. The stereotypes that were current in the nineteenth century are still commonplace *throughout* Argentina and among different generations, and one often hears that if the Argentines would only work as hard as the Italians, Argentina would get ahead.[23]

Profiting from the policies of Sarmiento and others, immigrants got ahead because they

> benefitted socially and economically from a hierarchy that had favored them ever since the nineteenth century, when the government first encouraged Europeans to settle in Argentina and work the land. . . . Argentina was there almost for the immigrants' taking, more a territory than a nation, with a numerically insignificant native population and an ineffective government. It was a place, some Italians thought, better suited to becoming an Italian colony than a sovereign nation.

In rural Argentina, especially, the population was small and there was little surrounding society to challenge the immigrants' ties to their homeland. Given these facts and, in addition, the official attitude toward Creoles and gringos, the lack of pressure on foreigners to become Argentine citizens, and the view that civilization was to be found in the cities rather than in the campo, it was no surprise that immigrant colonies became rather self-contained. In such a situation, it was not hard for immigrants to become isolated from Creoles, and for differences in values and life-styles to finally separate the two groups.[24]

In the village of the old-timers quoted above, geography, even in the spacious pampas, "divided and continues to divide the groups." Descendants of immigrants continue to live on the original land concessions that their families first rented and then purchased from the colonization company. "The few creoles who own land . . . have long been important landowners, distinct from the lower-class creoles who became the farmhands of the immigrants." These peon laborers tend to live in the village section of the colony, usually renting a small plot of land with a rancho hut on it from one of the gringo landowners. The few Creole peons who live on the agricultural and pastoral land of the colony live in the less desirable lower areas, while gringos live on the hilltops.[25]

The old-timers and their families lived out Sarmiento's prophecy that immigrants would prosper in Argentina. Meanwhile, though, the Creole peons' position deteriorated. Thus, it is not difficult to explain gringos' feelings of superiority to Creoles. Landowners and peons generally correspond to the two sides of the gringo-Creole (that is, lower-class Creole) dichotomy. Because many lower-class Creoles are peon laborers, the words "Creole" and "peon" are often used interchangeably, the ethnic group being equated with the occupation.[26]

If peons and landowners paused to consider their history, they would testify to its continuity.

> In the heyday of agricultural expansion in the nineteenth century, landowners expended little more compassion on their human work force than they did on their animals. The consensus among the old-timers is that the peons were ignorant and uncaring. Quite properly, therefore, they worked at the beck and call of the estancieros, of the weather, of international markets; they lived in mud shacks and ate their fatty beef with their work knives; they had a narrow vision of life's possibilities. . . . The situation is scarcely different today. Their status has improved little, they live in similar dwellings, and their work is no more secure, their options no less limited.[27]

Remarks by landowners, both young and old—"They never worked," "They were naive"—recall the long servile history of the peons. "They are the descendants of gauchos like the central figure of the nineteenth-century poem *Martín Fierro:* nomadic herders, prairie men" who were to have been transformed by the civilization of the immigrants, but who instead became their farmhands. "Even today, social and work situations have a degrading aspect for the peon, prompting porteños to comment that 'Entre Ríos is backward: peons still tip their hats to landowners.' But Entre Ríos holds no monopoly on prejudice toward peons and creoles," on prejudice toward ignorance, naiveté, and lack of progress.[28]

"The problem was, they were innocent," explained an old-timer in 1976, innocent of the new Argentina that was being created. He continued,

> They always said, 'Gringo here, gringo there. The gringos came to take away our land.' It's true. Old Costantino did this when creoles couldn't pay for their drinks at his store. They'd ask for a peso's worth of caña [rum] and he'd give them two pesos' worth. Then when the creoles couldn't pay, Costantino would take their land as payment and act as if he was doing them a favor. The creoles didn't understand they were being taken advantage of. The only thing they cared about was drinking rum, and when they finished they found they had no land.[29]

One of Sarmiento's purposes in promoting immigration was to end up with a population that would be able to exploit the land. Talking to gringos today, one hears the sentiment expressed long ago by Sarmiento and others, that the Creoles did not have a concept of exploiting the land either for their own profit or for Argentina's. A gringo old-timer tells the story of a peon to whom he had given a house and some land, food, and permission to milk the cows that were there for his family's use. "But the creole took all the milk he could get and sold it or gave it away to other people. Then he left and took all the farm tools with him." The gringo's conclusion was that, even with all this help, the Creole could not progress.[30]

This gulf is defined geographically, with foreigners and natives living separately. It is defined economically, gringos have prospered and the mass of lower-class Creoles have not. And it is defined socially, many rural communities becoming so dominated by gringos that Creoles have had to redefine their position in terms of values foreign to them. They have been put on the defensive about their supposed lack of interest in progress and productiveness.

Progress was the catchword of the nineteenth century. The particular mentality of Creoles or gringos hinged on their attitude toward their own and their community's progress.

> The oft-repeated comments of the gringo old-timers attest to the importance of the notion of progress. . . . 'The creoles never worked.' 'They could have progressed like we did; they had all the same chances.' 'But we worked hard, isn't that so? That's why we got ahead.' And so on. It is with explanations like these that gringos account for the gulf that has traditionally separated creoles and gringos.[31]

"In the face of all this criticism, creoles continue to view their own more immediate approach to life as preferable to the gringos' struggle for future wealth, at least as long as they have all they need to live in the present." "Creoles dislike gringos' denigration of the creole life-style and their desire to change it." As people point out, "the word 'gringo' was historically a little disrespectful. It is enough to stand along the sidelines of a soccer game . . . and hear taunts of 'Stupid gringos' hurled at one of the teams to know that this is still true."

"Gringos, for their part, have usually seen themselves as hardworking, interested in progress, and future-oriented," values that contributed to a superior moral sense that "made it important to keep the groups separate."[32] An old-timer recalls a time when Creoles and gringos ate together. "But at a certain point," he says,

> a difference in morality developed. It turned out that the creoles didn't feel right eating with us gringos, and then we had to put them outside or in another room. There were two types of creoles: the timid ones who were ashamed, and those who were brazenly unashamed and did impermissible things. The creoles had to be put in their place.[33]

This was certainly not a situation that could lead to the amalgamation of populations or the "civilizing" of natives.

In contrast to the desired goal of creating a civilized population in Argentina through intermarriage, gringo old-timers advised *against* marriage between Creoles and gringos. Creole women, it was felt, were unable or unwilling to teach their children the value of progress. There still remains a good deal of prejudice against intermarriage. Instances of mixed marriages continue to be part of the repertoire of village gossip and are cited as the reason why a gringo does not do as well economically as his peers and why his sons and even his grandsons do not show an entrepreneurial spirit. A Creole woman, after all, it is believed, cannot be expected to encourage the values of hard work and sacrifice in her husband and children.[34]

Sarmiento had been certain that with European immigration would come cities because civilization was synonymous with them. But in spite of massive immigration and the growth of cities, Argentina in many ways continues to resemble the republic of Sarmiento's time with its pampas relentlessly challenging the borders of its towns and cities, fragmenting the country. And the rural world, which nineteenth-century urban elites damned as barbarian and uncivilized, still has this reputation, with both its positive and negative connotations. Today, while campo children often envy their peers in the towns and cities and hope some day to live in a tall building, their parents have frequently rejected the more urban world and prefer the countryside, sometimes not making a trip to the nearest town for months at a time, and then only with reluctance. If they are Creole peons, they may feel unsure and uncomfortable—their campo culture showing, their lack of experience and vulnerability, their backwardness and lack of refinement all too visible. But even if they are gringos they may well reject the urban life, viewing it as a corrupting influence and resisting sending their children to school there. These are the descendants of immigrants, who, according to Sarmiento, were to have brought with them a disposition for the civilized life of the town. Instead, if Sarmiento were alive today, he would find that many of them live contentedly with a minimum of modern comforts and pride themselves on being as rustic as the campo itself.[35]

Contemporary Argentine society is not without its critics of the legacy of the times and policies of Sarmiento and his fellow statesmen—and this is the other side to the nineteenth-century's legacy of civilization and barbarism.

While Sarmiento did not really address himself to working out the details of broad immigration policies, every generation in Argentina has had to deal with a potentially volatile society composed of Creoles impoverished by a new economic situation in the republic and of newcomers—non-Spanish speakers, sometimes non-Catholics, non-campo people—with different values. But interestingly, in some areas of the republic, the "descendants of immigrants, themselves once considered progressive outsiders," have been replaced by a new group of outsiders who see themselves as the new breed of progressives. The more entrenched gringos with deeper roots in their villages now echo the old Creole plea—"to let their world remain the same so that they can continue their way of life."[36]

There are those who see a negative moral dimension to the immigrant's success in Argentina. Efforts initiated by some gringos to help Creole schoolchildren, to provide recreational activities for them, and to teach them technical skills are attempts to make gringos aware of their at least partial responsibility. And some gringos emphasize Creoles' generosity and willingness to do hard manual labor that gringos refuse to do and the injustice of gringo feelings of superiority. There are also gringos who see the distinction between Creole and gringo as diminishing. And there are now critics who maintain that gringos are not as progressive as they would like to seem. But the attitude of these critics just reaffirms that society continues to judge people on the basis of the old immigrant values of hard work and progress. Much has remained unchanged. Hearing the Creole taunts at soccer games, gringos readily respond with shouts of "worthless Indians," and even educated people frequently refer to "that gringo" and "that creole."[37]

Sarmiento could not have foreseen the divisions in society created by mass immigration. In the heady atmosphere of nineteenth-century liberalism and positivism, he had every confidence in his country's ability to change its politics and economy, its values and culture, and its ethnicity. As the villagers in Entre Ríos attest to so well, the individuals involved in working out the national immigration policy moved this transformation in their own way and continue to play an important role in the direction it takes. It has often been asserted that "Argentina is a country without Argentines," and, in fact, the ideal of Europe has never been out of sight for long. Argentina is thought of as a European country and was still advertising itself as such in Europe in the 1970s in order to appear attractive to prospective immigrants.[38] Thus continues the crisis of identity, the lack of national consensus among Argentines, in which the alluvial immigration of the nineteenth century played a major part.

NOTES

1. Dirección de Inmigración, Argentina, *Resumen estadístico del movimiento migratorio en la República Argentina, años 1857–1924* (Buenos Aires: Talleres Gráfico del Ministerio de Agricultura de la Nación, 1925).
2. Domingo F. Sarmiento, *Obras completas*, vol. 23, *Inmigración y colonización* (53 vols., Buenos Aires: Editorial Luz del Día, 1948–1956).
3. Carl E. Solberg, *Immigration and Nationalism: Argentina and Chile, 1890–1914* (Austin: University of Texas Press, 1970), 38.
4. Sarmiento, *Obras completas*, vol. 13, *Argirópolis*, 91. See also ibid., vols. 37–38, *Conflicto y armonías de las razas en América*.
5. See ibid., vol. 37, for this argument.
6. On the racial aspects of this policy, see George Reid Andrews, *The Afro-Argentines of Buenos Aires, 1800–1900* (Madison: University of Wisconsin Press, 1980), 103–107.
7. Solberg, *Immigration*, 18–19.
8. Domingo F. Sarmiento, *Civilización i barbarie. Vida de Juan Facundo Qiroga. I aspecto físico, costumbres, i abitos de la República arjentina* (Santiago: Imprenta del Progreso, 1845), 3.
9. Domingo F. Sarmiento, *Life in the Argentine Republic in the Days of the Tyrants, or Civilization and Barbarism. With a Biographical Sketch of the Author by Mrs. Horace Mann* (New York: Hafner Press, 1971), 46–48.
10. Sarmiento, *Obras completas*, vol. 5, *Viajes por Europa, África i América, 1845–1847*, 301.
11. Sarmiento, *Argirópolis*, 71.
12. Sarmiento, *Inmigración*, 176.
13. Sarmiento, *Life in the Argentine Republic*, 247.
14. David Rock, *Argentina, 1516–1982: From Spanish Colonization to the Falklands War* (Berkeley: University of California Press, 1985), 143. Sarmiento denounced campaigns to simplify Argentina's naturalization procedures.
15. Kristin H. Ruggiero, *And Here the World Ends: The Life of an Argentine Village* (Stanford: Stanford University Press, 1988), 7.
16. Ibid., 20.
17. Ibid., 15–16.
18. Ibid., 16.
19. Ibid., 19.
20. Ibid., 20.
21. Ibid., 21.
22. "The gaucho does not labor; he finds his food and raiment ready to his hand." Sarmiento, *Life in the Argentine Republic*, 22–23.
23. Ruggiero, *And Here the World Ends*, 22 and 68.

24. Ibid., 18–19.
25. Ibid., 19.
26. Ibid., 72.
27. Ibid., 67.
28. Ibid., 78.
29. Ibid., 20–21.
30. Quoted in ibid., 21.
31. Ibid., 66.
32. Ibid., 67.
33. Quoted in ibid., 19–20.
34. Ibid., 21.
35. Ibid., 86 and 124.
36. Ibid., 43–44.
37. Ibid., 67.
38. On Argentina's continuing pride in being a European, "white" nation, see Andrews, *Afro-Argentines,* 107 and 214–215.

Selected Bibliography

This bibliography is essentially a guide to the first American, English, French, and Spanish editions of the works of Sarmiento and to the first appearance of a foreword for an edited work of Sarmiento. Editions other than the first are included only if they have an intrinsic value of their own, or if the first edition could not be located. As a general rule, the reprints and later editions used by the contributors to this volume are not listed here. They are adequately identified in the endnotes. The bibliography does include some of the major works that discuss Sarmiento or significant issues of the period. Journal articles are not included.

WORKS BY SARMIENTO

Sarmiento, Domingo Faustino. *Ambas Américas, revista de educación, bibliografía i agricultura, bajo los auspicios de Domingo F. Sarmiento.* New York: Hallet and Breen, 1867–1868.

———. *Análisis de las cartillas, silabarios y otros métodos de lectura conocidos y practicados en Chile, por el director de la Escuela Normal.* Santiago de Chile: Imprenta del Progreso, 1842.

———. *The Argentine Republic. Resources, Character, and Condition. Letter from the Argentine Minister.* New York: n.p., 1865.

———. *Arjirópolis; o La capital de los estados confederados del Río de la Plata. Solución de las dificultades que embarazan la pacificación permanente del Río de la Plata, por medio de la convocación de un congreso, i la creación de una capital en la isla de Martín García, de cuya posesión (hoi en poder de la Francia) dependen la libre navegación de los ríos, i la independencia, desarrollo y libertad del Paraguay, el Uruguay i las provincias argentinas del litoral.* Santiago de Chile: Impr. de J. Belín i Cia., 1850.

———. *Argyropolis; Ou, la capitale des États Confédérés du Rio de la Plata, solution des difficultés qui empêchent la pacification définitive des provinces du Rio de la Plata, au moyen de la convocation d'un congrès national et de la création d'une capitale dans l'Ile de Martin-Garcia, aujourd'hui en possession de la France . . . pub. à Santiago de Chili.* Translated by J. M. B. Lenoir. 2d ed., revised and completed by Ange Champgobert. Paris: E. Belín, 1851.

———. *Argirópolis.* Edited by Ernesto Quesada. Buenos Aires: "La Cultura Argentina," 1916.

———. *Bosquejo de la biografía de D. Dalmacio Velez Saarsfield.* Buenos Aires: Impr. de la Tribuna, 1875.

———. *Campaña en el ejército grande aliado de Sud-América,* 1st installment, Santiago de Chile: Impr. de J. Belín, n.d.

———. *Campaña en el ejercito grande aliado de Sud America del teniente coronel D. F. Sarmiento.* Rio de Janeiro: Impr. Imp. y Const. de J. Villeneuve y Cia., 1852.

———. *Campaña en el ejército grande aliado de Sud América.* Edited by Tulio Halperín Donghi. Mexico City: Fondo de Cultura Económica, 1958.

———. *Campaña en el ejército grande.* Selections and foreword by Javier Fernández. Buenos Aires: Editorial Universitaria, 1962.

———. *Candidato á la presidencia de Chile para 1851, D. Manuel Montt.* Santiago de Chile: Impr. de J. Belín i Cia., 1851.

———. *El Carapachay; Imágenes de las islas del delta del Paraná.* Buenos Aires: Editorial Universitaria de Buenos Aires, 1974.

———. *Cartas confidenciales de Sarmiento a M. R. García (1866–1872).* Buenos Aires: Impr. de Coni Hermanos, 1917.

———. *Cartas de Sarmiento a la señora María Mann.* Buenos Aires: Impr. de la Universidad, 1936.

———. *Cartas y discursos políticos; itinerario de una pasión republicana.* Selections and foreword by José P. Barreiro. Buenos Aires: Ediciones Culturales Argentinas, Ministerio de Educación y Justicia, Dirección General de Cultura, 1965.

———. *Los caudillos; El general fray Félix Aldao. El último caudillo de la montonera de los llanos: El Chacho.* Buenos Aires: El Ateneo, 1928.

———. *Cien paginas á propósito de opiniones legales sobre la facultad de imponer en las herencias transversales ó las mandas en beneficio del alma.* Buenos Aires: Biedma, 1882.

———. *Las ciento y una. Polémico con Juan B. Alberdi. Precedida por la "Carta de Yungay" a d. Justo José de Urquiza.* Buenos Aires: "La Cultura Argentina," 1916.

———. *Las ciento y una. Polémico con Alberdi.* Foreword by Miguel Cane. 2d ed., Buenos Aires: Editorial Sopena, 1941.

———. *Chile: Descripciones, viajes, episodios, costumbres.* Selections and foreword by Narciso Binayán. Buenos Aires: Editorial Universitaria de Buenos Aires, 1961.

———. *El Ciudadano arjentino D. F. Sarmiento electo diputado á la lejislatura del estado de Buenos-Ayres: a sus electores.* Santiago de Chile: Imprenta de Julio Belín i Cia., 1854.

———. *Civilización i barbarie. Vida de Juan Facundo Qiroga. I aspecto fisico, costumbres, i abitos de la República arjentina.* Santiago de Chile: Imprenta del Progreso, 1845.

———. *Civilisation et barbarie; Moeurs, coutumes, caractères des peuples argentins. Facundo Quiroga et Aldao.* Translated and edited by A. Giraud. Paris: A. Bertrand, 1853.

———. *El civilizador; Síntesis del pensamiento vivo de Sarmiento.* Selections and foreword by Julio R. Barcos. Buenos Aires: Ediciones A. Zamora, 1961.

———. *Comentarios de la Constitución de la Confederación Arjentina, con numerosos documentos ilustrativos del texto.* Santiago: Impr. de J. Belín i Cia., 1853.

———. *Comentarios de la Constitución de la Confederación Argentina, con numerosos documentos ilustrativos del texto.* Foreword by Clodomiro Zavalía. Buenos Aires: Talleres Gráficos Argentina de L. J. Rosso, 1929.

——. *Condición del extranjero en América*. Foreword by Ricardo Rojas. Buenos Aires: Libreria "La Facultad," de J. Roldán, 1928.
——. *Conflicto y armonias de las razas en América*. Buenos Aires: S. Ostwald, 1883.
——. *Conflicto y armonias de las razas en América*. Edited by José Ingenieros. Buenos Aires: "La Cultura Argentina," 1915.
——. *Contra Rosas*. Buenos Aires: "El Ateneo," 1934.
——. *Convención de San-Nicolás de los Arroyos*. Santiago de Chile: Imprenta de Julio Belín i Cia., 1852.
——. *Correspondencia entre Sarmiento y Lastarria, 1844–1888*. Edited by María Luisa del Pino de Carbone. Buenos Aires: Privately printed, 1954.
——. *Cuatro conferencias: Espíritu y condiciones de la historia de América. La doctrina Monroe. Darwin. Bibliotecas populares*. Foreword by Aristóbulo del Valle. Buenos Aires: El Ateneo, 1928.
——. *Darwin, en una conferencia, seguido de El congreso de Tucumán y su espíritu*. Buenos Aires: Tip. de El Nacional, 1882.
——. *Sr. Dr. D. Salvador M. del Carril*. Buenos Aires: n.p., 1858.
——. *Derecho de ciudadania en el estado de Buenos Aires*. Santiago de Chile: Imprenta de Julio Belín y Cia., 1852.
——. *Diario des gastos, libreta llevada por Sarmiento en sus viajes, 1845–1847*. Unpublished manuscript. Edited by Antonio P. Castro. Buenos Aires: Museo Histórico Sarmiento, 1950.
——. *Diario de un viaje de Nueva York a Buenos Aires, de 23 de julio al 20 de agosto de 1868*. Santiago de Chile: Crux del Sur, 1944.
——. *Discurso de S.E. el Sr. Presidente de la República en la solemne inauguración del Observatorio Astronómico argentino, verificada en la ciudad de Córdoba, el 24 de octubre de 1871*. Córdoba: Imprenta del "Eco de Córdoba," 1871.
——. *Discurso en honor de la bandera nacional al inaugurar la estátua del general Belgrano, el 24 de setiembre de 1873*. Buenos Aires: Impr. de La Tribuna, 1873.
——. *Discurso inaugural de la Esposición nacional de Córdoba pronunciado por S.E. el Sr. Presidente de la República el 15 de octubre de 1871*. Buenos Aires: Imprenta Americana, 1871.
——. *Discurso presentado para su recepción en el Instituto Istórico de Francia*. Valparaiso: Imprenta Europea, 1848.
——. *Discursos parlamentarios*. Foreword by Alfredo L. Palacios. 2 vols. Buenos Aires: W. M. Jackson, 1933.
——. *Los discursos populares de D. F. Sarmiento, 1839–1883. (Arreglados por A. Belín Sarmiento)*. Buenos Aires: Impr. Europea, 1883.
——. *Documentos relativos a los sucesos ocurridos por motivo de las circulares con que señor Ministro del Interior comunicó a los Gobernadores su nombramiento al ministerio*. Buenos Aires: Imprenta de *El Nacional*, 1879.
——. *Educación común. Memoria presentada al Consejo universitario de Chile*. Buenos Aires: Impr. del Nacional, 1855.
——. *Educación común en el estado de Buenos Aires*. Santiago de Chile: Impr. de J. Belín i Cia., 1855.
——. *Educación de las mujeres y algunos documentos estranjeros i nacionales: Publicación que se hace de orden del ciudadano Melchor Urquidi*. Cochamba: Tipografía de Quevedo, 1861.
——. *De la educación popular*. Santiago de Chile: Impr. de J. Belín i Cia., 1849.
——. *De la educación popular*. Buenos Aires: Imprenta y Litografía "Mariano Moreno," 1896.
——. *Educación popular*. Foreword by R. Rojas. Buenos Aires: J. Roldán, 1915.
——. *Emigración alemana al Río de la Plata, memoria escrita en Alemania por D. F.*

Sarmiento, i enriquecida con notas sobre el Chaco i los paises adyacentes a los ríos interiores de la América del Sud, por el dr. Vappaüs. Translated from German by Guillermo Hilliger. Santiago: Impr. de J. Belín i Cia., 1851.

——. *Epistolario entre Sarmiento y Posse, 1845–1888.* Edited by Antonio P. Castro. 2 vols. Buenos Aires: Museo Histórico Sarmiento, 1946–1947.

——. *Epistolario intimo.* Buenos Aires: Ediciones Culturales Argentinas, Ministerio de Educación y Justicia, Dirección General de Cultura, 1963.

——. *Escritos sobre San Martín.* Selections and foreword by Rosauro Pérez Aubone. Buenos Aires: Instituto Nacional Sanmartiniano, 1966.

——. *La escuela sin la religión de mi mujer.* Buenos Aires: L. J. Rosso y Cía., 1918.

——. *Las escuelas: base de la prosperidad i de la república de los Estados Unidos. Informe al ministro de instrucción pública de la República Arjentina. Pasado por D. F. Sarmiento.* New York: D. Appleton, 1866.

——. *Espíritu y condiciones de la historia en América. Memoria leida el 11 de octubre de 1858 en el Ateneo del Plata por D. D. F. Sarmiento, nombrado director de historia.* Buenos Aires: Imprenta Argentina del "Nacional," 1858.

——. *Facundo; ó, Civilización i barbarie en les pampas arjentinas.* 4th ed. in Spanish, New York: D. Appleton and Co., 1868.

——. *Facundo; ó, Civilización i barbarie en las pampas argentinas.* 4th ed. in Spanish, Paris: Hachette, 1874.

——. *Facundo; Ó, Civilización i barbarie.* 3 vols. Montevideo: Tip. Americana, 1888–1889.

——. *Facundo.* Introduction by Joaquín V. González. Buenos Aires: L. J. Rosso, 1911.

——. *Facundo; civilización y barbarie en la República Argentina.* Foreword by R. Blanco-Fombona. Madrid: Editorial-América, 1916.

——. *Facundo.* Foreword by Ricardo Rojas. Buenos Aires: Librería "La Facultad," de J. Roldán, 1916.

——. *Facundo.* Translated by Marcel Bataillon; foreword by Anibal Ponce. Paris: Institut International de Cooperation Intellectuelle, 1934.

——. *Facundo.* Portuguese translation by Carlos Maul. 2d ed., Rio de Janeiro: Edição do Biblioteca Militar, 1938.

——. *Facundo; Edición crítica y documentada.* Foreword by Alberto Palcos. La Plata: Universidad Nacional de La Plata, 1938.

——. *Facundo.* Edited by Delia S. Etcheverry; introduction by Inés Cárdenas de Monner Sans. Buenos Aires: Ediciones Estrada, 1940.

——. *Facundo. Reseña de la historia cultural de la Argentina,* by Arturo Capdevila. Buenos Aires: W. M. Jackson, Inc., 1945.

——. *Facundo. Recuerdos de provincia.* Foreword and index of Americanisms by Juan Rómulo Fernández. Biographical notes by F. S. R. Madrid: Aguilar, 1950.

——. *Facundo; Ó, Civilización y barbarie en las pampas argentinas.* Edited by Raúl Moglia. Graphics by Nicasio. Buenos Aires: Ediciones Peuser, 1955.

——. *Facundo.* Edited by Emma Susana Speratti Piñero. Mexico City: Universidad Autónoma de México, 1957.

——. *Facundo.* Edited by Alberto Palcos. Enlarged reedition of the critical and documented edition published by the Universidad Nacional de La Plata, 1962. Buenos Aires: Ediciones Culturales Argentinas, 1962.

——. *Facundo; Ó, civilización y barbarie.* Foreword by Carlos Alberto Erro. Buenos Aires: SUR, 1962.

——. *Facundo, civilización y barbarie, vida de Juan Facundo Quiroga.* Introduction and chronological index by Raimundo Lazo. Mexico City: Editorial Porrúa, 1966.

——. *Facundo.* Introduction by Pedro Henríquez Ureña. 3d ed., Buenos Aires: Editorial Losada, 1969.

——. *Facundo; civilizacion y barbarie.* Introduction by Roberto Yahni. Madrid: Alianza, 1970.

——. *Facundo: civilización y barbarie.* Edited by Luis Ortega Galindo. Madrid: Editora Nacional, 1975.

——. *Facundo.* Introduction by Jorge Luis Borges. Buenos Aires: Librería El Ateneo Editorial, 1974.

——. *Fray Félix Aldao, esquisses historiques sur l'amérique du sud.* Translated and edited by M. Eugène Tandonnet. Bordeaux: Imprimerie d'Emile Crugy, 1847.

——. *El general San Martín.* Introduction by Fermín Estrella Gutiérrez. Buenos Aires: Editorial Kapelusz, 1950.

——. *Ideario.* Selections and foreword by Luis Alberto Sánchez. Santiago: Ediciones Ercilla, 1943.

——. *Informe del comisionado especial para la creación de una escuela modelo, decretada por la municipalidad de la ciudad de Buenos Aires.* Buenos Aires: Imprenta Argentina, 1857.

——. *Instrucción para los maestros de escuela, para enseñar a leer por el método gradual de lectura.* Santiago de Chile: Imprenta de los Tribunales, 1846.

——. *Introducción á las memorias militares y foja de servicios de Domingo F. Sarmiento.* Buenos Aires: Imprenta "Europa,"1884.

——. *Itinerario del primer cuerpo de ejército de Buenos Aires á las órdenes del jeneral D. Wenceslao Paunero. 1861.* Buenos Aires: Imprenta del "Comercio del Plata," 1862.

——. *Juicio crítico. Conflicto y armonias de las razas en América. Artículos publicados en el Comercial de Buenos Aires.* Buenos Aires: Imp. Inglesa de Lowe, Anderson y Cia., 1883.

——. *Juicios de Sarmiento sobre la mujer, 1888–1938.* Buenos Aires: Escuela Nacional Superior de Comercio de Ramos Mejía, 1939.

——. *Life in the Argentine Republic in the Days of the Tyrants; or, Civilization and Barbarism. With a Biographical Sketch of the Author, by Mrs. Horace Mann.* New York: Hurd and Houghton, 1868.

——. *Life in the Argentine Republic in the Days of the Tyrants; or Civilization and Barbarism. With a Biographical Sketch of the Author, by Mrs. Horace Mann.* London: n.p., 1868.

——. *Memoria enviada al Instituto histórico de Francia sobre la cuestión decima del programa de los trabajos que debe presentar la 1ª clase, "Quelle est la situation actuelle des républiques du Centre et du Sud de l'Amérique."* Santiago de Chile: Impr. de J. Belín i Cia., 1853.

——. *Memoria leida a la Facultad de humanidades [de la Universidad de Chile] el 17 de octubre de 1843.* Santiago de Chile: Impr. de La Opinión, 1843.

——. *Memorias.* Introduction by Luis de Paola. Buenos Aires: Ediciones Culturales Argentinas, Ministerio de Educación y Justicia, Dirección General de Cultura, 1963.

——. *Metodo de lectura gradual. Adoptado por la Facultad de [H]umanidades para la enseñanza pública.* Santiago de Chile: Imprenta de los Tribunales, 1846.

——. *Mi vida.* Edited by Julio Noé. 2 vols. Buenos Aires: A. Estrada y Cía., 1938.

——. *Don Manuel Montt, su época, y sus adversarios políticos.* Santiago de Chile: Impr. de la Sociedad, 1851.

——. *North and South America. A Discourse Delivered Before the Rhode-Island Historical Society, December 27, 1865. By His Excellency, Domingo Faustino Sarmiento,*

Argentine Minister to the United States. Providence, Rhode Island: Knowles, Antony & Co., Printers, 1866.

———. *Obras de D. F. Sarmiento.* 53 vols. Paris: Belín Hermanos, 1889–1909.

———. *Obras de D. F. Sarmiento.* 53 vols. Santiago de Chile: Imprenta Gutenberg, 1885–1903.

———. *Obras. Publicadas bajo los auspicios del gobierno arjentino.* 52 vols. Santiago de Chile: Impr. Gutenberg, 1887–1902.

———. *Obras de D. F. Sarmiento.* 53 vols. Buenos Aires: Moreno, 1887–1900.

———. *Obras de D. F. Sarmiento.* 53 vols. Paris: Belín Hermanos, 1895–1909.

———. *Obras completas.* 53 vols., Buenos Aires: Editorial Luz del Día, 1948–1956.

———. *Obras selectas.* Edited, revised, and with an introduction by Enrique de Gandía. 3 vols. Buenos Aires: Editorial "La Facultad," 193-.

———. *Observaciones con motivo de los artículos suscritos por J. B. A. en El Mercurio de Valparaiso, con el título de CUESTIONES AMERICANAS; i que son un examen de la Constitucion del Estado de Buenos-Aires, por Mariano E. de Sarratea, ciudadano arjentino, del Estado de Buenos-Aires.* Santiago de Chile: Imprenta de Julio Belín i Cia., 1854.

———. *Páginas confidenciales; Sus luchas, sus pasiones, sus triunfos, las mujeres en su vida.* Introduction by Alberto Palcos. Buenos Aires: Elevación, 1944.

———. *Páginas escogidas.* Edited by Carlos Alberto Erro. Buenos Aires: Ediciones Culturales Argentinas, 1963.

———. *El pensamiento vivo de Sarmiento,* by Ricardo Rojas. Buenos Aires: Editorial Losada, 1941.

———. *Polémica literaria.* Buenos Aires: Editorial Cartago, 1955.

———. *Política de Rosas.* Buenos Aires: El Ateneo, 1930.

———. *Proceso al Chacho de Domingo Faustino Sarmiento [y] José Hernández.* Introduction by León Pomer. Buenos Aires: Ediciones Caldén, 1968.

———. *Prospecto de un establecimiento de educación para señoritas. Primero escrito de Sarmiento.* Introduction by Victor M. Badano. Paraná: Impresora Argentina, 1942.

———. *Protestation contre le gouvernement du général Rosas à Buenos Ayres.* Translated by M. Ange de Champgobert. Paris: n.p., 1850.

———. *Recuerdos de provincia por el autor de Civilización i barbarie.* Santiago de Chile: Impr. de J. Belín i Cia., 1850.

———. *Recuerdos de provincia.* With an appendix on his death by Martín García Merou. Buenos Aires: "La Cultura Argentina," 1916.

———. *Recuerdos de provincia.* Foreword by Ricardo Rojas. Buenos Aires: Libreria "La Facultad," de J. Roldán y Cia, 1927.

———. *Recuerdos de provincia.* Foreword by Alberto Palcos. Buenos Aires: W. M. Jackson, 1944.

———. *Recuerdos de provincia.* Introduction by Jorge Luis Borges. Buenos Aires: Emecé Editores, 1944.

———. *Recuerdos de provincia.* Introduction by Carlos Alberto Erro. Buenos Aires: Editorial Norte, 1962.

———. *San Juan, sus hombres y sus actos, en la Regeneración Argentina. Narración de los acontecimientos que han tenido lugar en aquella provincia antes y después de la caida de Rosas.* Santiago de Chile: Imprenta de Julio Belín y Cia., 1852.

———. *D. F. Sarmiento, diputado al congreso nacional por San Juan, al jeneral Justo José de Urquiza, vencedor en Caseros.* Santiago de Chile: Imprenta de Julio Belín i Cia., 1852.

———. *Sarmiento, director de la Escuela normal, 1842–1845.* Foreword by Ricardo Donoso. Santiago de Chile: Imprenta Universitaria, 1942.

——. *A Sarmiento Anthology*. Translated by Stuart Edgar Grummon. Edited by Allison Williams Bunkley. Princeton: Princeton University Press, 1948.

——. *Sarmiento en el destierro; Edición ordenada, con notas y un estudio por Armando Donoso. Las polémicas del ostracismo. Contra la gramática. Réplicas a don Andrés Bello. La lengua popular y la literatura. Contra el romanticismo. Mi defensa.* Buenos Aires: M. Gleizer, 1927.

——. *Sarmiento y la educación pública.* Buenos Aires: Editorial Losada, 1962.

——. *Sarmiento-Mitre; Correspondencia, 1846–1868.* Buenos Aires: Impr. de Coni Hermanos, 1911.

——. *Una sentencia con cuerpo de delito y sin reo, sin rey, sin ley, sin delito, sin fuero, sin tradición, sin verdad, sin efecto. Autor (que lo firme el diablo, cuando las papas queman).* Buenos Aires: Imp. de "El Debate," 1885.

——. *Solución definitiva de hecho y de derecho de la cuestión nacional argentina.* n.p., n.d.

——. *El tirano José Virasoro.* Buenos Aires: Imprenta Argentina de *El Nacional,* 1860.

——. *Sarmiento's Travels in the United States.* Translated and edited by Michael Aaron Rockland. Princeton: Princeton Univerity Press, 1970.

——. *Viaje a Chile del canónigo Don Juan Maria Mastai-Ferreti oi sumo pontifice Pio, papa IX;* Translated from the Italian and with an index. Santiago de Chile: Impr. de la Opinión, 1848.

——. *Viajes en Europa, África i América.* 2 vols., Santiago de Chile: Impr. de J. Belín i Cia., 1849–1851.

——. *Viajes en Europa, África y América.* 2 vols. in 1. Buenos Aires: Impr. de Mayo, 1854.

——. *Viajes en Europa, África i América.* Introduction by Julio Noé. 3 vols. Buenos Aires: Administración: Vaccaro, 1922.

——. *Viajes.* Introduction by Alberto Palcos. 3 vols. Buenos Aires: Hachette, 1955–1957.

——. *Vida de Dominguito. In memoriam del valiente y deplorado captan Domingo Fidel Sarmiento muerto en Curupaití a los veinte años de edad.* Buenos Aires: Sociedad Tipográfica "El Censor," 1886.

——. *Vida de Dominguito.* Foreword by Antonio Sagarna. Buenos Aires: M. Gleizer, 1927.

——. *Vida de Dominguito.* Foreword by Gaspar Mortillaro. Buenos Aires: Editorial Araujo, 1938.

——. *Vida de Dominguito.* Foreword by Germán Berdiales, drawings by Alejandro Sirio. Buenos Aires: Instituto Amigos del Libro Argentino, 1954.

——. *La vida de Dominguito.* Edited by José Luis Lanuza. Buenos Aires: Ediciones Culturales Argentinas, Ministerio de Educación y Justicia, Dirección General de Cultura, 1963.

——. *Vida de N. S. Jesucristo, la tradujo y divulgó con su nombre el ilustre pedagogo como la mejor simiente de la paz social.* With an introduction by Ricardo Salas Edwards on Sarmiento's educational ideas. Santiago de Chile: Ediciones Ercilla, 1937.

——. *Vida de Abran Lincoln, décimo sesto presidente de los Estados Unidos. Precidida de una introducción.* New York: D. Appleton and Co., 1866.

——. *Vida de Abran Lincoln, décimo sesto presidente de los Estados Unidos. Precidida de una introducción.* 2d ed. New York: D. Appleton and Co. 1866.

——. *Vida y escritos del coronel D. Francisco J. Muñiz.* Buenos Aires: F. Lajouane, 1885.

——. *Vida de Facundo Quiroga, i aspecto fisico, costumbres i hábitos de la República*

Arjentina, seguido de apuntes biográficos sobre el jeneral frai Félix Aldao, por el autor de Arjirópolis. Seguida de un exánen crítico, traducido de la Revista de ambos mundo. 2d ed. Santiago de Chile: Impr. de J. Belín Cia., 1851.

——. *Vida de Juan Facundo Quiroga.* Introduction and bibliography by Benito Varela Jácome. Barcelona: Editorial Bruyuera, 1970.

——. *El Zonda de San Juan, 1839.* Republished for the Academia nacional de la historia. Foreword by Juan Pablo Echagüe. Buenos Aires: G. Kraft Ltda., 1939.

WORKS BY OTHERS

Alberdi, Juan Bautista. *La barbarie histórica de Sarmiento.* Buenos Aires: Ediciones Pampa y Cielo, 1964.

——. *Grandes y pequeños hombres del Plata.* Paris: Garnier Hermanos, 1912.

——. *Proceso a Sarmiento.* Foreword by León Pomer. Buenos Aires: Ediciones Caldén, 1967.

Alderete, Apolonio. *Sarmiento y la Crónica (el espíritu de una campaña periodistica).* Rosario: Ediciones Trabajo, 1971.

Álvarez, Florencio. *Sarmiento agricultor.* Buenos Aires: Editorial América, 1945.

Anderson Imbert, Enrique. *Una aventura amorosa de Sarmiento; Cartas de Ida Wickersham.* Buenos Aires: Editorial Losada, 1969.

——. *Genio y figura de Sarmiento.* Buenos Aires: Editorial Universitaria de Buenos Aires, 1967.

Arce, José. *Las manos llenas de verdades; Un episodio político electoral.* Buenos Aires: Museo Roca, 1966.

Arías Robalino, Augusto. *Tres ensayos.* Quito: Impr. de la Universidad Central, 1941.

Arrieta, Rafael Alberto. *Estudios en tres literaturas.* Buenos Aires: Editorial Losada, 1939.

Ayala, Eusebio. *Aspectos americanos de la personalidad de Sarmiento; Conferencia pronunciada el 11 de septiembre de 1939, en el Museo Histórico Sarmiento.* Buenos Aires: Museo Histórico Sarmiento, 1939.

Barrenechea, Ana María y Beatriz R. Lavandera. *Domingo Faustino Sarmiento.* Buenos Aires: Centro Editor de América Latina, 1967.

Belín Sarmiento, Augusto. *Epistolario de Sarmiento.* Buenos Aires: "Coni," 1925.

Bengoa, Juan León. *La vida gloriosa de Sarmiento; Film del hombre que realizó su sueño.* Montevideo: Sociedad Amigos del Libro Rioplatense, 1936.

Berdiales, Germán. *El maestro de América; Vida anecdótica de Sarmiento; de El Garrascal a Chungay, 1811–1849.* Buenos Aires: Editorial Acme, 1961.

Bilbao, Francisco. *Cartas de Bilbao á Sarmiento recopiladas por unos amigos de la verdad.* Buenos Aires: Imprenta Rural, 1875.

Blanco-Fombona, Rufino. *Grandes escritores de América.* (Siglo XIX). Madrid: Renacimiento, 1917.

Bosch Vinelli, Julia Beatriz. *Urquiza y su tiempo.* 2d ed., revised. Buenos Aires: Editorial Universitaria de Buenos Aires, 1980.

——. *Sarmiento y Urquiza; del unitarismo al federalismo.* Paraná: Imprenta y Casa Editora Coni, 1938.

Botana, Natalio R. *La tradición republicana.* Buenos Aires: Editorial Sudamericana, 1984.

Bravo, Héctor. *Sarmiento, pedagogo social; las concepciones sociales en la pedagogía de Sarmiento.* Buenos Aires: Editorial Universitaria de Buenos Aires, 1965.

Bucich, Antonio Juan. *Luchas y rutas de Sarmiento.* Buenos Aires: Talleres

"Gráficos Maggiolo," 1942.
Bunkley, Allison Williams. *The Life of Sarmiento*. Princeton: Princeton University Press, 1952.
Calle, Jorge Alberto. *El pasajero sugerente (glosario Sarmentino)*. Buenos Aires: M. Gleizer, 1925.
Campobassi, José Salvador. *La educación primaria desde 1810 hasta la sanción de la ley 1420*. Buenos Aires: Talleres Gráficos del Consejo N. de Educación, 1942.
———. *Sarmiento y Mitre; Hombres de Mayo y Caseros*. Buenos Aires: Editorial Losada, 1962.
———. *Sarmiento y su época*. 2 vols. Buenos Aires: Editorial Losada, 1975.
Carilla, Emilio. *El embajador Sarmiento, Sarmiento y los Estados Unidos*. Rosario: Universidad Nacional del Litoral, Facultad de Filosofía y Letras, Instituto de Letras, 1961.
———. *Lengua y estilo en Sarmiento*. La Plata: Universidad Nacional de La Plata, Facultad de Humanidades y Ciencias de la Educación, 1964.
Carsuzán, María Emma. *Sarmiento el escritor*. Buenos Aires: El Ateneo, 1949.
Castro, Antonio Pedro. *San Martín y Sarmiento; Conferencia pronunciada en el "Círculo Militar."* Buenos Aires: Museo Histórico Sarmiento, 1947.
———. *Sarmiento y Urquiza, dos caracteres opuestos, unidos por el amor a la patria; Interesante correspondencia*. Buenos Aires: Museo Histórico Sarmiento, 1954.
Castro, Isaac E. *Sarmiento ante la montonera*. Buenos Aires: Editorial Litex, 1970.
Castro, Juan Francisco. *Sarmiento y los ferrocarriles argentinos; Disertación pronunciada el 11 de setiembre de 1950*. Buenos Aires: Museo Histórico Sarmiento, 1950.
Chaparro, Félix A. *El logista Sarmiento*. Rosario: Tip. Llorden, 1956.
Correas, Edmundo. *Sarmiento and the United States*. Gainesville: University of Florida Press, 1961.
Corro, Gaspar Pío del. *Facundo y Fierro; La proscripción de los héroes*. Buenos Aires: Ediciones Castañeda, 1977.
Crowley, Francis G. *Domingo Faustino Sarmiento*. New York: Twayne Publishers, 1972.
Cúneo, Dardo. *Sarmiento y Unamuno*. 3rd ed., Buenos Aires: Editorial Pleamar, 1963.
Daliadiras, Héctor U. *Algo más sobre Sarmiento; á través de sus palabras y de sus obras*. 2d ed., Buenos Aires: Editorial Nuevo Orden, 1965.
Diego, Celia de. *Camino de luz y sombra; Obra teatral sobre la vida de Domingo Faustino Sarmiento, en los actos y un epílogo*. Buenos Aires: Talia, 1967.
Doll, Ramón. *Porqué fué unitario Sarmiento; Ensayo presentado al Primer Congreso de historia de Cuyo*. Mendoza: Ed. Di Bello, 1937.
Donoso, Armando. *Sarmiento en el destierro*. With notes and an essay. Buenos Aires: M. Gleizer, 1927.
Duarte, María P. de. *Anecdotario Sarmiento (300 anécdotas)*. Buenos Aires: Casa J. Peuser Ltda. 1927.
Echagüe, Juan Pablo. *Sarmiento crítico teatral*. Buenos Aires: "Coni," 1925.
———. *Paisajes y figuras de San Juan*. Buenos Aires: Editorial Tor, 1933.
———. *Seis figuras del Plata*. Buenos Aires: Editorial Losada, 1938.
Eggers-Lecour, Conrado E., ed. *Sarmiento; Estudio y antología*. Madrid: Compañía Bibliográfica Española, 1963.
Espinoza, Enrique. *El espíritu criollo*. Santiago de Chile: Babel, 1951.
Fariña Nuñez, Porfirio. *Los amores de Sarmiento*. Buenos Aires: Editorial Tor, 1935.
Fernández, Juan Rómulo. *Sarmiento (semblanza e iconografía)*. Buenos Aires: "Libreria del Colegio," 1938.

——. *Sarmiento, gobernador de San Juan.* Buenos Aires: n.p., 1964.

Font Ezcurra, Ricardo. *La unidad nacional. Edición definitiva aumentada con los artículos de Sarmiento en El progreso de Santiago de Chile.* Buenos Aires: Ediciones Theoría, 1961.

Franceschi, Gustavo Juan. *Sarmiento.* Buenos Aires: Editorial Criterio, 1938.

Franco, Luis Leopoldo. *Sarmiento entre dos fuegos.* Buenos Aires: Paidós, 1968.

Galvan Moreno, C. *Radiografía de Sarmiento, amplia visión de su vida y de su obra.* Buenos Aires: Editorial Claridad, 1938.

Gálvez, Manuel. *Vida de Sarmiento, el hombre de autoridad.* Buenos Aires: Emecé Editores, 1945.

Gamba, Carlos T. *Las gestas de la democracia. (Vidas heróicas). Los pueblos no quieren recordar. José Batlle y Ordóñez, Juan Montalve, Domingo Faustino Sarmiento, José Garibaldi, Víctor Hugo.* Montevideo: n.p., 1936.

García Martínez, José A. *Sarmiento y el arte de su tiempo.* Buenos Aires: Emecé Editores, 1979.

Chioldi, Américo Antonio. *Sarmiento en las crisis argentinas.* Buenos Aires: El Ateneo, 1948.

González, Joaquín Victor. *Mitre (con advertencia de Ricardo Levene).* Buenos Aires: "El Ateneo," 1931.

González Arrili, Bernardo. *Sarmiento, biografía.* Buenos Aires: J. Menéndez, 1938.

Guerra, José Guillermo. *Sarmiento, su vida i sus obras.* Santiago de Chile: Imprenta Elzeviriana, 1901.

Guerrero, César H. *Sarmiento, historiador y biógrafo.* Buenos Aires: El Ateneo, 1950.

——. *Mujeres de Sarmiento.* Buenos Aires: Privately printed, 1960.

——. *Domingo Soriano Sarmiento y su tocayo.* San Juan: Archivo Histórico y Administrativo, 1962.

——. *Sarmiento y "El Zonda."* San Juan: Museo Histórico y Biblioteca "Sarmiento," 1970.

——. *Sarmiento en su última visita a San Juan.* San Juan: Editorial Sanjuanina, 1973.

——. *Sarmiento, el pensador.* Buenos Aires: Ediciones Depalma, 1979.

Gutiérrez, Juan María. *Cartas de un porteño; Polémica en torno al idioma y a la Real academia española, sostenida con Juan Martínez Villergas, seguido de "Sarmenticidio."* Foreword by Ernesto Morales. Buenos Aires: Editorial Americana, 1942.

Hidalgo, Alberto. *Sarmiento y la cuestión de la Patagonia.* Rosario: Libreria y Editorial Ruiz, 1945.

Howe, Jennie E. *In Distant Climes and Other Years.* Buenos Aires: The American Press, 1931.

——. *En otros años y climas distantes.* Translated by Eduardo Rípodas. Buenos Aires: Raigal, 1951.

Iduarte, Andrés. *Sarmiento, Martí y Rodó.* Havana: Impr. "El Siglo XX," 1955.

Ingenieros, José. *Los iniciadores de la sociología argentina: Sarmiento, Alberdi y Echeverría.* Buenos Aires: P. Ingenieros, 1928.

Jitrik, Noé. *Muerte y resurrección de Facundo.* Buenos Aires: Centro Editor de América Latina, 1968.

Jones, Cyril A. *Sarmiento: "Facundo."* London: Grant and Cutler, 1974.

Jurado Padilla, Francisco. *Sarmiento y Vélez Sarsfield, una amistad patricia.* Foreword by Enrique Martínez. Córdoba: Impr. de la Universidad, 1948.

Katra, William H. *Domingo F. Sarmiento, Public Writer: (Between 1839 and 1852).* Tempe: Center for Latin American Studies, Arizona State University, 1985.

Lacay, Celina. *Sarmiento y la formación de la ideología de la clase dominante.* Buenos

Aires: Editorial Contrapunto, 1986.

Lagrange, Francisco. *Sarmiento y su época.* Córdoba: B. Cubas, 1918.

Landa, Augusto. *Sarmiento y el general Nazario Benavides; Conferencia pronunciada el 11 de septiembre de 1948.* Buenos Aires: Museo Histórico Sarmiento, 1951.

Levene, Ricardo. *Sarmiento, sociólogo de la realidad americana y argentina.* Buenos Aires: n.p., 1938.

———. *Fundación de escuelas públicas en la provincia de Buenos Aires durante el gobierno escolar de Sarmiento, 1856–1861, 1875–1881.* La Plata: Taller de Impresiones Oficiales, 1939.

Lobos, Porto. *Sarmiento y sus detractdores.* Córdoba: Biflignandi Ediciones, 1966.

Lorenzo-Rivero, Luis. *Larra y Sarmiento; Paralelismos históricos y literarios.* Madrid: Ediciones Guadarrama, 1968.

Lugones, Leopoldo. *Historia de Sarmiento. Estudio encargado por el presidente del Consejo nacional de educación, Dr. José M. Ramos Mexía.* 2d ed. Buenos Aires: Otero & Co., 1911.

———. *Historia de Sarmiento.* New ed., revised. Buenos Aires: Babel, 1931.

Luiggi, Alice Houston. *Sesenta y cinco valientes; Sarmiento y las maestras norteamericanas.* Foreword by Alberto Palcos. Buenos Aires: Editorial Agora, 1959.

———. *65 valiantes.* Gainesville: University of Florida Press, 1965.

Lusardo, João Baptista. *Sarmiento y el emperador don Pedro II; Conferencia pronunciada el 11 de septiembre de 1952.* Buenos Aires: Museo Histórico Sarmiento, 1954.

Martínez Estrada, Ezequiel. *Sarmiento.* Buenos Aires: Argos, 1946.

———. *Los invariantes histórico en el Facundo.* Buenos Aires: Viau, 1947.

———. *Meditaciones sarmientinas.* Santiago: Editorial Universitaria, 1968.

Maurín Navarro, Juan S. *La misión de Sarmiento en Chile en 1884 y la democratización de la cultura en Sud América.* Buenos Aires: Editorial "La Vanguardia," 1952.

Mayer, Jorge M. *Alberdi y su tiempo.* 2d ed., revised and enlarged, 2 vols. Buenos Aires: Distribudor Abeledo-Perrot, 1973.

Montt, Manuel S. *Sarmiento y Montt, una amistad internacional; Conferencia pronunciada el 11 de setiembre de 1951.* Buenos Aires: Museo Histórico Sarmiento, 1954.

Mortillaro, Gaspar. *Sarmiento en anécdotas, 1811–1888.* Buenos Aires: Ediciones de Sarmiento, 1961.

Moya, Ismael. *El americanismo en el teatro y la predica de Sarmiento.* Buenos Aires: Impr. de la Universidad, 1939.

Murray, Luis Alberto. *Pro y contra de Alberdi, y otros ensayos.* Foreword by Fermín Chavez. 2d ed., Buenos Aires: Editorial Sudestrada, 1969.

———. *Pro y contra de Sarmiento: Guía para maestros.* Foreword by Arturo Jauretche. Buenos Aires: A. Peña Lillo, 1974.

New York Chamber of Commerce of the State of New York. *Proceedings of the Chamber of Commerce of the State of New York, on Occasion of the Reception of Their Excellencies, Señor Joaquim Maria Nascentes de Azambuja, Minister of Brazil, and Señor Domingo Faustino Sarmiento, Minister of the Argentine Republic, to the United States, Thursday, November 1, 1866.* New York: J. W. Amerman, Printer, 1867.

Orgaz, Alfredo. *Tres ensayos sarmientinos.* Córdoba: Universidad Nacional de Córdoba, 1967.

Orgaz, Raúl Andrés. *Sarmiento y el naturalismo histórico.* Córdoba: Imprenta Argentina, Rossi, 1940.

Ortega Peña, Rodolfo, and Duhalde, Eduardo Luis. *Facundo y la montonera.*

Buenos Aires: Plus Ultra, 1968.

Palcos, Alberto. *Sarmiento, la vida, la obra, las ideas, el genio.* Buenos Aires: El Ateneo, 1929.

Paoli, Pedro de. *Sarmiento: Su gravitación en el desarrollo nacional.* Buenos Aires: Ediciones Theoría, 1964.

——. *Sarmiento y la usurpación del Magallanes; Réplica a las opiniones del Prof. José S. Campobassi.* Buenos Aires: Ediciones Theoría, 1968.

Patton, Elda Clayton. *Sarmiento in the United States.* Evansville, Ind.: University of Evansville Press, 1976.

Paz, José María. *Memorias postumas del brigadier general d. José M. Paz. Comprenden sus campañas, servicios y padecimientos, desde la guerra de la independencia, hasta su muerte, con variedad de otros documentos inéditos de alta importancia.* 4 vols. in 2. Buenos Aires: Impr. de la Revista, 1855.

Paz Soldán, Juan Pedro. *Domingo Faustino Sarmiento.* Buenos Aires: A. de Martino, 1911.

Pedroni, José B. *La hoja voladora.* Buenos Aires: Editorial Universitaria de Buenos Aires, 1961.

Peña, Milcíades. *Alberdi, Sarmiento, el 90; Límites del nacionalismo argentino en el siglo XIX.* Buenos Aires: Ediciones Fichas, 1970.

Pinilla, Norberto. *La polémica del romanticismo en 1842: V. F. López, D. F. Sarmiento, S. Sanfuentes.* Buenos Aires: Editorial Americalee, 1943.

Pisano, Natalio J. *La política agraria de Sarmiento: La lucha contra el latifundio.* Buenos Aires: Ediciones Depalma, 1980.

Ponce, Aníbal. *La vejez de Sarmiento. Amadeo Jacques. Nicolás Avellaneda. Lucio V. Mansilla. Eduardo Wilde. Lucio V. López. Miguel Cané.* Buenos Aires: Talleres Graficos Argentinos de L. J. Rosso, 1927.

——. *Sarmiento, constructor de la nueva Argentina.* Madrid: Espasa-Calpe, 1932.

Ponce, Manuel Antonio. *Sarmiento i sus doctrinas pedagójicas.* Valparaiso: Impr. i Lib. Americana de F. T. Lathrop, 1890.

Quiroga, Carlos Buenventura. *Sarmiento (hacia una reconstrucción del espíritu argentino).* Buenos Aires: Z. Zamora, 1961.

Ramella, Pablo A. *Sarmiento, Parlamentario; Conferencia pronunciada el 11 de septiembre de 1947.* Buenos Aires: Museo Histórico Sarmiento, 1947.

Ratto, Héctor Raúl, José Craviotto, and Humberto F. Burzio. *Sarmiento y la marina de guerra; Trabajos y conferencias.* Foreword by Humberto F. Burzio. Buenos Aires: Secretaría de Estado de Marina, Subsecretaría Departamento de Estudios Navales, 1963.

Rawson, Guillermo. *Polémicas con Sarmiento, discursos y escritos políticos.* Buenos Aires: El Ateneo, 1928.

Rebollo Paz, León. *Sarmiento, presidente.* Buenos Aires: n.p., 1968.

Richard Lavalle, Enrique. *Sarmiento.* 2d ed., Buenos Aires: Cabaut & Cia., 1911.

Rivas, Marcos P. *Sarmiento, mito y realidad.* Buenos Aires: Peña Lillo, 1961.

Rodríguez, Augusto G. *Sarmiento militar.* Foreword by D. Juan Pablo Echagüe. Buenos Aires: Ediciones Peuser, 1950.

Rojas, Ricardo. *El profeta de la pampa; Vida de Sarmiento.* Buenos Aires: Editorial Losada, 1945.

Romano Arena, José. *Sarmiento, educador (estudio objetivo-crítico).* Rosario: Imprenta Maxera & Cia., 1941.

Rosenthal, Mauricio. *Sarmiento y el teatro; La musa recóndita de un titán.* Buenos Aires: Editorial Kraft, 1967.

Sáenz Hayes, Ricardo. *La polémica de Alberdi con Sarmiento y otras páginas.* Buenos Aires: M. Gleizer, 1926.

Salomón, Noel. *Realidad, ideología y literatura en el Facundo de D. F. Sarmiento.* Amsterdam: Rodopi, 1984.

San Juan (city). Colegio de señoritas de la advocación de Santa Rosa de América. *Constitución del Colegio de señoritas de la advocación de Santa Rosa de América, el primer escrito de Sarmiento sobre educación; Reimpresión facsimilar, con advertencia de Ismael Bucich Escobar.* Buenos Aires: G. Kraft Ltda., 1939.

Sánchez de Bustamante, Samuel. *Sarmiento y las artes plásticas.* Mendoza: Universidad de Cuyo, 1965.

Santovenia y Echaide, Emeterio Santiago. *Sarmiento y su americanismo.* Buenos Aires: Editorial Américalee, 1949.

Sarmiento, Bienvenida. *Rasgos de la vida de Domingo F. Sarmiento.* Foreword and biography by Antonio P. Castro. Buenos Aires: Museo Histórico Sarmiento, 1946.

Schwamborn, Friedhelm. *Das Spanienbild Domingo Faustino Sarmientos.* Bonn: Romanisches Seminar der Universität Bonn, 1968.

Sociedad Sericícola Americana. *Esposición de los fines que se propone, sus sesiones i estatutos.* Santiago: J. Belín i Cia., 1848.

Stuardo Ortiz, Carlos. *El método de lectura gradual de Domingo F. Sarmiento; Datos para su historia y bibliografía.* Santiago de Chile: Impr. Universitaria, 1949.

Suárez, Matías E. *Sarmiento, ese desconocido.* Buenos Aires: Ediciones Theoría, 1964.

Suárez Urtubey, Pola. *La música en el ideario de Sarmiento.* Buenos Aires: Ediciones Polifonía, 1970.

Tamagno, Roberto. *Sarmiento, los liberales y el imperialismo inglés.* Buenos Aires: A. Peña Lillo, 1963.

Universidad Nacional de La Plata. Biblioteca. *Bibliografía sobre Sarmiento (piezas bibliográficas existentes en la Biblioteca pública de la Universidad. Con una nómina de las obras de Sarmiento pertenecientes a la institución).* La Plata: Talleres Gráficos Olivieri & Dominguez, 1938.

Universidad Nacional de La Plata. Facultad de Ciencias Jurídicas y Sociales. *Bibliografía de Sarmiento.* Foreword by Ricardo Rojas. Buenos Aires: Impr. de Coni Hermanos, 1911.

Universidad Nacional de La Plata. Facultad de Humanidades y Ciencias de la Educación. *Sarmiento: Homenaje de la Facultad de humanidades y ciencias de la educación.* 2d ed. La Plata: Universidad Nacional, 1939.

Universidad Nacional de La Plata. Facultad de Humanidades y Ciencias de la Educación. *Pueyrredón, Agrelo y Sarmiento, considerados como memorialistas (valor cierto de sus testimonios).* Foreword by Rómulo D. Carbia. La Plata: Universidad Nacional, 1930.

Universidad Nacional del Litoral. *Presencia y perennidad de Sarmiento.* Santa Fe: 1961.

Valdés, Carmelo B. *Domingo Faustino Sarmiento y su obra.* Introduction by Joaquín V. González. Buenos Aires: J. Lajouane & Cia., 1913.

Verdevoye, Paul. *Sarmiento, éducateur et publiciste entre 1839 et 1852.* Paris: Centre de Recherches de l'Institut d'Études Hispaniques, 1963.

Videla Morón, Mario E. *Reflexiones sobre el pasado sanjuanino e incursiones en el de Cuyo y Chile.* San Juan: Argentina Editorial Sanjuanina, 1965.

Villergas, J. M. *Sarmenticidio ó a mal Sarmiento buena podadera. Refutación, comentario, réplica, folleto ó como quiera llamarse esta quisicosa que, en respuesta à los viajes publicados sin ton ni son por un tal Sarmiento, ha escrito ratos perdidos un tal J. M. Villergas.* Paris: Agencia General de la Libreria Española y Extranjera, 1853.

Wilde, Eduardo. *Tiempo perdido.* Foreword by Domingo F. Sarmiento. Buenos Aires: El Ateneo, 1931.

Zinny, A. *Rasgos biográficos del ciudadano D. Domingo F. Sarmiento.* Buenos Aires: Imprenta Argentina, 1867.

Zorilla, Manuel M. *Al lado de Sarmiento y de Avellaneda; Recuerdos de un secretario.* 2d ed. Buenos Aires: Editorial Ayacucho, 1943.

Zuviria, José María. *Anales contemporáneos; Sarmiento, 1868-1874; Estudios sobre política Argentina.* Buenos Aires: Impr. de P. Coni, 1889.

Index